Andrew Robinson is the author of more than twenty-five books covering both science and the arts, s... ...hich are biographies. They include *The Last Man Who Knew Everything* (a biography of polymath Thomas Young), *Genius: A Very Short Introduction*, and *Einstein: A Hundred Years of Relativity*, which was described by the astronomer and writer Patrick Moore as 'by far the best book about Einstein that I have ever come across' in *BBC Sky at Night*. He is also a long-time contributor to magazines and newspapers, including the *Lancet*, *Nature* and *Science*.
http://www.andrew-robinson.org

Further praise for *Einstein on the Run*:

'Robinson's evocative account of a transitional phase in Einstein's life offers a valuable new perspective on this great scientist's personality.'
Sir Martin Rees, Astronomer Royal and former president of the Royal Society

'This book is an absolute page-turner, elegantly written and constantly fascinating; I found it very hard to put down.'
Stephen J. Blundell, author of *Magnetism: A Very Short Introduction*

'A well-researched and very readable book about a less well-known period in Einstein's life – his contact with England and English scientists.'
Dame Jocelyn Bell Burnell, Visiting Professor of Astrophysics, University of Oxford

'A scholarly and thoroughly entertaining new view of Einstein as a stateless Anglophile. A compelling read.'
Graham Farmelo, author of *The Strangest Man: The Hidden Life of Paul Dirac*

'Andrew Robinson's beautifully written book is a timely reminder of the values of affection, tolerance and justice that transcend national boundaries.'
Daniel Siemens, author of *Stormtroopers: A New History of Hitler's Brownshirts*

'I absolutely adore this book . . . Robinson is a very fine storyteller.'
Steven Gimbel, author of Einstein: *His Space and Times*

'This is a jewel of a book, to be read by anyone interested in Albert Einstein, his science, his peripatetic existence, his joys and travails.'
Diana Kormos-Buchwald, General Editor and Director, Einstein Papers Project

'The very first study of its kind. It wears its thorough and conscientious scholarship lightly on its sleeve – a splendidly entertaining read.'
Ze'ev Rosenkranz, editor of *The Travel Diaries of Albert Einstein*

'A compelling tale of Einstein's reception in Britain. Robinson casts in bold relief important insights into the nature and character of British and German societies in the interwar period.'
Robert Schulmann, joint author, *An Einstein Encyclopedia*

EINSTEIN ON THE RUN

HOW BRITAIN SAVED THE WORLD'S GREATEST SCIENTIST

ANDREW ROBINSON

YALE UNIVERSITY PRESS
NEW HAVEN AND LONDON

Cover images:
Albert Einstein addressing a group of fellow scientists in Harnack Haus, Berlin-Dahlem, *c.* 1933. Photo by George Rinhart/Corbis via Getty Images.
The public burning of 'un-German' books by members of the SA and university students on the Opernplatz in Berlin, 10 May 1933. United States Historical Memorial Museum, courtesy of National Archives and Records Administration, College Park.

First published in paperback in 2021

For information about this and other Yale University Press publications, please contact:
U.S. Office: sales.press@yale.edu yalebooks.com
Europe Office: sales@yaleup.co.uk yalebooks.co.uk

Set in Fournier MT by IDSUK (DataConnection) Ltd
Printed and bound in Great Britain by Clays Ltd, Elcograf S.p.A.

Library of Congress Control Number: 2019932771

ISBN 978-0-300-23476-3 (hbk)
ISBN 978-0-300-25499-0 (pbk)

A catalogue record for this book is available from the British Library.

10 9 8 7 6 5 4 3 2 1

For my wife, Dipli,
moromere, as ever

Contents

	List of Illustrations	*viii*
	Preface	*xi*
	Acknowledgements	*xiv*
Prologue	A Wanderer on the Face of the Earth	1
1	The Happiest Thought of My Life	9
2	Hats Off to the Fellows! From a Swiss Jew	43
3	A Stinking Flower in a German Buttonhole	85
4	God Does Not Play Dice with the Universe	119
5	A Barbarian among the Holy Brotherhood in Tails	145
6	The Reality of Nature and the Nature of Reality	189
7	On the Run	223
8	I Vill a Little T'ink	273
Epilogue	An Old Gypsy in a Quaint and Ceremonious Village	305
	Notes and References	*320*
	Bibliography	*335*
	Index	*341*

Illustrations

Einstein under guard in Norfolk, 1933. Archant Library, Norwich. 4

Solvay Congress in Brussels, 1911. 35

Einstein with Arthur Eddington, 1930. Winifred Eddington / from *The Life of Arthur Stanley Eddington* by A. Vibert Douglas. 51

Manuscript of an article on relativity by Einstein, 1919. Albert Einstein Archives, Jerusalem. 67

Einstein on his first visit to England, 1921. Ullstein Bild / Granger. 79

Drawing of Einstein by William Rothenstein, 1927. From *Twelve Portraits* by William Rothenstein. 92

Einstein and group at Government House, Jerusalem, 1923. Courtesy of École Biblique, Jerusalem. 106

Einstein and George Bernard Shaw at a dinner in London, 1930. Topical Press Agency / Hulton Archives / Getty Images. 116

Solvay Congress in Brussels, 1927. 133

Einstein during his doctoral ceremony in Oxford, 1931. Zuma Press, Inc. / Alamy Stock Photo. 148

Einstein's blackboard in Oxford, 1931. 161

Letter to the Rhodes trustees from Robert Gunther, 1931. Courtesy of Rhodes Trustees, Oxford. 162

Drawing of Einstein by F. Rizzi, 1933. Courtesy of Senior Common Room, Christ Church, Oxford. 171

Einstein and two men in Oxford, probably 1931. Albert Einstein Archives, Jerusalem. 176

Einstein seated in Oxford, 1931–33. Private collection. 183

Cartoon of Einstein by an unknown German artist, 1933. From *Einstein on Politics*, edited by David E. Rowe and Robert Schulmann. 194

Einstein in Christ Church quadrangle, Oxford, 1933. Trinity Mirror / Mirrorpix / Alamy Stock Photo. 203

Einstein's landing card at Dover, 1933. 207

Einstein at the Oxford Union, 1933. Gillman & Soame, Oxford. 210

Einstein with Winston Churchill, Chartwell, 1933. Leo Baeck Institute, New York. 232

Einstein with Oliver Locker-Lampson, London, 1933. Keystone Pictures USA / Alamy Stock Photo. 239

Cartoon of Einstein by Charles Raymond Macauley, 1933. From *Einstein on Politics*, edited by David E. Rowe and Robert Schulmann. 243

Einstein and wife with a Belgian police officer, 1933. Everett Collection Historical / Alamy Stock Photo. 247

Einstein on the front page of the *Daily Express*, 1933. Courtesy of Daily Express / Express Syndication. 252

Einstein alone in Norfolk, 1933. Leo Baeck Institute, New York. 253

Cartoon of Einstein by David Low, 1933. Courtesy of Caltech Archives, Pasadena. 255

Einstein with his bronze bust and Jacob Epstein, 1933. Bettmann / Getty Images. 259

Einstein speaks at the Albert Hall, London, 1933. Keystone Pictures USA / Alamy Stock Photo. 263

Cartoon of Einstein by Sidney 'George' Strube, 1933. Courtesy of Daily Express / Express Syndication. 269

Einstein in his study at Princeton, 1951. Ernst Haas / Getty Images. 279

Russell–Einstein Manifesto: cover of a recording by Bertrand Russell, 1955. Private collection. 302

Einstein in a stained-glass window of Christ Church Hall, Oxford. Courtesy of Christ Church, Oxford. 314

Cartoon by Herbert Lawrence Block, 1955. Herb Block Foundation, Washington DC. 318

Preface

Whenever we think of the world's best-known scientist, we generally picture him in relation to Germany, where Albert Einstein was born, or Switzerland, where he first became a physicist, or the United States, where he settled during his last two decades, or Israel, to which he willed his massive archives because of his Jewish sympathies.

Less often considered is Britain. Yet, it would be no exaggeration to say that Britain is the country that made Einstein into the worldwide phenomenon he is today. Profound and creative, Einstein's entanglement with Britain was both intellectual and emotional. In 1927, while he was living in Germany, he wrote to a British physicist in Oxford: 'in England . . . my work has received greater recognition than anywhere else in the world'. In 1933, while revisiting Britain, he remarked with uncharacteristic fervour to a London journalist: 'I love this country.' In 1937, having relocated from Europe to the United States, he told a refugee German physicist in Edinburgh that Britain was 'the most civilised country of the day'.

Einstein's relationship with Britain flourished for over half a century. In the 1890s, British theoretical and experimental physics, as epitomised by Isaac Newton, sparked his scientific development during his school and college education in Switzerland. In 1919, British astronomers confirmed his general theory of relativity, which made Einstein internationally famous. In 1933, Britain saved him from likely assassination by Nazi extremists by offering him refuge. And in 1955, Britain gave rise to his most enduring political statement: the Russell–Einstein Manifesto against the spread of nuclear weapons during the Cold War, initiated by the philosopher, mathematician and political activist Bertrand Russell – the last document signed by Einstein before his death.

All this was despite Einstein's never fluent, indeed at times comical, grasp of English, which he had not formally learned. 'It just won't stick to my ancient skull,' he confessed to his diary in 1931 (of course in German), after trying to study English on a long ocean voyage while going to lecture in the United States. 'Einstein's English was very simple, containing about 300 words pronounced in a very peculiar way,' noted his English-speaking physicist friend Leopold Infeld, a Polish refugee from Nazism who collaborated closely with Einstein at Princeton in the 1930s in the writing of their joint popular success, *The Evolution of Physics*. 'I cannot write in English, because of the treacherous spelling,' Einstein confessed in 1944 to another physicist, Max Born, an old friend from Germany who had studied in Cambridge as a young man and was comfortable with speaking and writing the language. 'When I am reading it, I only hear it and am unable to remember what the written word looks like.'

Even so, 'Einstein was an Anglophile,' declared three American scholars of Einstein – Alice Calaprice, Daniel Kennefick and Robert Schulmann – without hesitation or qualification in their study, *An Einstein Encyclopedia*, published by Princeton University Press in 2015. Nonetheless, Einstein specialists, including his many biographers, have tended to downplay his relationship with Britain because of its diversity and subtlety. I myself underrated it in my book, *Einstein: A Hundred Years of Relativity* – as did the book's nine expert contributors.

This book, *Einstein on the Run*, is the first to focus on Einstein and Britain. It brings together material that is both familiar and unfamiliar – some of it hitherto unpublished – from disparate parts of the Einstein archives. These archives at the Hebrew University in Jerusalem contain a total of around 30,000 documents, making them similar in size to the archives of Napoleon Bonaparte and several times the size of those of Newton and Galileo, according to the unique Einstein Papers Project at the California Institute of Technology. Since the 1980s, the project has overseen the publication of sixteen large volumes of *The Collected Papers of Albert Einstein* (*CPAE*), the latest of which concludes in 1929 – leaving about a third of his life still to be published. No wonder that Einstein still has the power to surprise and fascinate the world. As George Bernard Shaw said of him in a speech in London in 1930, at a dinner to honour Einstein: 'I rejoice at the new universe to which he has introduced us. I rejoice in the fact that he has destroyed all the old sermons, all the old absolutes, all the old cut and dried conceptions, even of time and space, which were so discouraging . . .'.

Acknowledgements

This book would not have been possible without the cooperation of the Albert Einstein Archives in Jerusalem, which made available to me Einstein's articles, lectures and letters, some of which are unpublished, plus related material and letters to Einstein. Its archivists, Barbara Wolff and Chaya Becker, were consistently helpful while I was researching both this book and *Einstein: A Hundred Years of Relativity*. My deepest gratitude goes to their colleague Or Orith Burla, who not only retrieved much archival material at my request but also suggested material I was not aware of and on occasion helped me to translate it from German into English. Her assistance with my research was generous, invaluable and particularly welcome to a freelance author.

I am also grateful to the fellows of Christ Church, Lady Margaret Hall and Nuffield College in Oxford, to the Rhodes House Trustees and to the English-Speaking Union, for permission to quote correspondence relating to Einstein's visits to Oxford, notably the Oxford diary of Margaret Deneke and the letters of Frederick Lindemann (Lord Cherwell).

Sebastian Born, on behalf of the Born family, generously granted permission to quote passages from the letters written by his grandfather Max Born to Einstein, originally published in English translation as *The Born–Einstein Letters*. 'I'm sure he would have been, and we are, happy that your work continues to reveal his thought and insight in these conversations with his great friend Einstein.'

Many archivists, based mainly in Britain, have been unusually helpful with my research. It is a pleasure to thank: Nicolas Bell (Trinity College, Cambridge), Judith Curthoys (Christ Church, Oxford), Gavin Fuller (Telegraph Media Group, London), Emma Huber (Taylor Institution Library, Oxford), Michael Hughes (Bodleian Library, Oxford), Clare Kavanagh (Nuffield College, Oxford), Suzanne Keyte (Royal Albert Hall, London), Oliver Mahony (Lady Margaret Hall, Oxford), Charlotte Oxendale (Rhodes House, Oxford), Niels Sampath (Oxford Union Library), Michael Simonson (Leo Baeck Institute, New York) and Anna Towlson (London School of Economics). Others include: Frank Baker (John Rylands Library, Manchester), Jessica Borge (King's College, London), Rosemary Dixon (Archant Library, Norwich), Melissa Downing (Rhodes House, Oxford), Heidi Egginton (Churchill Archives, Cambridge), Robyn Haggard (Museum of the History of Science, Oxford), Stephen Hebron (Bodleian Library, Oxford), Laura Hilton-Smith (Leeds University Library), Loma Karklins (Caltech Archives, Pasadena), Lee Macdonald (Museum of the History of Science, Oxford), Wilma Minty (Bodleian Library, Oxford), Alistair Murphy (Cromer Museum), Laura Outterside (Royal Society, London), Emma Quinlan (Nuffield College, Oxford), Ed Smithson (Nuffield College, Oxford), Jean-Michel de Tarragon (École Biblique, Jerusalem), Bridget Whittle (McMaster University, Hamilton) and Harry Wright (Friends House, London).

In the world of Einstein scholarship, it was a delight to discuss a range of issues with someone as well informed, open-minded and amusing as Robert Schulmann, former director of the Einstein Papers Project, author of influential books on Einstein and contributor to *Einstein: A Hundred Years of Relativity*, who shares my curiosity about Einstein's attitude to Britain. I also enjoyed interacting with Robert's former colleagues at the Einstein Papers Project: Alice Calaprice, editor of *The Ultimate Quotable Einstein*, who, despite her retirement from Princeton University Press, was always willing to answer my questions about Einstein quotations (genuine, probable and invented); and David Rowe, co-editor with Robert Schulmann of *Einstein on Politics*, who drew my attention to Antonina Vallentin's arresting account of Einstein in 1933, plus other sources. Among the current members of the Einstein Papers Project I am grateful to its director, Diana Kormos Buchwald, another contributor to *Einstein: A Hundred Years of Relativity*, for her general support, and to its assistant director, Ze'ev Rosenkranz, who took trouble to advise me on Einstein's travel diaries, his relationship to Palestine and other matters. In Oxford, Robert Fox was a generous source of information while he was researching an article on Einstein in Oxford for the Royal Society's journal, *Notes and Records*.

In the wider academic world, beyond Einstein studies, I owe a special debt to the physicist and historian of science Graham Farmelo, fellow author, biographer and journalist, who wrote excellent book reviews for me when I was literary editor of the *Times Higher Education Supplement*. Graham introduced me to Yale University Press.

Other friends and contacts inside and outside academe who deserve thanks for their advice on Einstein and/or Einstein-related matters are: Joanna Ashbourn, Jonathan Bowen (Edmund Bowen), Paul Cartledge, Jodie Collins (Oliver Locker-Lampson), David Dunmur (Frederick Lindemann), David Dutton (Austen Chamberlain), Josef Eisinger (Einstein's travel diaries), Mordechai Feingold (Isaac Newton), Nancy Greenspan (Max Born), Hanoch Gutfreund (The Hebrew University), Richard Hawkins (Samuel Untermyer), Gordon Johnson (Isaiah Berlin), David Levey,

Jonathan Locker-Lampson, Alex May (entries in the *Oxford Dictionary of National Biography*), Michael Musgrave (Marie Soldat), Cormac O'Raifeartaigh (Einstein's cosmology), David Robinson (Einstein's lecture at King's College, London), Tom Wakeford and Thomas Weber (Adolf Hitler).

At Christ Church, Oxford, my old friend James Lawrie organised a talk for me at the college on Einstein in Oxford in 2015, the centenary of general relativity, followed by an article in the college magazine, *Christ Church Matters*, commissioned by his colleague Simon Offen.

Among writers and journalists, various individuals in Norfolk kindly helped me in researching Einstein's stay near Cromer in September–October 1933, in particular Glenys Hitchings, Stuart McLaren, Steve Snelling and Del Styan. Stuart kindly supplied me with a copy of the rare souvenir booklet published (presumably by Oliver Locker-Lampson) to commemorate Einstein's speech at the Albert Hall meeting in October 1933. The BBC journalists David Edmonds and John Eidinow provided further information about this meeting regarding the role of Locker-Lampson. Thanks, too, to various editors who have recently published articles of mine about Einstein and related subjects, in particular: Sara Abdulla (*Nature*), Marina Benjamin (*Aeon*), Tushna Commissariat (*Physics World*), Barb Kiser (*Nature*), James McConnachie (*The Author*) and Valerie Thompson (*Science*).

It has been a distinct pleasure to work with the editorial staff of Yale University Press for the first time. My editor, Julian Loose – evidently fascinated by Einstein's personality and British adventures – was imaginatively involved with the book from its commissioning to its completion. Marika Lysandrou did sterling work on the illustrations. Rachael Lonsdale and Clarissa Sutherland were remarkably careful and efficient editors.

PROLOGUE

A Wanderer on the Face of the Earth

See him as he squats on Cromer beach doing sums, Charlie Chaplin with the brow of Shakespeare. . . . So it is not an accident that the Nazi lads vent a particular fury against him. He does truly stand for what they most dislike, the opposite of the blond beast – intellectualist, individualist, supernationalist, pacifist, inky, plump.

'Einstein' by John Maynard Keynes, *New Statesman and Nation*, October 1933

In September 1933 – a few months after exiling himself forever from his German home in Berlin where he had lived since 1914 – Einstein found himself unexpectedly dwelling alone in a thatched wooden holiday hut located in a wild rural area of Norfolk in eastern England, close to the sea near the coastal town of Cromer. He was far from being on holiday, however. The hut was a secret refuge to avoid a rumoured attempt at assassination by agents acting for the Nazi regime in Germany; Einstein was guarded with guns by a small group of local English people, led by a Conservative member of parliament who was also a decorated veteran of the First World War.

During March–April, shortly after Adolf Hitler came to power, Einstein had publicly criticised the repressive policies of the new National Socialist government; resigned from the Prussian Academy of Sciences in Berlin; applied for release from his Prussian (German) citizenship; and found a temporary home for himself and his wife on the coast of nearby Belgium. In response, he had been relentlessly attacked in the German press, and his scientific works had been publicly burned in Berlin. The government had confiscated his and his wife's bank accounts. Their summer villa near Berlin had reportedly been searched for arms – on the grounds that Einstein was treasonously spreading Communist-influenced 'atrocity propaganda' against Germany from abroad. One especially prominent anti-Semitic German publication about Jews, approved by the government's propaganda chief Josef Goebbels, showed a photograph of Einstein with the sinister caption in capital letters: '*BIS JETZT UNGEHAENGT*', that is, 'not yet hanged'.

Soon Einstein was widely thought to be public enemy number one of the Nazis. He was given round-the-clock police protection by the Belgian royal family. However, he tried to evade the policemen's watchful eyes and did not take rumours of an attack

Einstein under guard in rural England, September 1933. On the left is his English host, Commander Oliver Locker-Lampson MP, a veteran of the First World War; directly behind Einstein stands Marjory Howard, a secretary of Locker-Lampson; further away hovers Herbert Eastoe, a local gamekeeper. The world's press had recently announced that Nazi extremists had put a price on Einstein's head.

on him too seriously, despite his awareness of the disturbing history of political assassination in post-war Germany, which had claimed several lives including, most notoriously, that of Germany's foreign minister, Walther Rathenau, a friend of Einstein and a prominent Jew, who was murdered in Berlin in broad daylight in 1922. (Rathenau's photo was captioned 'executed'.) As a long-standing devotee of sailing, Einstein was indifferent to danger or death, to the extent that he refused to carry life-jackets or life-belts on board his sailing-boat – even though he had never learned to swim.

Then, on 30 August 1933, Nazi extremists shot an associate of Einstein in Czechoslovakia, the controversial German-Jewish philosopher Theodor Lessing, whose photo had also been captioned 'not yet hanged' – for which the assassins were immediately honoured in Germany. Within days, press reports appeared suggesting that Einstein was next in line, and mentioning a hefty financial reward placed on his head. Even so, Einstein shrugged his shoulders. He told a Paris-based correspondent: 'I really had no idea my head was worth all that.' As for the threat, 'I have no doubt it is really true, but in any case I await the issue with serenity.' To his hugely anxious wife, Elsa, he argued: 'When a bandit is going to commit a crime he keeps it secret' – according to a local press statement she made in early September, reported in the *New York Times*. Nonetheless, shortly after this, Elsa Einstein successfully insisted that her husband immediately go 'on the run' from possible Nazi retribution.

He discreetly departed from Belgium, took a boat across the English Channel and headed for London. But instead of going from London to his familiar berth in a historic Oxford college, he was soon settled in the depths of the English countryside.

There, in the holiday hut on Roughton Heath near Cromer, Einstein lived and toiled peacefully at mathematics – the unified field theory, based on his general theory of relativity, which would occupy him until his dying day – while occasionally stepping out for local walks or to play his violin. He had no library, of course, but this mattered relatively little to Einstein, who had long relied chiefly on his own thoughts and calculations; all he really missed was his faithful calculating assistant, who had stayed behind in Belgium. For about three weeks, Einstein was largely undisturbed by outsiders, except for a visit from the sculptor Jacob Epstein, who modelled a remarkable bronze bust of the hermit Einstein, today on occasional display at London's Tate Gallery.

From this undisclosed location, Einstein informed a British newspaper reporter in mid-September: 'I shall become a naturalised Englishman as soon as it is possible for my papers to go through.' However, 'I cannot tell you yet whether I shall make England my home.'

In early October, he emerged from hiding to speak at a meeting in London intended to raise funds for desperate academic refugees from Germany. Without our long fought-for western European freedom of mind, stated Einstein in front of a gripped audience overflowing the massive Albert Hall, 'there would have been no Shakespeare, no Goethe, no Newton, no Faraday, no Pasteur and no Lister'. Afterwards, on the steps of the hall, he told another newspaper reporter:

> I could not believe that it was possible that such spontaneous affection could be extended to one who is a wanderer on the face of the earth. The kindness of your people has touched my heart so deeply that I cannot find words to express in English what I feel. I shall leave England for America at the end of the week, but no matter how long I live I shall never forget the kindness which I have received from the people of England.

Einstein's flight from Nazi terror is easily understandable. But how was it that he came to take refuge in an obscure English hut? What was it about England, in particular, that appealed to Einstein as a sanctuary? And why – given his long and enriching relationship with Britain, dating back to his teenage encounters with British physics in Switzerland – would he leave the country for America, never to return to Europe?

CHAPTER ONE

The Happiest Thought of My Life

[B]efore Maxwell, people conceived of physical reality . . . as material points, whose changes consist exclusively of motions. . . . After Maxwell, they conceived of physical reality as represented by continuous fields, not mechanically explicable. . . . This change in the conception of reality is the most profound and fruitful one that has come to physics since Newton; but it has at the same time to be admitted that the programme has by no means been completely carried out yet.

Essay written by Einstein for the centennial celebration of the birth of James Clerk Maxwell, published by Cambridge University Press, 1931

On the walls of his apartment in 1920s Berlin, and later in his Princeton house, Einstein hung portraits of three British natural philosophers: the physicists Isaac Newton, Michael Faraday and James Clerk Maxwell – and no other scientists. Each of this trio he unquestionably revered. 'England has always produced the best physicists,' Einstein said in 1925 to a young Ukrainian-Jewish woman, Esther Salaman, attending his lectures on relativity in Berlin. He advised her to study physics at the University of Cambridge: the home of Newton in the second half of the seventeenth century and later the scientific base of Maxwell, founder of Cambridge's Cavendish Laboratory in the 1870s. As Einstein explained to Salaman: 'I'm not thinking only of Newton. There would be no modern physics without Maxwell's electromagnetic equations: I owe more to Maxwell than to anyone. But remember,' he warned her, 'in England everything is judged by achievement.'

While visiting England in 1930, immediately after stopping at Newton's birthplace in Woolsthorpe to pay tribute, Einstein remarked simply, before giving a lecture at the University of Nottingham: 'It is a pleasure and an honour to speak in the country in which my science, theoretical physics, was born.' In his last ever interview, two weeks before his death in Princeton, much of his conversation revolved around Newton's fascinating writings, scientific and theological, published and unpublished, without overlooking Newton's misanthropic personality – so different from Einstein's own. ('Newton is the Old Testament god; it is Einstein who is the New Testament figure . . . full of humanity, pity, a sense of enormous sympathy,' the Polish-born British mathematician Jacob Bronowski remarked in his 1970s BBC television series *The Ascent of Man*.)

EARLY YEARS IN GERMANY

Although England played little role in Einstein's childhood and adolescence in 1880s–90s Germany, some understanding of his early years is essential to appreciate his first receptive encounters with English physics, which he studied as a teenage autodidact in Germany from the early 1890s and then, more attentively, as a university student in Switzerland. Einstein's unconventional upbringing was what set him on the path not only to his theory of relativity and his quantum theory but also to his later, ultimately unfulfilled, pursuit of a unified field theory of gravity and electromagnetism.

There was no hint of any intellectual distinction in Einstein's family tree. His father, Hermann, was an easy-going businessman who was not very successful in electrical engineering and his paternal grandfather a merchant, while his mother, Pauline, a fine piano player but otherwise not gifted, also came from a business family which ran a profitable grain concern and was wealthy. Though both sides of the family were Jewish, neither was orthodox. Hermann and Pauline Einstein were thoroughly assimilated and non-observant Jews ('entirely irreligious', according to their son), who conversed in German, not Yiddish/Hebrew.

Nor was there much sign of distinction in Einstein as a child. Albert Abraham – the first name a common one among the ruling Hohenzollern dynasty, the second from Einstein's paternal grandfather – was born on 14 March 1879 in Ulm, in southern Germany, in the semi-rural province of the Swabians. Their 'speculative brooding', 'often roguish and occasionally coarse humour' and 'pronounced, individualistic obstinacy' Einstein would share, according to his biographer Albrecht Fölsing. He was a quiet baby, so quiet that his parents became seriously concerned and consulted a doctor about his not learning to talk.

But when a daughter, Maja, was born in November 1881, Albert apparently asked promptly: Where are the wheels of my new toy? It turned out that his ambition was to speak in complete sentences: first he would try out a sentence in his head, while moving his lips, and only then repeat it aloud. The habit lasted until his seventh year or even later. The family maidservant dubbed him 'stupid'.

His first school was a Catholic one in Munich, where the Einstein family had relocated in 1880. Albert was the only Jew in a class of about seventy students. But he seems to have felt anti-Semitism among the teachers only in the religious education classes, not in the rest of the school curriculum. Among the students, however, anti-Semitism was commonplace, and though it was not vicious, it encouraged Einstein's early sense of being an outsider, a feeling that would intensify throughout adulthood.

Academically he was good yet by no means a prodigy, both at this school and at his high school, the Luitpold Gymnasium. However, Einstein showed hardly any affection for his schooling and in later life excoriated the system of formal education current in Germany. He referred to his teachers as 'sergeants' and 'lieutenants', disliked physical training and competitive games – even intellectual games such as chess – and detested anything that smacked of the military discipline typical of the Prussian ethos of northern Germany. 'Constraint has always been his personal enemy. His whole youth was a battle against it,' wrote a friend and Einstein biographer, Antonina Vallentin, in 1954. 'When he uttered the German word for it, an abrupt word, with a particular sinister sound, *Zwang*, everything tolerant, humorous or resigned in his expression vanished.' In 1920, he even told a Berlin interviewer that the school matriculation exam should be abolished. 'Let us return to Nature, which upholds the principle of getting the maximum amount of effect from the minimum of effort, whereas the matriculation test does exactly the opposite.' As he astutely remarked in 1930 after he had become world famous: 'To punish me for my contempt of authority, Fate has made me an authority myself.'

Part of Einstein's problem lay in the heavy emphasis in the German Gymnasiums – as in British public schools of the period – on the humanities; that is, on classical studies and, to a lesser extent, German history and literature, to the detriment of modern foreign languages, such as French and English. Science and mathematics were regarded as the subjects with the lowest status.

But the main problem with school was probably that Albert was a confirmed autodidact, who preferred his own company to that of his teachers and fellow students. 'Private study' is a phrase frequent in his early letters and adult writings on education. It was clearly his chief means of becoming educated. His sister Maja recalled that even in noisy company her brother could 'withdraw to the sofa, take pen and paper in hand, set the inkstand precariously on the armrest, and lose himself so completely in a problem that the conversation of many voices stimulated rather than disturbed him'.

At a relatively early age, he began reading mathematics and science books simply out of curiosity; at college in Zurich he ranged very widely in his reading, including the latest scientific journals; and as an adult he never read books simply because they were said to be classics, only if they appealed to him. 'Einstein was more of an artist than a scholar; in other words, he did not clutter up his mind too much with other people's ideas,' according to the British mathematician and cosmologist Gerald Whitrow. Maybe there is a parallel here with Newton, an eclectic reader who nevertheless does not seem to have read many of the great scientific names of his own or earlier times.

His first scientific experience occurred as a child of four or five, according to Einstein, when his father showed him a magnetic compass. 'I can still remember,' he wrote half a century later, '– or at least believe I can remember – that this experience made a deep and lasting impression upon me. Something deeply hidden had to be behind things.'

Then, aged twelve, he experienced 'a second wonder of a totally different nature' while working through a book of Euclidian plane geometry. The 'lucidity and certainty' of the geometrical proofs, based on Euclid's ten simple axioms, made another deep impression, and set Einstein thinking for the rest of his life on the true relationship between purely mathematical forms and the same forms found in the physical world. Hence the strong appeal to him of Johannes Kepler's discovery that the planetary orbits are ellipses. The very word geometry, Einstein noted, was from the Greek for 'earth-measuring', which implied that mathematics 'owes its existence to the need which was felt of learning something about the behaviour of real objects'.

At the same time, Albert began reading two popular science books in German brought for him by a poor medical student, Max Talmud, who was given a weekly lunch by his parents – among the few Jewish customs the Einsteins did observe. These introduced him to the work of Newton and set him on course to be a scientist. They also convinced him – although they did not attack religion as such – that much of the Bible was untrue, and induced a 'suspicion against every kind of authority' which would last until his dying day.

At school, things came to a head in 1894. A new class teacher informed Einstein that 'he would never get anywhere in life'. When Einstein replied that surely he 'had not committed any offence', he was told: 'Your mere presence here undermines the class's respect for me.' For the rest of his life, Einstein would be known for a mocking (and self-mocking) way with words that was sometimes biting and always at odds with his later gentle image. When as an adult he chanced upon a German psychiatrist's book, *Physique and Character*, he was shaken by it and wrote down the following words in his diary, which he apparently thought applied to himself: 'Hypersensitivity transformed into indifference. During adolescence, inwardly inhibited and unworldly. Glass pane between subject and other people. Unmotivated mistrust. Substitute paper world. Ascetic impulses.'

At home, too, all was not going well. In 1893, after a battle with larger companies, the Einstein company had failed to get a contract for lighting an important part of Munich. The following year the company was liquidated and a new one set up in Italy, with a new factory. Maja moved there with her parents, but Albert was left alone in Munich with some distant relatives in order to take his matriculation exam. Meanwhile the beloved Einstein home in Munich was sold and quickly demolished by developers under his eyes.

The combination of disruptions at school and at home seems to have been too much for Albert, who would never refer to this unhappy period. Without consulting his parents, he got a doctor (Talmud's elder brother) to state that he was suffering from exhaustion and needed time off school, and convinced a teacher to give him a certificate of excellence in mathematics. The school authorities willingly released him. Then he headed south to Milan to face his surprised parents.

EDUCATION AND EMPLOYMENT IN SWITZERLAND

Einstein did not return to graduate, and a year later rejected his German nationality, presumably to avoid military service, becoming stateless until he was accepted as a Swiss citizen in

1901. Instead, after much private study at home in Italy in 1895, he sat the exam early for the Swiss Polytechnic in Zurich, probably the leading centre for the study of science in central Europe outside of Germany. He failed. However his brilliance in mathematics and physics was recognised, and he was encouraged to try again the following year after further schooling. On the advice of a Polytechnic professor, he went to a Swiss cantonal school in Aarau, which enjoyed a much less authoritarian atmosphere than the school in Munich. When he passed its final exam, which qualified him to begin study in Zurich in 1896, he wrote a revealing essay in (execrable) French on 'My plans for the future'. It announced his desire to study the theoretical part of physics because of 'my individual inclination for abstract and mathematical thinking, lack of imagination and of practical sense', and concluded significantly: 'Besides, I am also much attracted by a certain independence offered by the scientific profession.'

Switzerland now became integral to Einstein's life, during this formative intellectual period, which was also the time of his first love affair, with his fellow physics student Mileva Marić, whom he married in 1903. 'So far as he was ever at home, at any time in his life, it was in Bern and Zurich, before the First World War,' wrote the British novelist C. P. Snow after discussions with Einstein in the late 1930s. Judging from his youthful letters, his love of the soaring, solitary splendour of the alpine peaks influenced his scientific theorising. After he eventually became a professor in Zurich, Einstein's students remembered him standing in the middle of a snowstorm under a street lamp at the foot of the Zurichberg, handing his unfurled umbrella to a companion and jotting down formulae for ten minutes while snowflakes fell on his notebook. Much later, in *The Evolution of Physics*, he wrote:

> creating a new theory is not like destroying an old barn and erecting a skyscraper in its place. It is rather like climbing a mountain, gaining new and wider views, discovering unexpected connections between our starting-point and its rich environment. But the point from which we started out still exists and can be seen, although it appears smaller and forms a tiny part of our broad view gained by the mastery of the obstacles on our adventurous way up.

Thus, in the mid-1890s, Einstein would start from Newton's laws of force and motion and Maxwell's equations of electromagnetism and ascend to the heights of the field equations of general relativity twenty years later, not by overturning Newton or Maxwell but rather by subsuming them into a more comprehensive theory, somewhat as the map of a continent subsumes a map of an individual country.

The main source for Einstein's thinking in his early Zurich years are his love letters to Mileva. They were peppered with references to his wide scientific reading. But there is not much technical detail, probably because Mileva avoided science in her replies. So it is hard to penetrate the evolution of Einstein's ideas. Perhaps the most revealing glimpse came in 1899, when he wrote to her of Maxwell's theories about how electromagnetic light waves move through space – the hypothetical medium then known as the 'luminiferous ether' – as follows: 'I'm convinced more and more that the electrodynamics of moving bodies as it is presented today doesn't correspond to reality, and that it will be possible to present it in a simpler way.' According to the novice Einstein, 'The introduction of the term "ether" into theories of electricity has led to the conception of a medium whose motion can be described, without, I believe, being able to ascribe physical meaning to it.' Soon, his scepticism about the ether would turn to outright rejection of Maxwell's concept as a physical entity.

What *is* clear, however, is Einstein's dissatisfaction with some of the science teaching at the Swiss Polytechnic. He paid tribute to his professors of mathematics, particularly Hermann Minkowski, although he failed to apply himself to mathematics assiduously. (Minkowski remembered his student Einstein as a 'lazy dog' in a letter to Max Born, while himself developing special relativity mathematically after 1905, as we shall see.) But he regarded his physics professors as behind the times and unable to cope with challenges to their authority. Even allowing for the fact that Einstein was extremely precocious in theoretical physics for a student of the late 1890s, it is astonishing that no course was offered to him and his fellow Zurich students on Maxwell's equations, which had been published as long ago as the 1860s. Despite the experimental physicist Heinrich Hertz's justification of Maxwell's electromagnetic theory in 1888, the electromagnetic field was still considered too recent and controversial for students.

After four years of study, most of it 'private', Einstein graduated in 1900 with a diploma entitling him to teach mathematics in Swiss schools. His aim was to become an assistant to a professor at the Polytechnic, write a doctoral thesis and enter the academic world. But now his 'impudence', 'my guardian angel' (to quote another letter to Mileva), of which Einstein had made little secret at university, told against him.

The next two years would be very tough indeed for Albert and Mileva (who had failed to acquire a diploma). He was not offered an assistantship, unlike some other students. Nevertheless he thought continually about physics and began to publish theoretical papers in a well-known physics journal; he also completed a thesis, but it was not accepted by the University of Zurich.

When he wrote letters to notable professors offering his services, they were ignored. (One of the professors, the chemist Wilhelm Ostwald, ironically would be the first scientist to nominate Einstein for a Nobel prize, a mere nine years later!) Soon Albert was virtually starving, dependent on casual school teaching, and at risk of malnutrition. Then Mileva became pregnant, failed the Polytechnic exam again, and gave birth to a daughter, which had to be hushed up. Einstein's parents had always hotly opposed his proposed marriage and refused their consent; it was not given until his father lay dying in 1902, his business in bankruptcy, although his mother would never accept the marriage. Only Einstein's unshakeable confidence in his own scientific prowess, encouraged by Mileva's single-minded devotion, could have carried him through these desperate two years.

Rescue came in 1902 from a fellow student at Zurich, Marcel Grossmann, who would also play a significant role in the mathematics of general relativity. 'He a model student; I untidy and a daydreamer. He on excellent terms with the teachers and grasping everything easily; I aloof and discontented, not very popular,' Einstein later confessed in a condolence letter to Grossmann's widow.

Grossmann's father secured Einstein a job at the Federal Swiss Office for Intellectual Property – the Patent Office – in Bern. He was a friend of the office's long-standing director, who was looking for a patent examiner with the ability to understand inventions in the burgeoning electrical industry. Einstein's knowledge of electromagnetic theory, and his considerable practical exposure to electrical devices through his family's engineering business, were deemed sufficient. On 23 June 1902, he reported for duty as a 'technical expert, third class' – the most junior post of its kind. The Swiss Patent Office would become the somewhat unlikely setting that would allow Einstein to make his name as a physicist with his quantum, relativity and atomic theories during his 'miraculous year', 1905. 'It gave me the opportunity to think about physics,' he later reflected. 'Moreover, a practical profession is a salvation for a man of my type; an academic career compels a young man to scientific production, and only strong characters can resist the temptation of superficial analysis.'

Part of the reason for Einstein's profound success was surely his wide and precocious reading in science, fuelled by his voracious curiosity allied to his unusual power of concentration, as already noted. In addition, he had an analytical ability worthy of Sherlock Holmes. John Rigden, a physicist, remarked in *Einstein 1905: The Standard of Greatness* that Einstein 'was intrigued rather than dismayed by apparent contradictions, whether they consisted of experimental results that conflicted with theoretical predictions' – as shown in his paper on quantum theory – 'or theories with formal inconsistencies' – as demonstrated in his paper on relativity.

In a related vein, Jürgen Renn and Robert Schulmann, two historians of science, identified Einstein's unwillingness to adopt received ideas simply on the authority of a scientist's reputation – even if the scientist was Newton or Maxwell. For example, Einstein examined the highly influential works of Ernst Mach, a leading physicist of his formative years. Mach did not accept the concept of either the ether or the atom, neither of which had been experimentally observed in the late nineteenth century. Though Einstein did not share Mach's positivist philosophy, he liked Mach's scepticism. '[Einstein] would carefully study Mach's arguments against burdening physics with unnecessary concepts,' noted Renn and Schulmann, 'and eventually discard the ether concept, while accepting Mach's criticism of atomism as a challenge and trying to provide evidence for the existence of atoms.' This Einstein effectively achieved in his 1905 paper on atomic theory. It explained the puzzling phenomenon of 'Brownian movement' – the erratic fluctuations of microscopic particles suspended in a fluid, such as fine pollen in water, observed by a British botanist, Robert Brown, in 1827 – in terms of the kinetic motion of atoms and molecules. According to this kinetic theory, the invisible fluctuations of atoms/molecules produce visible fluctuations of particles via collisions between atoms/molecules and particles.

A third clue to Einstein's success is that he relished debate, even if his ideas got torn apart. About a year after arriving in Bern, he formed a small club with two friends of his own age, Conrad Habicht and Maurice Solovine. As a joke they gave it a high-sounding name, the Olympia Academy, with Einstein as president, and arranged to meet in the cafés of the city, at music recitals, on long walks at the weekend or in the Einsteins' small apartment. Besides reading Mach together, the 'three intellectual musketeers' argued in detail about a recently published book, *Science and Hypothesis*, by the mathematician Henri Poincaré, and debated the thoughts of David Hume, Baruch de Spinoza and other philosophers, while also tackling some classic literary works. Sometimes Einstein would play his violin. They also stuffed themselves with as much good food as they could afford, and generally horsed around. Once, Habicht had a tin plate engraved by a tradesman and fixed it to the Einsteins' door. It proclaimed: 'Albert Ritter von Steissbein, President of the Olympia Academy' – meaning roughly 'Albert Knight of the Backside' or maybe something worse (since the rhyming word *Scheissbein* means 'shit-leg'!). Albert and Mileva 'laughed so much they thought they would die,' according to Solovine. Decades later, Einstein remembered the Olympia Academy in a letter to Solovine as being 'far less childish than those respectable ones which I later got to know'. Its discussions, and Einstein's talks with a few other close friends in Bern, were unquestionably a key stimulus to him in 1902–5.

The most important of all these friends was probably Michele Besso (who was not an 'Olympian'), six years older than Einstein, a well-read, quick-witted and affectionate man whose career as a mechanical engineer did not prosper because of a natural indecisiveness. Einstein got to know him at a musical gathering in his first year in Zurich and would remain in touch for six decades until Besso's death just a month before Einstein's own. In 1904, at Einstein's suggestion, Besso joined the Patent Office too, and soon the two friends were walking back and forth from the office discussing physics. Earlier, Besso had been the person who had interested the student Einstein in Mach. Now he became the catalyst in the solving of the relativity problem.

Sometime in the middle of May 1905, Einstein tells us that he went to see Besso for a chat about every aspect of relativity. After a searching discussion, Einstein returned to his apartment, and during that evening and night he saw the solution to his difficulties. The following day he went back to Besso and straightaway told him, without even saying hello: 'Thank you. I've completely solved the problem. An analysis of the concept of time was my solution. Time cannot be absolutely defined, and there is an inseparable relation between time and signal velocity.' Einstein's sincere gratitude can be felt in his published acknowledgement to Besso for his 'steadfastness' and for 'many a valuable suggestion' in his 1905 paper on relativity – especially given the astonishing fact that this paper contains not a single bibliographical reference to established scientists!

SPECIAL RELATIVITY

So how did Einstein come up with special relativity? The physicist Stephen Hawking, in his millennial essay 'A Brief History of Relativity', observed that Einstein 'started from the postulate that the laws of science should appear the same to all freely moving observers. In particular, they should all measure the same speed for light, no matter how fast they were moving.' Let us try to unpack these tricky ideas a little.

Near the beginning of Einstein's 1916 introduction to relativity for the general reader, published in English translation in 1920, he described a simple but profound observation. You stand at the window of a railway carriage which is travelling uniformly, in other words at constant velocity, not accelerating or decelerating – and let fall a stone on to the embankment, without throwing it. If air resistance is disregarded, you, though you are moving, see the stone descend in a straight line. But a stationary pedestrian, that is someone 'at rest', who sees your action ('misdeed' says Einstein) from the footpath, sees the stone fall in a parabolic curve. Which of the observed paths, the straight line or the parabola, is true 'in reality', asked Einstein? The answer is – both paths. 'Reality' here depends on which frame of reference – which system of coordinates in geometrical terms – the observer is attached to: the train's or the embankment's. One can rephrase what happens in relative terms as follows, said Einstein:

> The stone traverses a straight line relative to a system of coordinates rigidly attached to the carriage, but relative to a system of coordinates rigidly attached to the ground (embankment) it describes a parabola. With the aid of this example it is clearly seen that there is no such thing as an independently existing trajectory (lit. 'path-curve'), but only a trajectory relative to a particular body of reference.

Another, somewhat less familiar, situation involving relativity that bothered Einstein concerned electrodynamics. An electric charge at rest produces no magnetic field, while a moving charge – an electric current – generates a magnetic field (circular lines of magnetic force around a current-carrying wire), as first described by Faraday. Imagine a stationary electrically charged object with an observer A, also at rest relative to the object; the observer will measure no magnetic field using a compass needle. Now add an observer B moving uniformly to the east. Relative to B's reference system, the charged object (and observer A) will appear to be moving west uniformly; B, using a sensitive compass, will detect a magnetic field around the moving charged object. So, from A's point of view, there is no magnetic field around the charged object, while from B's uniformly moving point of view there *is* a magnetic field.

Anomalies of this kind intrigued Einstein. He was determined to resolve them. It was his deeply held view that throughout the physical world the laws of mechanics, and indeed the laws of science as a whole, must be the same – 'invariant' in scientific language – for all observers, whether they are 'at rest' or moving uniformly. For Einstein believed that it made no physical sense to postulate such a thing as Newton's absolute space or Maxwell's ether: a universal frame of reference to which the movement of all bodies could be tacitly referred. Instead, he argued, the position in space of a body must always be specified relative to a given system of coordinates. We may choose to describe our car as moving down a motorway at a velocity of 110 kilometres per hour, but this figure has no absolute significance; it defines our position and speed relative only to the ground and takes no account of the Earth's rotational position and velocity around its axis or Earth's orbital position and velocity around the Sun.

But if this new postulate about the invariance of the laws of nature was actually correct, it must apply not only to moving bodies but also to electricity, magnetism and light, the electromagnetic wave of Maxwell and Hertz, which was known from experiment to move at a constant velocity in a vacuum of about 300,000 kilometres per second, supposedly relative to the ether. This posed a severe problem. While Einstein was contented enough to relinquish the ether, which had never satisfied him as a concept, the constancy of the speed of light was another matter altogether.

In 1895 (maybe while preparing at home in Milan to take the entry exam for the Swiss Polytechnic), Einstein had reflected on what would happen if one chased light and caught up with it. Contra Newton, he now concluded: 'If I pursue a beam of light with the velocity c (velocity of light in a vacuum), I should observe such a beam of light as a spatially oscillatory electromagnetic field at rest. However, there seems to be no such thing, whether on the basis of experience or according to Maxwell's equations.' To catch up with light would be as impossible as trying to see a chase scene in a movie in freeze-frame: light exists only when it moves, the chase exists only when the film's frames move through the projector. Were we to travel faster than light, Einstein imagined a situation in which we should be able to run away from a light signal and catch up with previously sent light signals. The most recently sent light signal would be detected first by our eyes, then we would see progressively older light signals. 'We should catch them in a reverse order to that in which they were sent, and the train of happenings on our Earth would appear like a film shown backwards, beginning with a happy ending.' The idea of catching or overtaking light was clearly absurd.

Einstein therefore formulated a radical second postulate: the speed of light is always the same in all coordinate systems, *independent* of how the emitting source or the detector moves. However fast his hypothetical vehicle might travel in chasing a beam of light, it could never catch it: relative to him the beam would always appear to travel away from him at the speed of light.

This could be true, he eventually realised, only if time, as well as space, was relative and not absolute. In order to make his first postulate about relativity compatible with his second about the speed of light, two 'unjustifiable hypotheses' from Newtonian mechanics had therefore to be abandoned. The first – absolute time – was that 'the time-interval (time) between two events is independent of the condition of motion of the body of reference'. The second – absolute space – was that 'the space-interval (distance) between two points of a rigid body is independent of the condition of motion of the body of reference'.

Thus the time of the person chasing the light wave and the time of the wave itself are not the same. Time flows for the person at a rate different from that of the wave. The faster the person goes, the slower his time flows, and therefore the less distance he covers (since distance travelled equals speed multiplied by duration of travel). As he approaches the speed of light, his watch gets slower and slower until it almost stops. In Hawking's words, relativity 'required abandoning the idea that there is a universal quantity called time that all clocks would measure. Instead, everyone would have his or her own personal time.' For space there is a difference, too, between the person and the light wave. The faster the person goes, the more his space contracts, and therefore the less distance he covers. As he approaches the speed of light, he shrinks to almost nothing. Depending on how close the person's speed is to the speed of light, he experiences a mixture of time slowing and space contracting, according to Einstein's equations of relativity.

These ideas seem extremely alien because we never travel at speeds of even a tiny fraction of the speed of light, so we never observe any 'relativistic' slowing of time or contraction of space – though we are familiar with the effect of perspective when two people walk away from each other and each sees the other person as diminished in height. Our human motions seem to be governed entirely by Newton's laws of motion (in which the speed of light, *c*, is a quantity that does not even appear). Einstein himself had to struggle hard in 1905 – hence his need for an intense discussion with Besso – to accept these relativistic concepts so remote from everyday experience.

With space contraction, he at least had the knowledge of a comparable earlier proposal by the physicists Hendrik Lorentz and George FitzGerald, though this had a different theoretical basis from his own and relied on the existence of the ether, a concept which Einstein had of course rejected. But the abandonment of absolute time, too, required a still greater leap of the imagination. Poincaré had questioned the concept of simultaneity in 1902 in *Science and Hypothesis*: 'Not only do we have no direct experience of the equality of two times, but we do not even have one of the simultaneity of two events occurring in different places.' Indeed, Poincaré seems to have come very close to a theory of relativity just before Einstein, but apparently drew back because its implications were too disturbing to the foundations of physics. Simultaneity is a very persistent illusion for us on Earth because we so easily neglect the time of propagation of light; we think of light as 'instantaneous' relative to other familiar phenomena like sound. 'We are accustomed on this account to fail to differentiate between "simultaneously seen" and "simultaneously happening"; and, as a result, the difference between time and local time is blurred,' wrote Einstein.

QUANTUM THEORY

Yet, despite the strangeness of its predictions, relativity was built on the mechanics of Newton modified by the electrodynamics of Maxwell, as Einstein was at pains to emphasise. Most modern physicists regard relativity theory as revolutionary, but Einstein himself did not, and reserved 'revolutionary' to describe his paper on the quantum theory. Ironically, although the quantum paper was published in April 1905 before his relativity paper in June 1905, his relativity paper does not refer to the quantum theory; the relativity paper treats electromagnetic radiation purely as a wave and never so much as hints that it might consist of particles or quanta of energy. Presumably Einstein recognised that one big new idea per paper would be indigestible enough for most physicists. Perhaps, too, his isolating of the two ideas in two separate papers reflected his own doubts about the quantum concept. Nevertheless, with these two papers he became the first physicist to accept what is today the orthodoxy in physics: light can behave both like a wave (in relativity theory) *and* like a particle (in quantum theory).

Newton had been divided about the relative merits of waves and particles, on the whole favouring the latter in his 'corpuscular' theory of light, which dominated physics until convincing new evidence for the wave theory was discovered by Thomas Young (yet another English physicist admired by Einstein) soon after 1800. As for gravity, Newton had no idea at all as to how such a continuous influence might arise from discrete (in other words discontinuous) masses. Indeed, the debate about whether nature is fundamentally continuous or discontinuous runs through science – from the atomic theory of ancient Greece right up to the present day with its opposing concepts of analogue and digital, and the wave/particle 'duality' of subatomic entities like the electron. Russell is supposed to have asked: Is the world a bucket of molasses or a pail of sand? In mathematical terms, asked the physicist Rigden, 'Is the world to be described geometrically as endless unbroken lines, or is it to be counted with the algebra of discrete numbers? Which best describes Nature – geometry or algebra?'

Quantum theory, the modern corpuscular theory, was born with the new century, in 1900, as a result of the work of the physicist Max Planck, although it would remain in limbo until 1905, when Einstein's paper would endow it with its true significance. Planck considered the energy of heat that had been measured emerging from a glowing cavity, termed a 'black body' because the hole leading to the cavity behaves almost as a perfect absorber and emitter of energy with no reflecting power (like a black surface). Planck tried to devise a theory to explain how the heat energy of a black body varied over different wavelengths and at different temperatures of the cavity. But he found that if he treated the heat as a continuous wave, this wave model did not agree with experiment. Only when he assumed that the energies of the 'resonators' (atoms) in the walls of the cavity that were absorbing and emitting heat were not continuous but could take only discrete values, did theory match experiment. Instead of continuous absorption and emission of energy, energy was exchanged between heat and atoms in packets or quanta. Moreover, the size of a quantum was proportional to the frequency of the resonator, which meant that high-frequency quanta carried more energy than low-frequency quanta. As a believer in nature as a continuum, and as an innately conservative man, Planck did not feel at all comfortable with what his calculation had told him, but in 1900 he reluctantly published his theoretical explanation of black-body radiation.

Einstein was bolder than Planck. He was twenty years younger and had less stake than Planck in classical nineteenth-century physics. Probably encouraged by his disbelief in the ether, Einstein decided that it was not just the exchange of energy between heat/light and matter (i.e. absorption and emission) that was quantised – *light itself was quantised*. In his introduction to his April 1905 paper he radically stated: 'According to the assumption to be contemplated here, when a light ray is spreading from a point, the energy is not distributed continuously over ever-increasing spaces, but consists of a finite number of energy quanta that are localised in points in space, move without dividing, and can be absorbed or generated as a whole.' Instead of moving particles, Einstein visualised a light beam as moving packets of energy. When this avant-garde concept was finally accepted by reluctant physicists in the 1920s, the packets were termed 'photons'.

Had there been no experimental support for Einstein's assumption of quantised light, it would have met with an even more sceptical reaction than it in fact did. But fortunately there was at least some significant laboratory evidence. Though it was not detailed, Einstein audaciously interpreted the evidence with the quantum theory he had elaborated in the first part of his paper. The success of his theoretical explanation of the 'photoelectric effect' in his 1905 paper (which won him the Nobel prize) meant that light quanta could not be totally ignored, even if they were gravely distrusted.

The photoelectric effect had been discovered by Hertz around 1888 while investigating electromagnetic waves. Hertz noticed that in a spark gap the spark gained in brightness when illuminated by ultraviolet (high-frequency) light. With the discovery of X-rays in 1895, and of the electron in 1897, followed by the experiments of Philipp Lenard (a former assistant to Hertz), it was soon accepted that high-frequency light could knock electrons out of the surface of a metal producing photoelectrons, so-called cathode rays. 'I just read a wonderful paper by Lenard on the generation of cathode rays by ultraviolet light. Under the influence of this beautiful paper I am filled with such happiness and joy that I absolutely must share some of it with you,' Einstein wrote to his fiancée Mileva in 1901. It may have been this paper by Lenard that started Einstein speculating on the quantised nature of light. For Lenard's published data were in major contradiction with those expected from classical physics.

With the wave theory of light, the more intense the light, the more energy it must have and the greater the number of electrons that should be ejected from the metal. This was observed by Lenard – yet *only* above a certain frequency of light. Below this frequency threshold, no matter how intense the light, it knocked out no electrons. Moreover, above the threshold, electron emission was observed even when the light was exceedingly weak. With the quantum theory, however, Einstein realised such behaviour was to be expected. *One* quantum of light (later called a photon) would knock out *one* electron, but only if the quantum carried enough energy to extract it from the surface of the metal. Since, as Planck had shown, the size of a quantum depended on its frequency, only quanta of a sufficiently high frequency or higher would knock out electrons – hence the existence of the threshold frequency. Moreover, even a very few quanta (a very weak intensity of light) would still eject a few electrons, provided that the quanta were above the threshold in frequency.

So truly revolutionary was this discontinuous view of nature, which owed almost nothing to earlier physics, that light quanta took much more experimentation and a lot of fresh thinking to be accepted by other physicists. This happened only in the late 1920s. So we shall leave the quantum theory for now, and return to it much later, after following the next phase in Einstein's struggle with relativity.

GENERAL RELATIVITY

In 1908, Einstein's former mathematics professor at Zurich, Minkowski, reformulated relativity mathematically and introduced the new concept of 'space-time'. He enthusiastically announced:

> The views of space and time which I wish to lay before you have sprung from the soil of experimental physics and therein lies their strength. They are radical. Henceforth space by itself, and time by itself, are doomed to fade away into mere shadows, and only a kind of union of the two will preserve an independent reality.

More prosaically, events in four-dimensional space-time are analogous to points in three-dimensional space. There is an analogy, too, between the interval separating events in space-time and the straight-line distance between points on a flat sheet of paper. The space-time interval is absolute, in other words its value does not change with the reference frame used to compute it. In conventional space and time the stone falling from a uniformly moving train has two trajectories – straight down and parabolic – depending on whether it is observed from the train or from the embankment. But in the geometry of space-time it has only *one* trajectory, which Minkowski dubbed its 'world line'.

'Since the mathematicians pounced on the relativity theory I no longer understand it myself,' Einstein apparently sighed on studying Minkowski's treatment. As a physicist he was at this time somewhat ambivalent about pure mathematics. Even in his introduction to relativity for the general reader, he felt obliged to warn that mathematical talk of a 'four-dimensional space-time continuum' had nothing at all to do with the occult or with inducing 'mysterious shuddering'. Yet, Einstein did admit that without Minkowski's mathematics, the general theory of relativity might never have grown out of its infant state. ' "Analytic" or "algebraically expressed" geometry is fundamental to modern theoretical physics, because of its ability to take the imagination way beyond everyday physical constraints,' according to mathematician Robyn Arianrhod in *Einstein's Heroes: Imagining the*

World through the Language of Mathematics. 'Newton used an early form of it (in his calculus) to visualise aspects of the mechanism that keeps "the stars in their courses"; Maxwell used it to imagine Faraday's invisible fields; and Einstein used it to imagine the whole cosmos.'

The following year, 1909, with the growing fame of relativity, Einstein's academic career took off. After seven years he left the Patent Office in Bern to become a (non-tenured) professor of theoretical physics at the University of Zurich; was the guest of honour at the next annual meeting of German scientists in Salzburg; and received his first honorary degree in Geneva at the age of just thirty. In early 1911, he moved to Prague as a full professor, but stayed only sixteen months before moving back to Zurich in 1912, now as full professor of theoretical physics. While based in Prague, in late 1911 he attended the first Solvay Congress in Brussels and lectured about his quantum theory on terms of equality with the world's greatest scientists: Lorentz, Planck and Poincaré – already known to him – as well as Marie Curie, Ernest Rutherford, Walther Nernst and others. Nernst's student, Frederick Lindemann, secretary of the Congress – who as a future professor of physics at the University of Oxford would host Einstein in England – meeting him for the first time, recalled Einstein as 'singularly simple, friendly and unpretentious. He was invariably ready to discuss physical questions, even with a mere post-graduate student, as I then was. . . . But his pre-eminence among the eighteen greatest theoretical physicists of the day, who were there assembled, was clear to any unprejudiced observer.' Finally, in the spring of 1914, Einstein left Switzerland – while remaining a Swiss citizen – and arrived in Berlin where he was elected a member of the Prussian Academy – thereby reacquiring, in effect, German citizenship – on the understanding that he could devote his entire time to research.

Solvay Congress in Brussels, Belgium, 1911: a gathering of the greatest scientists in the world at this time. Einstein, then only thirty-two years old, who gave the concluding address on his revolutionary quantum theory, stands second from right. Among the seated scientists are Walther Nernst (far left), Hendrik Lorentz (fourth from left), Marie Curie (second from right) and Henri Poincaré (far right). Those standing include Max Planck (second from left), Arnold Sommerfeld (fourth from left), Frederick Lindemann (fifth from left), James Jeans (fifth from right) and Ernest Rutherford (fourth from right).

At this point, the relativity theory of 1905 began to be known as 'special' relativity, to distinguish it from the later, more general theory, following Einstein's own terminology introduced in 1915. Of course the 'general' theory subsumes the 'special' theory, indeed it reduces to the special theory under conditions of uniform motion with constant velocity (as with the example of the train and the falling stone). In such an idealised universe, without gravity, special relativity alone is sufficient. But in the real physical universe, which is pervaded by gravity and accelerations due to gravity as well as various other kinds of forces, there is no such thing as absolutely uniform motion, only approximations to it, so we need the more general theory.

Einstein's aim was to make his 1905 relativity theory valid for *all* moving coordinate systems. Then, as he noted ironically, there would be an end to the violent disputes that had racked human thought since Copernicus, because 'The two sentences, "the Sun is at rest and the Earth moves," or "the Sun moves and the Earth is at rest," would simply mean two different conventions concerning two different coordinate systems.' In 1905, he had done away with Newton's concepts of absolute space and absolute time. Now, using the concept of space-time introduced by Minkowski and radically developed by Einstein with the help of his mathematician friend Grossmann, Einstein would devise a more sophisticated theory which would also do away with gravity's inexplicable instantaneous action at a distance, while at the same time retaining Newton's laws of motion and his inverse-square law of gravitational attraction as a first approximation to physical reality.

The initial inkling of how to generalise relativity struck Einstein in 1907, and it is a moment reminiscent of Newton's contemplation of the falling apple, though trickier to comprehend. 'I was sitting on a chair in my Patent Office in Bern.

Suddenly a thought struck me: if a man falls freely, he would not feel his weight,' Einstein later recalled. In other words, if you were to jump off a rooftop or better still a high cliff, you would not feel gravity. 'I was taken aback. The simple thought experiment made a deep impression on me. It was what led me to the theory of gravity.' He called this 'the happiest thought of my life'.

To drive home the point, he imagined that as you fall, you let go of some rocks from your hand. What happens to them? They fall at the same rate as you, side by side. If you were to concentrate only on the rocks (admittedly difficult!), you would not be able to tell if they were falling to the ground. An observer on the ground would see you and the rocks accelerating together for a smash, but to you the rocks, relative to your reference frame, would appear to be 'at rest'.

Or imagine being inside a moving lift while standing on a weight scale. As the lift descends, the faster it accelerates, the less you will feel your weight and the lighter will be the weight reading on the scale. If the lift cable were to snap and the lift to go into free fall, your weight according to the scales would be zero. Then gravity would not exist for you in your immediate vicinity. In other words, the existence of gravity is *relative* to acceleration.

From such thinking, which became intensive only after he moved to Prague in 1911, Einstein restated a venerable idea that has become known as his 'equivalence principle' – the idea that gravity and acceleration are, in a certain sense, equivalent. It encompasses the fact, first observed by Galileo Galilei, that gravity accelerates all bodies equally. In more scientific language, inertial mass (as defined by Newton's second law of motion) equals gravitational mass (as defined by gravity). Newton had simply assumed this equivalence as self-evident in formulating his gravitational equation, but Einstein felt that by understanding the physical reason for the equivalence he could gain insight into how to include gravity in relativity theory. Modern physicists have different ways to state the equivalence principle. For example, it is 'the idea that the physics in an accelerated laboratory is equivalent to that in a uniform gravitational field', according to Tony Hey and Patrick Walters.

For the next few years Einstein became obsessed with thoughts of accelerating closed boxes. On a Swiss Alpine hike with Marie Curie, her two daughters and their governess in the summer of 1913, Einstein toiled along crevasses and up steep rocks without seeing either, stopping periodically to discuss science. Once, Eve Curie remembered with amusement, Einstein seized her mother's arm and burst out: 'You understand, what I need to know is exactly what happens in a lift when it falls into emptiness.' At a packed lecture in Vienna the following month, he entertained an audience of scientists by asking them to imagine two physicists awakening from a drugged sleep to find themselves standing in a closed box with opaque walls but with all their instruments. They would be unable to discover, he said, whether their box was at rest in the Earth's gravity or was being uniformly accelerated upwards through empty space (in which gravity is taken to be negligible) by some mysterious external force.

In a similar example, Einstein imagined a small hole in the wall of a lift which is being accelerated upwards by an external force. A light ray enters the lift through the hole. The ray travels to the opposite wall of the lift. But as it does so, the lift moves upwards. The ray therefore meets the opposite wall at a point a little below its point of entrance. For an observer outside the lift, there is no difficulty: the lift is accelerating upwards and so the light ray is bent downwards into a slight curve. (Had the lift been moving uniformly, the ray would have appeared to travel in a straight line.) But for an observer *inside* the lift who believes that the lift is at rest and that it is gravity that is acting on the lift, the curved ray poses a problem. How can a ray of light be affected by gravity? Well, said Einstein, it must be: 'A beam of light carries energy and energy has mass' – as shown in his famous equation $E = mc^2$, derived from his 1905 theory of relativity. 'But every inertial mass is attracted by the gravitational field, as inertial and gravitational masses are equivalent. A beam of light will bend in a gravitational field exactly as a body would if thrown horizontally with a velocity equal to that of light.'

The deflection of light by Earth's gravity would be far too small to measure, Einstein realised. But deflection might be measurable, he reasoned, when light from distant stars passed close to a massive body like the Sun. Furthermore, the equivalence principle dictated that the light emitted *from* the Sun should feel the drag of solar gravity too. Its energy must therefore fall slightly, which meant that its frequency must fall and therefore its wavelength must get longer (since light's velocity must remain constant, and the velocity of a wave equals its frequency multiplied by its wavelength). So light from atoms in the surface of the Sun, as compared with light emitted by the same atoms in interstellar space, should be shifted towards the red – longer wavelength – end of the visible spectrum when observed on Earth. The deflection of starlight by the Sun and the red shift of solar radiation were therefore possible tests of relativity.

But in order to introduce gravity into relativity, a major problem confronted Einstein in trying to apply the equivalence principle to the flat space-time visualised by Minkowski. The problem can be perceived, at least dimly, from a paradox about a simple merry-go-round that bothered Einstein. When a merry-go-round is at rest, its circumference is equal to π times its diameter. But when it spins, its circumference travels faster than its interior. According to relativity, the circumference should therefore shrink more than the interior (since space contraction increases with velocity), which must distort the shape of the merry-go-round and make the circumference less than π times the diameter. The result is that the surface is no longer flat; space is curved. Euclid's geometry, based on flat surfaces and straight light rays, no longer applies. Einstein is said to have had a nice analogy for this curvature, which he gave to his young son, when the boy asked his father why he was so famous: 'When a blind beetle crawls over the surface of a curved branch, it doesn't notice that the track it has covered is indeed curved. I was lucky enough to notice what the beetle didn't notice.'

In the mid-nineteenth century, the mathematician Bernhard Riemann had invented a geometry of curved space in which, said Einstein, 'space was deprived of its rigidity, and the possibility of its partaking in physical events was recognised'. Now Einstein – initially with the help of his mathematician friend Grossmann but after he moved to Berlin in 1914 almost entirely alone – used Riemann's geometry to create a new geometry of curved space-time. 'His idea was that mass and energy would warp space-time in some manner yet to be determined,' explained Hawking. Gravity would no longer be an interaction of bodies through a law of forces; it would be a *field* effect that emerged from the way in which mass curved space. When a marble is propelled across a flat, smooth trampoline on which sits a large and heavy ball, the marble follows a curved path around the depression caused by the ball. In the Newtonian view, a gravitational force emanates from the ball and somehow compels the marble to move in a curve. But according to general relativity it is the curvature of space – or rather space-time – that is responsible; there is no mysterious force. 'Matter tells space-time how to curve, and curved space tells matter how to move' – to quote a well-known summary of Einstein's general theory of relativity by the physicist John Archibald Wheeler.

The light 'corpuscles' in a light ray from a distant star grazing the Sun on its way to our eyes could be interpreted like marbles moving past a ball. In 1911, before he had mastered curved spacetime, Einstein had calculated the expected deflection of starlight on the basis of Newton's law of gravitation. In 1915, however, having completed general relativity, he recalculated the deflection as *twice* the size of his 1911 calculation based on Newton. If the magnitude of the actual deflection were to be measured by astronomers, it would test which gravitational theory was correct: Newton's or Einstein's. 'The examination of the correctness or otherwise of this deduction is a problem of the greatest importance, the early solution of which is to be expected of astronomers,' wrote Einstein in his introduction to relativity in 1916. It was to be British astronomers who would answer his challenge, in 1919, and launch Einstein as a new star visible across planet Earth.

CHAPTER TWO

Hats Off to the Fellows! From a Swiss Jew

[T]he English have behaved much more nobly than our colleagues here. . . . How magnificent their attitude has been towards me and relativity theory in comparison! . . . I can only say: Hats off to the fellows!

Letter from Einstein to Fritz Haber, March 1921

Despite Einstein's deep admiration for English physics, his theory experienced a surprisingly indifferent reception in England following its publication in Germany: as special relativity in 1905, followed by general relativity in 1915–16. Hardly any English mathematicians and physicists adopted it in the period 1905–19; as Rutherford remarked as late as 1932, 'The theory of relativity by Einstein, quite apart from any question of its validity, cannot but be regarded as a magnificent work of art.' Even their German opposite numbers viewed general relativity more with awe than comprehension. Einstein's friend Born decided never to attempt any work in the field. 'The foundation of general relativity appeared to me then, and it still does, the greatest feat of human thinking about Nature, the most amazing combination of philosophical penetration, physical intuition and mathematical skill,' Born recalled in 1955 on the fiftieth anniversary of special relativity, looking back on his bemused reaction in 1915. 'But its connections with experience were slender.' In a presumably unconscious echo of Rutherford, Born concluded: 'It appealed to me like a great work of art, to be enjoyed and admired from a distance.'

Less surprisingly, all English thinkers in the humanities were baffled by Einstein's theory. To them, 'Einstein had really offended against common sense, the limited yardstick with which men measure the exterior world,' observed Einstein's English biographer, Ronald Clark.

RELATIVITY AT OXFORD AND CAMBRIDGE

At the University of Oxford, for instance, as late as 1919, Einstein's theory was openly considered to be wrong on technical grounds by the Waynflete Professor of Metaphysical Philosophy, J. A. Smith. He said as much in a tense public debate in Oxford with Lindemann, Dr Lee's Professor of Experimental Philosophy (i.e. physics). After Smith had spoken, a second Oxford philosopher, H. W. B. Joseph, announced that he agreed with Smith's conclusion, though on purely philosophical rather than technical grounds, apparently based on his own unshakeable faith that the space we inhabit must be Euclidean. No wonder that Lindemann had recently been appointed professor with a remit to rescue physical science at Oxford from the doldrums. It was then dominated by Greats (the Oxford term for classical studies), as epitomised by the approach to relativity of these two philosophers, and also by a story later recalled by Lindemann. When once he happened to express his misgivings about the inferior position of science in Oxford to the wife of the warden of All Souls College, she assured him that 'he should not worry because a man who had got a first-class degree in classics and philosophy could get up science in a fortnight'!

One of the members of the audience for this 1919 Oxford debate, Roy Harrod, described it four decades later in delicious and devastating detail in his memoir of Lindemann, *The Prof.* At the time, Harrod was a mere undergraduate in humanities, whose tutor happened to be Joseph; in later years, he would become a distinguished colleague of Lindemann and Einstein at Christ Church. His memoir expressed undisguised scorn for Smith, who discussed certain mathematical equations and physical assumptions. 'How came it that this distinguished purveyor of Greats wisdom, himself neither a mathematician nor a physicist, supposed that he could find, not on the plane of philosophy, but on the plane of physics itself, a technical error in the assumptions behind a theory that had been minutely scrutinised for some time by the greatest minds in the world?' As for Harrod's tutor Joseph, 'he did not show the slightest sign of his ever having seriously tried to understand either what the theoretical considerations were, or what the experimental results had been, that had led these distinguished physicists to the need to expound these tiresome theories of the relativity of space and time'.

Nevertheless, Harrod honestly admitted that Lindemann – himself a recent convert to relativity – struggled, and largely failed, to win the debate, despite some support from scientists in the audience. 'It was a hot-house Oxford product', to which Lindemann, as an Oxford newcomer, had no access. At one point, he was reduced to telling Joseph with an ironic facial expression (perhaps regarding Joseph's Euclidean convictions), 'Well, if you really suppose that you have private inspiration enabling you to know that . . .' – and leaving this provocation dangling in the charged atmosphere of the debating chamber. 'The Prof really never got to grips with his argument; he did not know how to do so; none of the real points of interest in relation to relativity had been touched on; the whole game must have seemed to him to be perfectly futile.'

Even at the University of Cambridge – the home of Newton, Maxwell, Sir J. J. Thomson and (later) Rutherford – the initial response to Einstein's theory was not much more perceptive. When Rutherford was told in 1910 by the German physicist (and future fellow Nobel laureate) Wilhelm Wien that 'No Anglo-Saxon can understand relativity!', he laughingly replied: 'No! They have too much sense.' According to *Masters of Theory: Cambridge and the Rise of Mathematical Physics* by the historian Andrew Warwick, 'In Cambridge during the period 1905 to 1920, Einstein's work was, by turns, ignored, reinterpreted, rejected, and, finally, accepted and taught to undergraduates' – eventually under the leadership of an astronomer, Sir Arthur Eddington, rather than a physicist.

Indeed, only one British physicist is known to have corresponded directly with Einstein about relativity before 1919:

G. F. C. Searle, a demonstrator in experimental physics at the Cavendish Laboratory in Cambridge and a regular pre-war visitor to German physicists. In 1907, Einstein sent Searle a copy of his 1905 paper on special relativity from his position at the Patent Office in Bern. When Searle eventually replied in 1909, after a period of illness, he confessed to Einstein: 'I have not been able so far to gain any really clear idea as to the principles involved or as to their meaning and those to whom I have spoken in England about the subject seem to have the same feeling.'

One of Searle's unnamed advisers was probably the Cambridge-educated James Jeans, who gave no particular importance to Einstein's relativity in his book *The Mathematical Theory of Electricity and Magnetism*, published in 1908. Another was likely to have been a mathematician, Ebenezer Cunningham, also Cambridge educated, who published *The Principle of Relativity* in 1914. In this book Cunningham alluded to Einstein's theory as follows, though without mentioning Einstein's name: 'The principle of relativity then does not deny the existence of an aethereal medium; that is only the interpretation of an individual. What it does do is to emphasise the insufficiency of the existing conceptions of the aether, and to set up a criterion by which suggestions as to the nature of the aether may be examined.' At this time Cunningham and his fellow British physicists strongly objected to Einstein's attempt, from 1905 onwards, to abandon the revered aether/ether: a concept first postulated by Aristotle as a fifth element composing the heavenly realm, along with earth, fire, water and air.

The chief stumbling-block in these English reactions to relativity between 1905 and 1919 was that English physicists, following the discovery of electromagnetic waves by Hertz in 1888 and of the electron by Thomson in 1897, had chosen to adopt an exclusively electronic theory of matter (known as the

ETM), accompanied by a firm belief in the existence of the ether. In Hertz's emphatic words: 'Take electricity out of the world, and light vanishes; take the luminiferous ether out of the world, and electric and magnetic forces can no longer travel through space.' *Aether and Matter*, an influential work published in 1900 by Cunningham's teacher, Joseph Larmor, Lucasian Professor of Mathematics at Cambridge (the chair once held by Newton), argued that matter was electrically constituted and contracted minutely in its direction of motion through the ether according to the relativistic theory of Hendrik Lorentz. When another of Larmor's students, G. H. Livens, published *The Theory of Electricity* in 1918, he included a short section on 'Relativity', but did not associate the concept especially with the name of Einstein! In fact, Livens opened with the comment that 'the whole electrodynamic properties of matter can be explained on the basis of a stationary aether and electrons' – that is, using Larmor's ETM, not involving relativity.

Yet, this Cambridge-based theory of the whole mass of the atom as being electromagnetic in origin plainly failed to incorporate the non-electrical force of gravity. This failure induced gradually increasing doubts among the followers of the ETM, including Cunningham. 'Quietly obeying the law of the inverse square, [gravitation] heeded not the bustle and excitement of the new physics of the atom, but remained, independent and inevitable, a constant challenge to rash claimants to the key of the universe,' Cunningham eventually felt obliged to concede in the leading scientific journal, *Nature*, in December 1919 – after the experimental verification of Einstein's general relativity, which of course included both light and gravity and also rejected the existence of the ether. 'The electrical theory seemed on the way to explain every property of matter yet known, except the one most universal of them all. It could trace to its origins the difference between copper and glass, but not the common fact of their weight; and now the aether began silently to steal away,' Cunningham confessed. (Persistent experimental attempts to demonstrate the ether's existence, beginning with the classic experiment of two American physicists, Albert Michelson and Edward Morley, in 1887, and continuing in the period 1902–5 and after, always failed to detect it, although this experimental fact played little, if any, direct role in Einstein's development of relativity.)

ENTER ARTHUR EDDINGTON

The 1919 sea-change in English attitude towards Einstein's theory had its origins in the depths of the First World War, in June 1916, when Einstein sent a copy of his newly published summary of general relativity, spelling out some of its cosmological implications, from Berlin to Willem de Sitter, professor of astronomy at the University of Leiden in the politically neutral Netherlands. De Sitter was a foreign correspondent of the Royal Astronomical Society in England, who wished to maintain wartime scientific contacts between England and Germany. He passed on Einstein's copy to the secretary of the Society, Eddington, who was Plumian Professor of Astronomy and Experimental Philosophy at Cambridge. An excited Eddington, despite his minimal knowledge of German, and without any direct contact with Einstein, invited de Sitter to write three expository articles, which Eddington published in the *Monthly Notices* of the Royal Astronomical Society in 1916–17: the first technical introduction to general relativity for English scientists written in English. These articles whetted their appetite for Eddington's own, highly mathematical, *Report on the Relativity Theory of Gravitation*, commissioned by the Physical Society and published in 1918. 'The long train of

Einstein with astronomer Sir Arthur Eddington at the Cambridge Observatory, 1930. Eddington led the British solar eclipse observations in 1919, which confirmed Einstein's general theory of relativity and made him internationally famous.

events set in motion by de Sitter and continued by Eddington was to have repercussions quite as formidable in their own way as the bloody battles being waged on the Western front,' commented Clark in his Einstein biography.

Why did Eddington respond favourably to Einstein's theory – unlike his mathematician and physicist colleagues at Cambridge, such as Cunningham, Jeans, Larmor and Searle? There appear to have been several reasons for Eddington's exceptionalism.

He shared the mathematical education typical of Cambridge in the early Edwardian period, where he was an undergraduate from 1902 to 1905. However, unlike the majority of students, Eddington also studied differential geometry under his tutor Robert Herman, its acknowledged master at Cambridge. This discipline enabled Eddington to penetrate the mathematics of general relativity with much greater confidence than his Cambridge contemporaries.

More important, though, was Eddington's chosen field of study. Rather than the electromagnetic theory studied by Larmor et al., astronomy and cosmology were what appealed to Eddington. After graduating from Cambridge, and a brief, unsuccessful encounter with experimental electronics in the Cavendish Laboratory, he moved in 1906 to the Royal Greenwich Observatory as chief assistant to the Astronomer Royal – Sir Frank Dyson, from 1910 – before returning to Cambridge as Plumian Professor in 1913.

Astronomers and cosmologists, unlike experimental physicists, were certain to be attracted to general relativity. In the first place, their field was directly affected by the theory's astronomical predictions, such as the deflection of starlight by the gravity of the Sun. Second, the business of positional astronomy did not require the ether. Indeed, Eddington's first book, *Stellar Movements and the Structure of the Universe*, published in 1914, did not refer to the ether. 'Unlike the case of British electromagnetic theory, therefore, the ether could be abandoned, or simply ignored, in astronomy, without devaluing the professional practice of the discipline and without requiring any retraining on the part of the astronomers,' wrote Warwick. As a result:

> Far from regarding [Einstein's] theory as a threat to Cambridge views on geometry and electrodynamics, Eddington saw it as a new, physical explanation of gravitation that attributed gravitational effects with a finite rate of propagation, explained a puzzling anomaly in Mercury's motion, opened exciting avenues of research concerning the large-scale structure of the universe, and made further predictions that were testable by astronomers.

In addition to its scientific appeal, general relativity also attracted Eddington for what might be called political reasons, connected with the disaster of the First World War. Both he and Einstein were pacifists: Eddington because of his religious upbringing since birth as a Quaker, Einstein because of his lifelong dislike of German authoritarianism.

In October 1914, two months after the outbreak of the war, ninety-three leading Germans from the world of the arts, humanities and sciences had enthusiastically signed what would become a notorious document during and after the war, entitled 'Manifesto to the Cultured World'. In November 1919, after the announcement of Eddington's eclipse observations, *The Times* noted approvingly that Einstein had *not* been one of the document's signatories.

Published in the leading German dailies, the manifesto was also translated into ten languages throughout the world. It protested 'the lies and defamations with which our enemies are trying to besmirch Germany's pure cause in the hard life-and-death struggle forced upon it'. It denied that Germany had started the war, defended

Germany's breach of Belgium's neutrality, dismissed the stories of atrocities committed by Germany's troops as fabrications, and proclaimed that Germany's cultural legacy – Goethe, Beethoven and Kant were mentioned by name – and its current militarism, were one. Among the scientists who signed it, in addition to two Nobel laureates, Wien and Lenard, were three colleagues and friends of Einstein: Planck, Nernst and Haber.

As a Swiss citizen, Einstein had not been asked for his signature (and was of course exempt from German military service). Yet he now decided to make his first-ever public political statement by signing a counter-manifesto drafted by a well-known German physician and physiologist, Georg Friedrich Nicolai, whose patients included the imperial family. This 'Manifesto to the Europeans', though it openly rejected the 'Manifesto of the 93', did not analyse the causes of the war and attribute guilt. Instead, in deliberately restrained language, it urged educated people everywhere to try to 'create an organic unity out of Europe. . . . Should Europe, too, as Greece did earlier, succumb through fratricidal war to exhaustion and destruction? For the struggle that is raging today will hardly leave a victor but only vanquished behind.' Nicolai circulated the counter-manifesto among the staff at the University of Berlin in late 1914. Many indicated agreement (some, including Planck, were having regrets about signing the nationalist manifesto) – but only two others apart from Einstein, one of whom was an unknown, were willing to sign the appeal. A distressed and isolated Nicolai gave up, and the counter-manifesto did not appear in print until 1917 – and then in Zurich, not Berlin. Nicolai's career was ruined by it; German ultra-nationalists regarded him as a traitor and succeeded in having him banned from teaching in 1920.

Meanwhile, among the patriots, Wien sent round his own circular. It called upon his German academic colleagues to avoid quoting scholars from the enemy camp in Britain, even in footnotes, unless such quotations were indispensable. Einstein's influential physicist colleague, Arnold Sommerfeld, declared himself pleased to sign the appeal in a letter to Wien written on Christmas Day 1914 – of all inappropriate days – while German and Allied troops were fraternising in a truce in the trenches. Two decades later, under Adolf Hitler, German academic references to the work of Jewish physicists, especially Einstein's, were *verboten*, unless they were derogatory. But in the Nazi case this was by government fiat, with serious penalties for transgression. What is particularly dispiriting about German scientific self-censorship in the First World War is that it was entirely voluntary.

The national self-delusion was perfectly encapsulated in a vignette from Einstein the following year. After every meeting of the Berlin University Senate, he remarked in 1915 to a Swiss colleague, laughing aloud, all the professors would meet in a restaurant and 'invariably' the conversation would begin with the question: 'Why are we hated in the world?' Then there would be a discussion in which everyone would supply his own answer while 'most carefully steering clear of the truth'.

In Britain, Eddington, after the introduction of military conscription in 1916, was in a more challenging situation than the technically Swiss Einstein in Germany, since he was a British citizen. Some British Quaker conscientious objectors in Cambridge (such as Cunningham) were sent to work in agriculture or minesweeping, others to prison. Russell, an active pacifist (though not a Quaker), who eventually went to prison, remembered the Cambridge colleges during this stressful period as melancholy places: 'dead, except for a few Indians and a few pale pacifists and bloodthirsty old men hobbling along victorious in the absence of youth. Soldiers are billeted in the courts and drill on the grass; bellicose parsons preach to them in stentorian tones from the steps of the hall.'

Eddington made no secret of his conscientious objection and expected to suffer the official consequences. He informed a tribunal:

> To assert that it is our religious duty to cast off the moral progress of centuries and take part in the passions and barbarity of war is to contradict my whole conception of what the Christian religion means. Even if the abstention of conscientious objectors were to make the difference between victory and defeat, we cannot truly benefit the nation by wilful disobedience to the divine will.

However, he was rescued from agricultural labour or even prison by Dyson, the Astronomer Royal – and by the happy chance of the forthcoming total solar eclipse in May 1919, which both Dyson and Eddington realised could be used to test general relativity. In March 1917, despite the exigencies of war, Dyson persuaded the British government to give £1,000 to investigate the eclipse (assuming that by May 1919 the war was over), under the auspices of a Joint Permanent Eclipse Committee of the Royal Society and the Royal Astronomical Society, of which Dyson was chairman. He was determined that Eddington should be the expedition's leader. In 1918, Dyson wrote in support of Eddington:

> I should like to bring to the notice of the tribunal the great value of Prof. Eddington's researches in astronomy, which are, in my opinion, to be ranked as highly as the work of his predecessors at Cambridge – Darwin, Ball, and Adams. They maintain the high position and traditions of British science at

> a time when it is very desirable that they be upheld, particularly in view of a widely spread but erroneous notion that the most important scientific researches are carried out in Germany.

He added: 'Under present conditions the eclipse will be observed by very few people. Prof. Eddington is peculiarly qualified to make these observations, and I hope the tribunal will give him permission to undertake this task.'

The tribunal agreed. In effect, Eddington was exempted from military conscription in order to undertake scientific research judged to be of national importance. Although his religious objections to the war were officially ignored, the members of the tribunal did declare that they were convinced he was a genuine conscientious objector. For Eddington, who presciently foresaw his proving of Einstein's scientific theory as an important, 'pacifist' opportunity to restore post-war Anglo-German relations, the tribunal's statement was sufficient recognition of his religious objections. He accepted its decision.

SOLAR ECLIPSE EXPEDITIONS AND RELATIVITY

In early 1919, following the armistice of November 1918, planning of the British eclipse expeditions began in earnest. The solar eclipse was predicted to occur on 29 May in front of the Hyades, a cluster of bright stars in the constellation Taurus. A series of test photographs of the Hyades, against a reference frame of other stars, was taken by Eddington through telescopes in Britain in January and February 1919. Comparison of these baseline measurements of each star's position with future corresponding measurements made during the darkness of the eclipse, when these stars were just visible at the limb of the Sun, should enable astronomers to determine whether the deflection of the stars' light by the Sun conformed to the prediction of Newton's theory of gravitation or to the prediction of Einstein's general relativity (that is, a deflection of starlight twice that of Newton's theory).

In March, the four astronomers assigned to make the observations – Eddington and E. T. Cottingham in Principe, an island off the coast of West Africa, and A. C. D. Crommelin and C. R. Davidson in Sobral, a city in northeastern Brazil – met for a final briefing in Dyson's study at Flamsteed House in Greenwich. At one point Cottingham asked: 'What will it mean if we get double the Einstein deflection?' 'Then,' said Dyson, 'Eddington will go mad and you will have to come home alone.' The psychological validity of this story is supported by the fact that in later years Eddington told the young astrophysicist Subrahmanyan Chandrasekhar that he was so utterly convinced by Einstein's theory in 1919, 'had he been left to himself, he would not have planned the expeditions'!

The following morning, both parties set off from England by ship. Eddington and Cottingham, after two weeks' delay in Portugal waiting for a steamer, arrived in Principe on 29 April, exactly a month before the predicted date of the solar eclipse on 29 May. After a lot of hard work under mosquito netting, building waterproof huts for their equipment, setting up the telescopes and instruments, taking test photographs from 16 May, and even hunting monkeys interfering with the equipment, they were ready for the moment of truth.

But cloudy weather, obscuring the solar disc, was against them – not to speak of high temperatures, affecting photographic development. The great day, 29 May, began with heavy rain, which ceased only around noon. The eclipse – scheduled to reach totality at 2.15 p.m. – had already started by the time the two astronomers got their first glimpse of the Sun. According to Eddington's diary:

> About 1:30 when the partial phase was well advanced, we began to get glimpses of the Sun, at 1:55 we could see the crescent (through cloud) almost continuously, and there were large patches of clear sky appearing. We had to carry out our programme of photographs in faith. I did not see the eclipse, being too busy changing plates, except for one glance to make sure it had begun, and another half-way through to see how much cloud there was. We took 16 photographs. . . . They are all good pictures of the Sun, showing a very remarkable prominence; but the cloud has interfered with the star-images. The first ten photographs show practically no stars. The last six show a few images which I hope will give us what we need; but it is very disappointing.

Only on 3 June did they get their first scientific results:

> We developed the photographs two each night for six nights after the eclipse, and I spent the whole day measuring. The cloudy weather upset my plans, and I had to treat the measures in a different way from what I intended; consequently I have not been able to make any preliminary announcement of the result. But one good plate that I measured gave a result agreeing with Einstein and I think I have got a little confirmation from a second plate.

This, writes Eddington's biographer, 'was a moment which Eddington never forgot. On one occasion in later years he referred to it as the greatest moment in his life.' Turning to Cottingham in Principe, he said – recalling their conversation in

Dyson's Greenwich study – 'Cottingham, you won't have to go home alone.' To Dyson Eddington sent a noncommittal telegram: 'Through cloud. Hopeful.'

Soon after his return from West Africa, Eddington attended a dinner of the Royal Astronomical Society. In an affectionate parody of Edward FitzGerald's *Rubáiyát of Omar Khayyám*, the 'Astronomer-Poet of Persia', he confidently announced:

Oh leave the Wise our measures to collate.
One thing at least is certain, LIGHT has WEIGHT
One thing is certain, and the rest debate –
Light-rays, when near the Sun, DO NOT GO STRAIGHT.

More seriously, Eddington developed four more photographic plates from Principe. He detected in them Einstein's value for the deflection of light, though within a rather large margin of error. As for the photographs taken in Sobral, these were all brought back to England only in late August 1919 for development and measurement. The first set to be developed showed a deflection half that of the Principe photographs, that is, Newton's value – to the surprise and dismay of Eddington in September. But fortunately, the second set of Sobral photographs, which had been taken through a technically better telescope and could be developed only in October, supported Einstein's value with total unambiguity and excellent accuracy. 'They gave a final verdict,' wrote Eddington, 'definitely confirming Einstein's value of the deflection, in agreement with the results obtained in Principe.' Although Eddington's results would long remain controversial, amidst unsubstantiated allegations by some scientists that he had fudged his measurements in favour of Einstein's theory, subsequent evidence for general relativity has shown that Eddington and the other expedition astronomers were undoubtedly honest victims of adverse weather in Principe and some inadequate technology in Sobral.

During this five-month-long scientific assessment, Einstein, sitting in Berlin, was naturally anxious for news from the British expeditions. He was still not in direct contact with Eddington, so he asked his close physicist friend at Leiden (de Sitter's university), Paul Ehrenfest, for up-to-date information. On 22 September, another physicist friend at Leiden, Lorentz, replied by telegram, to the effect that Eddington had confirmed a deflection lying somewhere between Newton's and Einstein's values: a consequence of Eddington's uncertainty prior to the development of the Sobral plates in October (of which Einstein was unaware).

Despite this doubtful experimental result, Einstein – like Eddington – had all along been convinced that general relativity was true. He showed Lorentz's telegram to a doctoral student, and told her: 'I knew all the time that the theory was correct.' But supposing the result had been equivocal or contradicted his theory, the student asked. 'In that case I'd have felt sorry for God, because the theory is correct,' Einstein famously replied. Almost thirty years later, when Planck died, Einstein told a friend, after warmly praising Planck, 'but, you know, he didn't really understand physics. During the eclipse of 1919, Planck stayed up all night to see if it would confirm the bending of light by the gravitational field of the Sun. If he had really understood the way the general theory of relativity explains the equivalence of inertial and gravitational mass, he would have gone to bed the way I did.'

Not until 23 October did Einstein receive private but explicit confirmation of his theory by the eclipse observations. It came on a visit to Leiden, when a colleague showed Einstein a letter written by Eddington after he had measured the photographic plates from Sobral. Immediately, Einstein informed Planck of the experimental evidence, and also reported happily to his mother in Switzerland: 'The result is now definite and means an exact confirmation of my theory.'

GENERAL RELATIVITY CONFIRMED

Public confirmation occurred in London on 6 November 1919, when the observations were presented as the sole item on the agenda of the joint meeting of the Royal Society and the Royal Astronomical Society. So important was the occasion that the audience was virtually a roll-call of the greatest names in British physics, astronomy and mathematics. Alfred North Whitehead, mathematician and philosopher, who had come specially from Cambridge, described the scene:

> The whole atmosphere of tense interest was exactly that of the Greek drama. We were the chorus, commenting on the decree of destiny in the unfolding development of a supreme incident. There was a dramatic quality in the very staging – the traditional ceremonial, and in the background the picture of Newton to remind us that the greatest of scientific generalisations was now, after more than two centuries, to receive its first modification. Nor was the personal interest wanting; a great adventure in thought had at length come safe to shore.

First the Astronomer Royal, Dyson, who had launched the whole enterprise in March 1917, outlined the course of the two expeditions to West Africa and Brazil and the essentials of the photographic plates taken on 29 May 1919. Dyson declared: 'A very definite result has been obtained that light is deflected in accordance with Einstein's law of gravitation.' Then Eddington, speaking for the Principe expedition, and Crommelin, speaking for the Sobral expedition, presented their observations in detail. Finally, the presidents of the two scientific societies supported Dyson and Eddington. Thomson, the president of the Royal Society – and thus the successor to Newton – said of general relativity:

> this result is not an isolated one; it is part of a whole continent of scientific ideas. . . . This is the most important result obtained in connection with the theory of gravitation since Newton's day, and it is fitting that it should be announced at a meeting of the Society so closely connected with him. . . . If it is sustained that Einstein's reasoning holds good . . . then it is the result of one of the highest achievements of human thought.

A leader article published in *The Times* on 7 November, the day after the meeting, summed up: 'It is confidently believed by the greatest experts that enough has been done to overthrow the certainty of ages and to require a new philosophy of the universe, a philosophy that will sweep away nearly all that has hitherto been accepted as the axiomatic basis of physical thought.' Three headlines in the newspaper – 'Revolution in science', 'New theory of the universe' and 'Newtonian ideas overthrown' – were followed by six headlines in the *New York Times* on 10 November, including 'Lights all askew in the heavens', 'A book for 12 wise men' and 'No more in all the world could comprehend it, said Einstein when his daring publishers accepted it.'

Thomson's awed, but slightly sceptical, praise was to be expected from physicists in England, given the Cambridge school's commitment to the electronic theory of matter (ETM), based on an ether concept that Einstein's relativity rejected. One of them, the physicist, inventor and writer Sir Oliver Lodge, author of *The Ether of Space*, left the meeting early, even though he had been expected to speak in the discussion. Later in the month, Lodge expressed his fear in a lecture that 'Einstein's theories would dominate all physics and the next generation of mathematical physicists would have a terrible time'. Even Dyson, surprisingly, shared some of the sceptical feeling – unlike his friend and fellow astronomer, Eddington. Despite being the chief organiser of the expeditions in 1919, Dyson wrote in December to another astronomer in the United States: 'I was myself a sceptic, and expected a different result. Now I am trying to understand the principle of relativity and am gradually getting to think I do.'

Indeed, general relativity would remain legendarily recondite and incomprehensible for a long time to come among scientists, even many astronomers and physicists. A famous story, originally told by Eddington, relates that as the November 1919 meeting was dispersing, a physicist who had published a textbook on special relativity in 1914 came up to him and said: 'Professor Eddington, you must be one of the three persons in the world who understands general relativity.' When Eddington demurred, his colleague persisted 'Don't be modest, Eddington,' and received the reply: 'On the contrary, I am trying to think who the third person is.'

Moreover, the author of the challenging new theory, Einstein, was still a virtually unknown personality in England. (Not even Eddington had met him.) To the press, he was a complete blank. The first report of the meeting in *The Times*, 'Revolution in science', referred only to 'the famous physicist, Einstein', and did not give his first name or the fact that he worked in Berlin. Was he a German, a Swiss, a Jew, or some unfamiliar fusion of all three? Where did he really belong? The following day, 8 November, *The Times* briefly introduced him thus:

> Dr Albert Einstein, whose astronomical discoveries were described at the meeting of Royal Society on Thursday as the most remarkable since the discovery of Neptune, and as propounding a new philosophy of the universe, is a Swiss Jew, 45 years of age. He was for some time Professor in Mathematical Physics at the Polytechnic in Zurich, and then Professor at Prague. Afterwards he was nominated a member of the Kaiser Wilhelm Academy for Research in Berlin, with a salary of 18,000 marks (£900) per annum, and no duties, so that he should be able to devote himself entirely to research work.
>
> During the war, as a man of liberal tendencies, he was one of the signatories of the protest against the German manifesto of the men of science who declared themselves in favour of Germany's part in the war, and at the time of the Armistice he signed an appeal in favour of the German revolution. He is an ardent Zionist and keenly interested in the proposed Hebrew University at Jerusalem, and has offered to cooperate in the work there.

Not only did this report get Einstein's age significantly wrong (he was actually forty years old in 1919), it also failed even to hint at Einstein's open admiration for Newton, Faraday, Maxwell and other British physicists, while dwelling on his attitude to the recent war and his Jewishness. An amused Einstein responded accordingly, citing his status as a 'Swiss Jew' as an example of relativity when contributing a substantial article on 'Time, space, and gravitation' to the newspaper in late November. He remarked:

> The description of me and my circumstances in *The Times* shows an amusing feat of imagination on the part of the writer. By an application of the theory of relativity to the taste

> of readers, today in Germany I am called a German man of science, and in England I am represented as a 'Swiss Jew'. If I come to be regarded as a *bête noire*, the descriptions will be reversed, and I shall become a Swiss Jew for the Germans and a German man of science for the English!

However, *The Times* – which had been notably bellicose during the recent war under its proprietor, Lord Northcliffe – was not so amused. 'He is famous just now,' it commented with a touch of anti-German asperity. 'We concede him his little jest. But we note that, in accordance with the general tenor of his theory, Dr Einstein does not supply any absolute description of himself.'

FAME FOR GENERAL RELATIVITY AND ITS AUTHOR

By now, the University of Cambridge was electrified by Einstein's theory. Gone were the empty colleges and the malaise of war, and in their place had emerged a busy and optimistic inquisitiveness. When Eddington gave a lecture on relativity in the hall of Trinity College, his own – and Newton's – college, on 2 December, the queue for admittance stretched half-way across the Great Court, reported *Nature*:

> and during the lecture the hall was entirely filled with dons and students listening breathlessly to hear an intelligible account, if one could be given, of the new theory. The keen interest was due, no doubt, largely to curiosity stimulated by the newspaper accounts of the subject, but also partly to the feeling, to which at last some hope of satisfaction can be given, that a further great unifying principle is needed in natural philosophy.

(1)

Was ist Relativitäts-Theorie?

Dem Ersuchen Ihres Mitarbeiters, für die „Times" etwas über „Relativität" zu schreiben, komme ich gerne nach. Denn nach dem beklagenswerten Zusammenbruch der früheren regen internationalen Beziehungen der Gelehrten ist mir dies eine willkommene Gelegenheit, meinem Gefühl der Freude und Dankbarkeit den englischen Astronomen und Physikern gegenüber auszusprechen. Es entspricht ganz den grossen und stolzen Traditionen der wissenschaftlichen Arbeit in Ihrem Lande, dass bedeutende Forscher viel Zeit und Mühe, Ihre wissenschaftlichen Institute grosse materielle Mittel aufwendeten, um eine Folgerung einer Theorie zu prüfen, die im Lande Ihrer Feinde während des Krieges vollendet und publiziert worden ist. Wenn es sich bei der Untersuchung des Einflusses des Gravitationsfeldes der Sonne auf die Lichtstrahlen auch um eine rein objektive Angelegenheit handelte, so drängt es mich doch, den englischen Fachgenossen meinen persönlichen Dank für ihr Werk zu sagen; denn ohne dasselbe hätte ich die Prüfung der wichtigsten Konsequenz meiner Theorie wohl nicht mehr erlebt. —

Man kann in der Physik Theorien verschiedener Art unterscheiden. Die meisten sind konstruktive Theorien. Diese suchen aus einem relativ

Einstein's handwritten German draft of an article attempting to explain relativity published in London in *The Times* in November 1919 under the title 'Einstein on his theory: Time, space and gravitation'. This first page begins by expressing his 'joy and gratitude towards the astronomers and physicists of England' for their efforts in testing the implications of 'a theory which was perfected and published during the war in the land of your enemies'.

Oxford was almost equally fascinated. Now the classicists and philosophers who had challenged Lindemann (in person) and Einstein (*in absentia*) earlier in 1919 were compelled to listen to the physicists and astronomers, whether they liked it or not. That December, the world's very first extensive account of Einstein's theory in English aimed at both scientists and non-scientists was published in Oxford. Written by a little-known, German-speaking physicist at the university, Henry Brose, *The Theory of Relativity: An Introductory Sketch based on Einstein's Original Writings including a Biographical Note* was reprinted by its publisher, Basil Blackwell, an astonishing four times over the next four months – such was the curiosity aroused by the solar eclipse expeditions.

Soon, *Punch* magazine compared Einstein's sudden, mysterious celebrity to the simultaneous, if less mysterious celebrity of the sculptor Epstein, in a witty verse:

Einstein and Epstein are wonderful men,
 Bringing new miracles into our ken.
Einstein upset the Newtonian rule;
 Epstein demolished the Pheidian School.
Einstein gave fits to the Royal Society
 Epstein delighted in loud notoriety.
Einstein made parallels meet in infinity
 Epstein remodelled the form of divinity.

An Einstein Society was started by British Members of Parliament. 'Its formation was due more to the curiosity of those of us who had unexpectedly survived the First World War than to any profound scientific search,' recalled one of its members, Sir Colin Coote, who subsequently became editor of the *Daily Telegraph*.

Meanwhile, across the Atlantic Ocean, the leading popular-science magazine *Scientific American* offered a prize of $5,000 for the best essay from any part of the globe explaining Einstein's theories of relativity. During 1920, there were 300 submissions from all parts of Europe and North America, and from India, South Africa and South America. The winner was an Englishman, Lyndon Bolton, who had long been employed as a senior examiner in the British Patent Office – a curious coincidence with Einstein's Patent Office job in Switzerland when he conceived special relativity in 1905.

In his very first letter to Einstein, written at the time of his December 1919 Cambridge lecture, Eddington enthused:

> All England has been talking about your theory. . . . There is no mistaking the genuine enthusiasm in scientific circles and perhaps more particularly in this University. It is the best possible thing that could have happened for scientific relations between England and Germany. I do not anticipate rapid progress towards official reunion, but there is a big advance towards a more reasonable frame of mind among scientific men, and that is even more important than the renewal of formal associations.

Eddington quickly became a fluent and entertaining lecturer on relativity, who captivated large popular audiences in both person and writing. But his students and fellow specialists saw a different side of him, which was often confused and hesitant, as he wrestled with difficulties in the theory during the very process of lecturing. A student parodied the beginning of a typical Eddington lecture with a touch of cruelty as follows: '[He] gave a moan and then stopped for what seemed a very long time. He then moaned again and stopped again for a very long time. Then he shook his head vigorously and said: "No! That's wrong." ' An American professor specialising in relativity, W. H. Williams, captured this bemusement more affectionately in 'The Einstein and the Eddington', a poem based on Lewis Carroll's 'The Walrus and the Carpenter', written for a faculty club dinner in Eddington's honour (quoted here in extract):

The time has come, said Eddington,
To talk of many things;
Of cubes and clocks and meter-sticks,
And why a pendulum swings,
And how far space is out of plumb,
And whether time has wings.
I learned at school the apple's fall
To gravity was due,
But now you tell me that the cause
Is merely G mu nu.
I cannot bring myself to think
That this is really true.
. . .
And space, it has dimensions four,
Instead of only three.
The square on the hypotenuse
Ain't what it used to be.
It grieves me sore, the things you've done
To plane geometry.
You hold that time is badly warped,
That even light is bent;
I think I get the idea there,
If this is what you meant:
The mail the postman brings today,
Tomorrow will be sent.

...
The shortest line, Einstein replied,
Is not the one that's straight;
It curves around upon itself,
Much like the figure eight,
And if you go too rapidly
You will arrive too late.
But Easter day is Christmas time
And far away is near,
And two and two is more than four
And over there is here.
You may be right, said Eddington,
It seems a trifle queer.

Another letter to Einstein in late 1919, this one from an English physicist much less well known than Eddington – living in industrial Sheffield rather than establishment Cambridge – struck a remarkably similar note to Eddington's letter. Regarding the eclipse observations: 'People here have been talking of nothing else for the past few weeks.' And regarding their potential impact on Anglo-German relations: 'Now that I am back in my home country, it is my dearest wish to work towards healing the deep wounds inflicted on the hearts of mankind by this war as quickly as possible and towards reviving opportunities for continued collaboration.'

Its author, Robert Lawson, a Quaker scientist (like Eddington), had attended a lecture by Einstein, followed by a lively discussion, in Vienna in 1913, while working as a post-graduate student in the Radium Institute. At the outbreak of war in 1914, Lawson had been confined as an enemy alien. But then, for four years, his Austrian physicist colleagues at Vienna University had looked after him and enabled him to continue his experiments, for which Lawson was deeply grateful, despite his difficult living conditions. After he explained this background to Einstein in two introductory letters, they immediately struck up a relationship. Einstein replied to Lawson: 'thank God, the solar eclipse and the theory of relativity have nothing in common with politics. In this work, English men of science have behaved splendidly throughout, and to my delight your letter shows me that the feelings of English colleagues have not been influenced as much by the war as one might have feared.' Within the last few days, he added, he had received 'a very charming letter' from Eddington, which had greatly pleased him. Using these favourable circumstances he planned to work as much as possible towards reconciliation between German and English colleagues.

Lawson forthwith proposed that he should translate Einstein's German introduction to relativity, published in 1916, into English; and Einstein quickly agreed. He had never been satisfied by his book, which was too demanding for the general reader. (He liked to quote against himself a remark once made by Planck, that 'Einstein believes his books will become more readily intelligible if every now and again he drops in the words "Dear reader"'.) However, its English version, *Relativity: The Special and the General Theory*, published in London in August 1920 – nine months after the pioneering Oxford introduction by Brose – was a bestseller: it was reprinted six times in nineteen months, and remains in print a century later. This short book is probably still the best non-academic treatment of relativity, thanks to Lawson's careful and creative work, with the active assistance of Einstein.

Some idea of Lawson's achievement can be divined from a letter sent to him by the book's forthcoming publisher, Methuen, which Lawson passed on to Einstein with great amusement in February 1920. The publisher requested Lawson:

> When you send in the matter for the prospectus of Einstein's book I shall be glad if you will make the description of its contents as intelligible as possible to the ordinary man. Our travellers tell us that there is complete ignorance in the public mind as to what Relativity means. A good many people seem to think that the book deals with the relations between the sexes. Perhaps you would explain the meaning of the word and say something about the epoch-making character of the book and how Einstein's discovery affects Newton's law. Most people have heard of Newton and his apple and that will give some kind of clue.

At this time, such a formidable level of public ignorance of relativity would still have been mildly surprising to Einstein. But not for much longer. From 1920 onwards, as the 'relativity circus' got going and his fame spread around the world, the very incomprehensibility of Einstein's theory made newspapers all the hungrier for information about the personality behind it. And once he was contacted and interviewed – initially by *The Times* and the *New York Times* in November 1919 – Einstein rapidly proved to be a deft, witty, occasionally mischievous and often eminently quotable populariser of his own ideas. Never, or at least hardly ever, did he lay down the law as a recognised authority and expect others to defer; rather he showed a genuine humility and willingness to learn from those he respected. While he was not by nature a great teacher, because he had too many original ideas, Einstein had a gift for making himself understood (though generally in German). For press reporters, a willing Einstein interview almost always made for excellent copy. Even he, though, could not transform relativity into more than a tantalising concept for the non-mathematically minded. During the 1920s, it became widely believed that 'Einstein taught everything is relative, including truth; that all observations are subjective; that anything is possible', according to the authors of *Einstein as Myth and Muse*. In his later years, besieged with requests from journalists and the public, Einstein was reduced to telling his secretary to give casual enquirers the following light-hearted explanation of relativity: 'An hour sitting with a pretty girl on a park bench passes like a minute, but a minute sitting on a hot stove seems like an hour.'

FIRST VISIT TO ENGLAND

Consider the earliest national newspaper coverage of Einstein's first visit to England in 1921, accompanied by his second wife, Elsa, on his way back to Germany from giving lectures in the United States. At the University of Manchester, a major centre for physics (home to Rutherford before he moved to Cambridge, and also to Rutherford's collaborator and Einstein's friend, Niels Bohr), Einstein accepted an honorary doctorate in science and delivered a lecture on 9 June 1921 to an audience of about 1,000 staff, students and others, on 'Relativity'. Speaking in German, he stuck closely to science, and did not allow himself even a single sentence on the philosophical implications of his discoveries, 'though that would, no doubt, have been appreciated by his audience', noted a serious report of the lecture in the *Manchester Guardian*.

But his wise forbearance did not prevent the newspaper from publishing the following additional commentary by an anonymous staff writer:

> Einstein himself has become, with amazing rapidity, the hero not only of the scientist and the scholar, but also of the populace. The reason is not hard to seek. The man in the street, a traveller between life and death, is compact of all elements,

> and is neither wholly devoid of science nor of poetry. He may have few ideas in either, but he probably cherishes what he has, and whatever touches them nearly is of moment to him.
>
> Professor Einstein's theory of Relativity, however vaguely he [the man in the street] may comprehend it, disturbs fundamentally his basic conceptions of the universe and even of his own mind. It challenges somehow the absolute nature of his thought. The very idea that he can use his mind in a disinterested way is assailed by a conception which gives partiality to every perception. And with this keen thrust at personal things, the idea of Relativity stretches out to the very conceptions of the universe, as can be seen from the mere titles of the closing chapters in Professor Einstein's little book on the subject.
>
> Definite ideas emerge, even, on the shape of the universe itself, and the finite and the infinite are made to lie down comfortably together by deductions from the relativity of our daily observations. Everything, it has been said, assimilates to the nature of music. Professor Einstein is a musician in his leisure moments, and his science seems to bear some relation to that art, in which everything is thought of in terms of movement and relation, and the fixed only as something arbitrary.

To put it politely, this brief editorial is a feeble parody, rather than an informed appraisal, of why Einstein's relativity matters to non-scientists. Yet, it does have at least this much historical value: it demonstrates beyond doubt the gulf of misunderstanding between the public and Einstein's science, to which the man himself was constantly exposed after he became famous – even in his favourite country for physics.

From Manchester, on the day after the lecture, Einstein and his wife moved south to London. Their host, Lord Richard

Haldane, bade them welcome to his house at Queen Anne's Gate for the duration of their stay in the capital. Having attended a meeting of the Royal Astronomical Society, at which Eddington gave an account of the solar eclipse expeditions in 1919, the Einsteins had dinner at the Haldanes with Eddington, Dyson, Thomson, Whitehead, the Archbishop of Canterbury (Randall Davidson) and others, and met George Bernard Shaw during an after-dinner reception. At some point, Archbishop Davidson said cautiously to Einstein of relativity: 'Lord Haldane tells us that your theory ought to make a great difference to our morals.' But Einstein refused to be drawn (as in his Manchester lecture), and replied simply: 'Do not believe a word of it. It makes no difference. It is purely abstract – science.' After dinner, Davidson's wife explained to Einstein's wife how a friend had been speaking of Professor Einstein's theory 'especially in its mystical aspect'. Elsa broke into laughter and cried: 'Mystical! Mystical! My husband mystical!'

Haldane, born in Edinburgh into a distinguished family (including scientists), had studied philosophy with honours at the University of Edinburgh and then at Göttingen University in the 1870s. The combination gave him both a lifelong sympathy for Germany and the German language – which he spoke fluently – and an urge to write books on philosophy, including *The Reign of Relativity*, published at the time of Einstein's visit. (This treatise, arguing that the principle of relativity 'will be found to date back to the days of ancient Greece', though none too relevant to physics and somewhat ponderous in style, nevertheless went through three impressions in four months during 1921.) After a career as a successful barrister, Haldane entered politics in 1885 as a Scottish Liberal, in due course serving as secretary of state for war from 1905 to 1912 – during which he negotiated with the arrogant Kaiser Wilhelm II and also attempted to reduce the armed rivalry between Britain and Germany – and then as lord chancellor from 1912 to 1915, until he was hounded from office after a wartime propaganda campaign alleging that he had pro-German sympathies. 'In a post-war Britain drained of most things except bitterness, Haldane was therefore in a delicate position vis-à-vis the Germans,' wrote Clark. 'It was certainly courageous of Einstein to have come so willingly to London; it was equally courageous of Haldane to be his host.'

Although Einstein and Haldane appeared very different in background, interests and achievements, Einstein undoubtedly appreciated Haldane for his character and practicality, if not so much for his philosophy. (As Einstein ironically remarked in the mid-1920s about philosophers of relativity, 'the less they know about physics the more they philosophise'.) Long after Haldane's death in 1928, Einstein paid this warm tribute in a letter to Haldane's biographer: 'Lord Haldane was a man of kind and subtle feelings as is so rare in the case of men of quite unusual energy and working capacity,' who somehow 'gave the impression of a person whose leading motive was to serve in humility the causes he thought worthy.' By way of example, Einstein recalled an occasion during his visit to England when Haldane told him of a trip to a mining district that he was due to make in order to give a popular lecture to the miners. 'I never had the feeling that there was anything worthwhile for which he would not easily find the necessary time and strength.'

The highlight of Einstein's London visit was his lecture at King's College on 13 June in the afternoon – after Einstein, accompanied by Haldane, had laid a wreath on the grave of Newton at Westminster Abbey in the morning. Arranged in April by Haldane with the principal of King's, Sir Ernest Barker, the lecture was an unpredictable occasion – symbolised by the fact that Einstein left it to the college to decide his fee (£90), and then elected to donate almost half of this for the relief of distressed students in the universities of central Europe. 'I was almost terrified by the commotion which his lecture excited, but I was still more elated by its success,' Barker wrote in his memoirs, published in 1953. 'Feeling against Germany was very much stronger after the war of 1914–18 than it has been since the war of 1939–45; and there were fears that the lecture might be disturbed or even prevented. Those fears proved groundless; but they were succeeded by other and opposite fears' – of being overwhelmed by the potential audience. There was a great demand for tickets, 'and we now began to fear that the lecture would be disturbed, or even prevented, by an uncontrollable crowd of would-be listeners – listeners, by the way, who would probably understand nothing, being ignorant alike of German and of relativity, but would none the less be eager to listen.'

In the event, the lecture hall was packed out but orderly, with scores of students standing all round the walls. Yet, according to a detailed and scientifically well-informed eye-witness report in the *Nation & Athenaeum*, there was no welcoming applause after Haldane got to his feet and introduced Einstein with the words: 'You are in the presence of the Newton of the twentieth century, of a man who has effected a greater revolution in thought than that of Copernicus, Galileo, and even Newton himself.' The report continued:

> One felt the slight shock in the air. For, after all, is not Einstein a German? But Lord Haldane, smiling, wary, and implacable, drove the point home. They had to swallow it whole: the dose was not minimised, however indecent the truth might appear that the greatest scientific man the latter centuries have produced is a German Jew. One glanced at Einstein: he was patient, dreamy, looking at nothing.

Einstein on his first visit to England, June 1921. He is being photographed in London at the home of his host Lord Richard Haldane (second from left), a former lord chancellor, lifelong Germanophile and author of a bestselling philosophical study of relativity.

And then Lord Haldane, still with the resolute smile, went on to speak of Einstein's violin playing. The audience relaxed; everybody felt relieved. He had the technique of a first-class professional, we were told, and more understanding of what he played than most first-class professionals. One glanced again at Einstein. He was beaming. He sat twisting his fingers in embarrassed pleasure, his face shining with delight. So he is, after all, susceptible to flattery.

Now Einstein himself began to speak, in German, without notes, blackboard or mathematical formulae, and also without hesitation or repetition. He opened with a heartfelt, but also politically astute, tribute to English physics:

> It is a special joy for me to be able to speak in the capital of the country from where the most important ideas of theoretical physics were brought into the world. I think of the theories of the motion of masses and of gravitation, which Newton gave us, and of the concept of the electromagnetic field by Faraday and Maxwell, which provided physics with a new foundation. One may well say that the theory of relativity brought a kind of conclusion to Maxwell's and Lorentz's grand framework of ideas by trying to extend the physics of fields to all of its phenomena, gravitation included.

Then he turned to the subject of the evening's lecture: relativity. He wanted to emphasise, he said, that relativity was a theory that was not speculative in origin, but rather had arisen from his desire to adapt theoretical physics to observable facts as closely as possible. Hence relativity was the natural development of a path that could be followed over the centuries. Its abandonment of certain concepts of space, time and motion, hitherto regarded as fundamental, 'must not be perceived as voluntary, but only as enforced by observed facts'.

Here, one might have expected a reference to the recent confirmation of general relativity by the 'observed facts' of the 1919 eclipse expeditions. But, strangely, these were never mentioned by Einstein himself, either in the various reports of the lecture or in its published version.

The silence from the audience continued. Then at some point Einstein paused and said, in German: 'My lecture is already a little long.' There came a storm of encouraging applause from all parts of the hall. 'I shall take that as an invitation,' he said, smiling, and the applause was redoubled. 'But my further remarks will not be so easy to follow,' he continued, and everybody laughed with him. At the end of the lecture, his ovation lasted for several minutes – 'and surely not least for his courage', noted a German-Jewish listener, recalling the occasion in a letter to *The Times* in 1933, after the rise of Nazism.

At a grand dinner for Einstein that evening in King's College, Barker said in his speech:

> We welcome you twice, for discovering a new truth which has added to the knowledge of the universe, and for coming to us from a country that was lately our enemy to knit again the broken threads of international science. If at your command the straight lines have been banished from our universe, there is yet one straight line which will always remain – the straight line of right and justice. May both our nations follow this straight line side by side in a parallel movement, which, in spite of Euclid, will yet bring them together in friendship with one another and with the other nations of the world.

Among those present was Lindemann, who was meeting Einstein in person after a gap of ten years (since their first meeting at the Solvay Congress in Brussels in 1911). The following morning, 14 June, Lindemann whisked the Einsteins away from London by car in order to give Einstein his first glimpse of Oxford. An announcement in *The Times* on 15 June stated: 'Professor Einstein paid a private visit to Oxford yesterday as the guest of Dr Lindeman [*sic*], of Wadham College. A tour was made of the principal University buildings, and the Professor returned to London in the evening.'

Unfortunately, neither Einstein nor Lindemann recorded any impressions of the visit. It must have been brief, since the Einsteins in fact returned to London earlier than mentioned that day, by an afternoon train. Presumably Lindemann, probably at Einstein's request, did not introduce him to any of his colleagues and friends, so that the Einsteins could have enough time to see the buildings. They did not meet even the university's vice-chancellor. As Lindemann commented in a scribbled letter from Oxford to Haldane: 'I enclose a note [for Einstein] which the vice-chancellor just brought here. He said he much regretted not having known of Einstein's visit in time to offer him some hospitality.' Then Lindemann congratulated Haldane on hosting Einstein in England: 'Whatever anyone may hold about political matters, there is no doubt that international cooperation is absolutely essential in scientific questions and you have, I feel sure, done more to re-establish good relations by your reception of Einstein than anybody else could have done by years of endeavour.' To which Haldane responded the following day after talking to Einstein in London: 'They both enjoyed greatly their visit to Oxford and to yourself.' He added: 'Yes. I think that the German ambassador was right when he said to me on Monday evening [after Einstein's London lecture] that the reception of

Einstein in England would do something towards making the way smoother for the approach to better international relations. Our people have behaved in a manner worthy of them.'

Certainly Einstein's view chimed with Haldane's (and Lindemann's). A few days after returning to Germany on 17 June, he wrote to thank Haldane with transparently sincere emotion: 'The wonderful experiences in England are still fresh in my mind and yet like a dream. The impression this land with its wonderful intellectual and political tradition left on me was a profound and lasting one, even larger than I had expected.' He was extremely grateful, he said, for his 'extraordinary reception', and especially for the fact that influential individuals in England had expressed an open desire for international understanding. He concluded by thanking Haldane personally, together with Haldane's sister, 'from the bottom of my heart' for their generous hospitality, kindness and friendliness.

'There is no doubt that your visit has had more tangible results in improving the relations between our two countries than any other single event,' Haldane replied. 'Your name is a power in our country.'

CHAPTER THREE

A Stinking Flower in a German Buttonhole

A funny lot, these Germans. To them I am a stinking flower, and yet they keep putting me into their buttonhole.

Comment by Einstein in his travel diary in Argentina,
April 1925

Einstein's growing fame and generous personal welcome in England in 1919–21 must have been a piquant experience for him. For back home in Germany, in striking contrast with England, this same period saw the birth of a vociferous anti-relativity movement – among a few notable scientists and some philosophers but also among the general public – culminating in the publication in 1931 of an anti-relativity book in German with the revealing title, *A Hundred Authors against Einstein*. Although this was not essentially an anti-Semitic publication, the anti-relativity movement coincided with increasing abuse of Einstein as a Jew, accentuated by his declared sympathy from 1921 onwards for the Zionist goal of establishing a Jewish national home in Palestine, in addition to abuse of his increasing sympathy for international pacifism.

As a result, during the first half of the 1920s, Einstein found himself in a disturbing position. He was promoted and hailed as an important cultural ambassador for the Weimar Republic when he travelled and lectured in many countries – ranging from the United States and then England in 1921 to Japan in 1922, Palestine in 1923 and South America in 1925. Yet he was also fiercely attacked by many Germans, at home and abroad, and even placed at risk of assassination by right-wing extremists – as had happened to Walther Rathenau in 1922. In Argentina, for example, the German ambassador reported to his masters in Berlin on Einstein's 1925 visit: 'For the first time, a world-famous German scholar came here, and his naïve, kindly, perhaps somewhat unworldly manner had an extraordinary appeal for the local population. One could not find a better man to counter the hostile propaganda of lies, and to destroy the fable of German barbarism.' And yet, the ambassador admitted, the local German community in Argentina had boycotted all Einstein-related events because its members objected to his pacifism. Several times in this period, Einstein seriously contemplated leaving Germany for good. Such personal tribulations gave him advance warning – ahead of most other Germans – of what to expect from the Nazi Party a decade later.

The anti-relativity movement – dubbed the 'Anti-relativity Company' by Einstein – was started in 1920 by a graduate engineer and covert anti-Semite with journalistic and political ambitions and hidden financial backing, Paul Weyland. For scientific respectability Weyland recruited Ernst Gehrcke, an experimental physicist at the Reich Physical and Technical Institute and professor at the University of Berlin, who had been attempting to refute relativity in print since 1911. Neither Weyland nor Gehrcke was of much distinction. But they were soon supported by the physics Nobel laureate Lenard, who had won the prize in 1905. Even before the First World War, Lenard resented what he saw as insufficient British recognition of his experimental physics. During the war he apparently wrote to a physicist colleague fighting at the front 'expressing his hope that the defeat of the English would make amends for their never having cited him decently', noted Philip Ball in *Serving the Reich*, his history of German physics under the Nazis. Antagonistic by nature, Lenard became an anti-Semite after the war, and a follower of Hitler as early as 1924. 'He invented the difference between "German" and "Jewish" physics,' commented Born much later; and after 1933 (along with another Nobel laureate, Johannes Stark), he would set about cleansing German science of Jews. (In his book, *German Physics*, published in 1936, Lenard wrote: 'In contrast to the intractable and solicitous desire for truth in the Aryan scientists, the Jew lacks to a striking degree any comprehension of truth.') Einstein's very public appreciation by English physicists, combined with his Jewishness, infuriated Lenard from the start. 'This, however,' Ball suggested with black humour, 'was no more than one could expect from a nation of vulgar materialists – Lenard would surely have sympathy with Napoleon's remark about shopkeepers – who knew nothing of the heroic selfless Germanic *Kultur*.'

During August 1920, the movement announced twenty meetings to be held in the biggest towns in Germany. With its headquarters in Berlin, Weyland and his sponsors hired the Berlin Philharmonic Hall for a set-piece opening demonstration against both relativity and its internationally celebrated author, scheduled for 24 August. Einstein, and some distinguished physicist friends, made an unscheduled appearance by hiring a box to watch the proceedings – and be watched by the audience. 'As the speakers went on, attacking relativity, omitting, distorting, unbalancing, appealing to the good Aryan common sense of their audience and invoking its members not to take such stuff seriously, the clown that lies not far below genius began to show itself,' noted Einstein's biographer Clark. Sometimes Einstein was observed to burst into laughter and clap his hands in mock applause. At the end of the meeting he told his friends: 'That was most amusing.' But behind this façade he was really furious, because Weyland and Gehrcke had accused him not only of scientific charlatanry and self-advertisement but had also implied that he had plagiarised the work of an obscure Pomeranian schoolmaster, Paul Gerber. For two days after the event, he first toyed with the notion of abandoning Germany, as was reported in the Berlin press. In an interview, he remarked: 'I feel like a man lying in a good bed, but plagued by bedbugs.'

Stung by the public meeting's accusations, Einstein hit back with an article published on 27 August, headlined 'My response. On the Anti-relativity Company', in the columns of a liberal daily newspaper, the *Berliner Tageblatt* – an unprecedented forum for a respected university scientist in the more staid scientific world of those days. He began:

Herr Weyland and Herr Gehrcke recently delivered a first lecture in this tenor at the Philharmonic; I myself was present. I am very well aware that both speakers are not worthy of an answer from my pen, because I have good reason to believe that motives other than the striving for truth are at the bottom of this business. (If I were a German nationalist with or without a swastika instead of a Jew with liberal international views, then . . .). I only answer because well-meaning circles have repeatedly urged me to make my opinion known.

First, I want to note that today, to my knowledge, there is hardly a scientist among those who have made substantial contributions to theoretical physics who would not admit that the theory of relativity in its entirety is founded on a logical basis and is in agreement with experimental facts which to date have been reliably established. The most important theoretical physicists – namely, H. A. Lorentz, M. Planck, Sommerfeld, Laue, Born, Larmor, Eddington, Debye, Langevin, Levi-Civita – support the theory, and most of them have made valuable contributions to it. As a pronounced opponent of the theory of relativity among physicists of international reputation I would have to name only Lenard. I admire Lenard as a master of experimental physics; but he has not yet produced anything outstanding in theoretical physics, and his objections to the general theory of relativity are of such superficiality that up to now I did not think it necessary to answer them in detail. I intend to make up for this.

I have been accused of running a tasteless advertising campaign for the theory of relativity. But I can say that all my life I have been a friend of well-chosen, sober words and of concise presentation. Highfalutin phrases and words give me goose bumps whether they deal with the theory of relativity or with anything else. I have often made fun of effusions that are now finally attributed to me. Besides, I am happy to let the *Herren* of the Company have their fun.

Having gone on to deal with some of Gehrcke's scientific objections to relativity (including his egregious omission of the celebrated confirmation by foreign astronomers of general relativity in 1919), Einstein concluded his salvo with a reference to Holland and Britain: 'Seeing how the theory and its creator are slandered in such a manner in Germany will make a strange impression in foreign countries, especially with my Dutch and British colleagues H. A. Lorentz and Eddington, gentleman who worked intensively in the field of relativity and repeatedly gave lectures on this subject matter.' The accuracy of his prediction is revealed by an internal memo dated 2 September 1920 from the German chargé d'affaires in London to the foreign ministry in Berlin: 'The attacks on Prof. Einstein and the agitation against the well-known scientist are making a very bad impression over here,' it reported. 'At the present moment in particular Prof. Einstein is a cultural factor of the first rank, as Einstein's name is known in the broadest circles. We should not drive out of Germany a man with whom we could make real cultural propaganda.'

Einstein's best friends in Germany were horrified by his newspaper article, and told him so. Ehrenfest could not believe that some of its phrases were from the pen of Einstein himself. Sommerfeld reported that various people had told him the article did not seem worthy of the Einstein they personally knew, though Sommerfeld supported Einstein's aggressive comparison of his critics with 'bedbugs'. Born and his wife felt that Einstein had been 'goaded into that rather unfortunate reply in the newspapers'. To which Einstein responded: 'Don't be too hard on me.

Drawing of Einstein by William Rothenstein, 1927. Rothenstein was principal of the Royal College of Art in London and a leading British portraitist. Einstein sat for the artist in his study in Berlin, where there was a single framed print on the wall, according to Rothenstein: a portrait of the physicist James Clerk Maxwell.

Everyone has to sacrifice at the altar of stupidity from time to time, to please the Deity and the human race.'

In truth, the article's tone was an expression of Einstein's lifelong 'impudence' towards authority (to recall the word he used of his graduate student self, back in 1901). And it would define the tenor of his contradictory relationship with politics in Germany, whether under Kaiser Wilhelm or the Weimar Republic. Although he felt a deep loyalty to German science, about Germany itself Einstein was always ambivalent. As he had written in 1915 in a contribution to a wartime patriotic book requested by the officers of the Berlin Goethe League: 'The state, to which I belong as a citizen, plays not the slightest role in my emotional life; I regard a person's relations with the state as a business matter, rather like one's relations with a life assurance company' – a comment which the League had refused to publish.

JEWISHNESS AND ANTI-SEMITISM

No doubt Einstein's Jewishness contributed to his ambivalence, although its role is difficult to analyse, not least because it altered over time. While trying to get established as a scientist in his twenties Einstein knew very well that his search for an academic post had been hampered by his Jewishness. A 1901 letter from his future wife, Mileva, to her best friend makes it plain: 'you know that my darling has a very wicked tongue and on top of it he is a Jew'. That said, in Switzerland Einstein was not confronted with 'the virulent anti-Semitism common among German students of this period', as Ze'ev Rosenkranz noted in *Einstein before Israel*. However, discreet anti-Semitism was evident in Einstein's first successful academic appointment, at the University of Zurich in 1909. The dean of the department wrote confidentially:

> Herr Dr Einstein is an Israelite, and . . . the Israelites are credited among scholars with a variety of disagreeable character traits, such as importunateness, impertinence, a shopkeeper's mind in their understanding of their academic position, etc., and in numerous cases with some justification. On the other hand, it may be said that among the Israelites, too, there are men without even a trace of these unpleasant characteristics and that it would therefore not be appropriate to disqualify a man merely because he happens to be a Jew.

Einstein's own attitude at this time was summarised in his private comment on the Jews from wealthy families in Zurich who were *Privatdozents* (teaching assistants – the position for which he himself was rejected in 1907) but who continued to aspire to be professors, purely for reasons of social acceptance, despite being repeatedly passed over for promotion. 'Why are these fellows, who make out very comfortably by private means, so anxious to land state-paid positions? Why all that humble tail-wagging to the state?' Their subservience showed a lack of proper pride, he felt.

Although Einstein's parents and immediate family believed in pursuing a high degree of Jewish assimilation into German society, he himself was less persuaded, and moved further and further away from this view with age. His Jewish friend Haber's desire to be a Prussian – to the extent of having himself baptised a Protestant in the 1890s – was quite beyond the pale for Einstein, who never felt that he 'was Jewish, but wished he weren't and tried to pretend that he wasn't' (as was said of the physicist J. Robert Oppenheimer, Einstein's colleague at Princeton). Nor did he agree with another Jewish friend, Born, who came from a highly assimilated family and regarded the anti-Semitic expressions and measures of pre-1918 Germany as 'unjustified humiliations'. Einstein's basic view, prior to the appalling excesses of the Nazi period, was that anti-Semitism, though unquestionably unpleasant, was to be expected in any multi-ethnic society, and was 'not to be got rid of by well-meaning propaganda. Nationalities want to pursue their own path, not to blend. A satisfactory state of affairs can only be brought about by mutual toleration and respect.' (As Born admitted in the 1960s: 'History has shown that Einstein was the more profound.')

The corollary to this attitude, for Einstein, was that Jews should build up their own sense of self-assurance and look after their own kind, rather than seeking acceptance and help from their host societies. In 1920, he therefore declined to attend a meeting organised by the Central Association of German Citizens of the Jewish Faith intended to help fight anti-Semitism in academic circles. 'I am neither a German citizen, nor is there anything in me which can be designated as "Jewish faith",' Einstein informed the organisers. 'But I am a Jew and am glad to belong to the Jewish people, even if I do not consider them in any way God's elect. Let us calmly leave anti-Semitism to the non-Jew and retain our love for people of our own kind.'

Einstein felt that he was bound to other Jews by tribal ties, not by ties of religion. Hence the German word, *Stammesgenossen*, he would typically use when referring to fellow Jews, meaning 'tribal companions', rather than the more orthodox 'co-religionists'. His earliest use of it appears to have been in 1914 in a letter he sent from Berlin rejecting an invitation from the Academy in St Petersburg to visit Tsarist Russia, because of the Russian empire's history of anti-Jewish pogroms: 'It goes against the grain to travel without necessity to a country where my tribal companions were so brutally persecuted.' He used the term again in 1921, while arguing with Haber about why, by contrast, he was willing to visit the United States as part of a Zionist fund-raising mission for settling Jews in Palestine: 'Naturally, I am needed not for my abilities but solely for my name, from whose publicity value a substantial effect is expected among the rich tribal companions in Dollaria.'

FOR AND AGAINST ZIONISM

His growing feeling of solidarity with the Jewish tribe was, of course, what first sparked Einstein's interest in Zionism. In his Berlin-based talks in 1919–20 with a German-Jewish writer, Alexander Moszkowski, published as *Conversations with Einstein* soon after, Zionism was not even mentioned (nor was Judaism). It was the anti-Semitism Einstein experienced in Germany after August 1920 that sharpened his commitment and drew him towards the Zionist fold.

However, being Einstein – a self-confessed 'lone traveller' – he never formally joined the Zionist organisation. 'The Zionists' always remained 'them' for Einstein, noted Rosenkranz; 'they did not make the all-important transition to "us"'. Freedom and independence always came first for him; tribal loyalty second. From 1921 onwards, he would be selfless in helping the Zionists to raise money, especially for the Hebrew University in Jerusalem, but he would not toe the Zionists' line when he disagreed with their nationalism, especially their antagonism towards the Arab population in Palestine.

His very personal, dichotomous amalgam of commitment and rejection led Einstein both to admire and to condemn Chaim Weizmann, the leader of Zionism from the 1920s and the first president of the state of Israel. The prickly synergy between the two men involved not only Jewish tribalism and German nationalism but also British colonial politics, and even science. (Weizmann struggled to understand relativity but joked that after Einstein had explained it to him many times, 'I was fully convinced that he understood it.') According to Sir Isaiah Berlin, a Jew born in Russia who made his career as a political philosopher at the University of Oxford, who knew both Weizmann and Einstein personally:

> Weizmann's relationship with Einstein, despite their deep mutual admiration for each other, remained ambivalent; Weizmann was inclined to regard Einstein as an impractical idealist inclined to utopian attitudes in politics. Einstein, in his turn, looked on Weizmann as too much of a *Realpolitiker*, and was irritated by his failure to press for reforms in the [Hebrew] University away from what he regarded as an undesirable American collegiate pattern. Nevertheless, they remained allies and friends to the end of their lives.

Weizmann, like Berlin, was a Russian-born Jew, whose twin careers in science and politics were made by England. He emigrated there, via Germany, in 1904; established himself as a biochemist at the University of Manchester; became a British citizen in 1910; and retained British citizenship until his appointment as the first president of Israel in 1948. During the First World War he was a key scientist for the Allied cause – like Haber for imperial Germany – with his discovery of a particular strain of bacterium that could synthesise acetone, a compound vital for the manufacture of the explosive cordite. Throughout the war Weizmann worked in British government service, and became director of the Admiralty's laboratories from 1916 to 1919, initially under A. J. Balfour, the first lord of the Admiralty.

He had been actively interested in Zionism since the 1880s and had first visited Jerusalem in 1907. While undertaking his war-related research, Weizmann also laboured to promote Zionist interests in Palestine with the support of the British government.

In 1916, Balfour left the Admiralty for the Foreign Office. By mid-1917, Weizmann's influence through Balfour was such that the issue of Palestine was discussed in the war cabinet. In November 1917, the Balfour Declaration of the British government's support for a Jewish national home in Palestine was announced in a letter to Lord Rothschild, a leader of the British Jewish community. In early 1919, Weizmann represented the Zionist organisation at the Versailles peace conference. In the following year, the British Mandate of Palestine was created out of the former territory of the Ottoman Empire; it would last until the creation of Israel, led by Weizmann, in 1948.

Soon after this key British political development in 1920, Weizmann began to cultivate Einstein as an ally of the Zionist cause. It was a propitious moment to do so, coming in the wake of the anti-relativity movement and the rise of German anti-Semitism against Einstein, plus the confirmation of general relativity in November 1919 (news of which was first communicated to Einstein in Berlin by the Central Zionist Bureau in London) that made Einstein a worldwide political asset for Jews. By 1921, 'Einstein and the Zionist movement very much needed each other', according to Rosenkranz. 'Indeed, his personal needs and their organisational needs coalesced to form a highly advantageous constellation for both parties.'

In February that year, Weizmann – who was yet to meet Einstein in person – sent a telegram from England to Germany addressed to a key Zionist in Berlin, Kurt Blumenfeld. Weizmann knew that Blumenfeld had been courting Einstein since early 1919 without fully persuading him of the merits of Zionism. 'I was to stir up Einstein,' Blumenfeld reported in his memoirs, and convince him to accompany Weizmann to the United States in order to raise funds from American Jews, particularly for the proposed Hebrew University.

When Blumenfeld went to see Einstein with Weizmann's telegram, he initially met with a refusal. Einstein said he was not fully convinced by the idea of the Jerusalem university. 'Besides, I consider that the role which is expected of me is an unworthy one. I am not an orator. I can contribute nothing convincing, and they only need my name which is now in the public eye.'

Blumenfeld chose not to respond to this, and instead read the telegram aloud again. Then he added: 'Weizmann represents Zionism. He alone can make decisions. He is the president of our organisation, and if you take your conversion to Zionism seriously, then I have the right to ask you, in Dr Weizmann's name, to go with him to the United States and to do what he at the moment thinks is necessary.'

To Blumenfeld's 'boundless astonishment', this exhortation to obey authority proved unexpectedly powerful. Einstein answered: 'What you say now is right and convincing. With argument and counter-argument we get no further. To you Weizmann's telegram is a command. I realise that I myself am now part of the situation and that I must accept the invitation. Telegram Weizmann that I agree.'

When this news was announced by the Zionist organisation, there was universal opposition in Germany, particularly among Jews. Einstein's friend Haber wrote him a heartfelt and eloquent four-page letter begging him to change his mind. According to Haber, Einstein's affiliation to Zionism would damage, not assist, the prospects of German Jews:

> To the whole world you are today the most important of German Jews. If at this moment you demonstratively fraternise with the British and their friends, people in this country will see this as evidence of the disloyalty of the Jews. Such a lot of Jews went to war, have perished, or become

> impoverished without complaining, because they regarded it as their duty. Their lives and death have not liquidated anti-Semitism, but have degraded it into something hateful and undignified in the eyes of those who represent the dignity of this country. Do you wish to wipe out the gain of so much blood and suffering of German Jews by your behaviour? . . . You will certainly sacrifice the narrow basis upon which the existence of academic teachers and students of the Jewish faith at German universities rests.

Replying by return, Einstein admitted some reservations about the timing and nature of the US visit, yet argued for its fundamental validity on grounds that went beyond the particular situation of assimilated German Jews such as Haber: 'Despite my internationalist beliefs I have always felt an obligation to stand up for my persecuted and morally oppressed tribal companions as far as is within my power.' Therefore much more was involved in his decision than an act of loyalty or disloyalty. The establishment of a Jewish university 'fills me with particular joy, having recently seen countless instances of perfidious and loveless treatment of splendid young Jews, with attempts to cut off their chances of education'.

In the event, during Einstein's visit to the United States in April–May 1921 – his very first overseas trip – and in his other world travels during the 1920s, Einstein's Jewishness received less attention abroad than it did in Germany (with the obvious exception of his visit to Palestine), except in Jewish and Zionist circles in those countries. In England, for example, in June 1921, it was naturally prominent when Einstein addressed the Manchester University Jewish Students' Society on the subject of the Jerusalem university. But it went unmentioned in newspaper reports on his lectures on relativity in Manchester and

London (and also in Lord Haldane's lengthy philosophical book, *The Reign of Relativity*). So much so, in fact, that a commentator in the *Jewish Chronicle* felt obliged to complain:

> Recall Einstein's visit a week or two ago. He was acclaimed as the greatest mind of our age; his simplicity of demeanour, his ability to produce sweet music were favourably commented upon. But not once did I see it stated that Einstein is a Jew. I do not think that this point needs stressing. Jews may sometimes produce a great genius: other peoples may sometimes do no less. But when (in breach of the ninth commandment) the mass of the public is informed in season and out of season that Jews are revolutionaries, that they are a disruptive element in modern society, that the British Empire itself is in danger of their secret machinations, it is only fair surely to expect that when a popular hero who is a Jew appears on the horizon, his Jewishness should be pointed out. Why is it that this small point is overlooked?

In 1922, Jewishness was certainly a factor in triggering Einstein's visit to faraway Japan. On 24 June, his friend Rathenau was gunned down in a Berlin street. Immediately, Einstein realised that he too, as a prominent Jewish liberal in Germany's public life like Rathenau, was at risk. At first he considered leaving the country for good, as he had considered doing in 1920 at the time of the 'Anti-relativity Company' event. Four days later, however, after the initial panic had subsided, Einstein decided to stay in Germany, but resign from his public offices and avoid public appearances, such as the centenary celebration conference of the Society of German Scientists and Physicians, scheduled for September. 'For, I am supposedly among the group of persons being targeted by nationalist assassins,' he informed Planck, one of the conference organisers, in a letter from Kiel on 6 July. 'I have no secure proof, of course; but the prevailing situation now makes it appear thoroughly credible.' After disappearing from view in Berlin as far as possible, at the beginning of October Einstein and his wife were able to get away from Germany for almost six months, during which Einstein lectured to large and respectful audiences in Japan, at the invitation of a Japanese publisher that had first been extended to him in 1921.

While the Einsteins were there in December 1922, the trial of the would-be assassins of Rathenau took place in Berlin. One of the witnesses, a German-Jewish journalist, Maximilian Harden, testified in court that 'The great scholar Albert Einstein is now in Japan because he does not feel safe in Germany.' This comment was picked up from a news agency report by the *Japan Advertiser*, causing embarrassment to the German ambassador to Japan, Wilhelm Solf. He requested Einstein by cable to allow him to deny the story by cable publicly. But as Einstein conveyed to Solf in a letter, the true situation was somewhat more complicated than it appeared. He explained: 'Harden's statement is certainly awkward for me, in that it aggravates my situation in Germany; nor is it completely correct, but neither is it completely wrong. Because people who know the situation in Germany well are indeed of the opinion that a certain threat to my life does exist.' He then admitted that his own assessment of the threat had changed as a result of the murder of Rathenau. Before the murder, 'A yearning for the Far East led me, in large part, to accept the invitation to Japan'; after the murder, 'I was certainly very relieved to have an opportunity for a long absence from Germany, taking me away from the temporarily heightened danger without my having to do anything that could have been unpleasant for my German friends and colleagues.'

VISIT TO PALESTINE

Even more complicated was Einstein's relationship with Palestine, which he visited on the way back to Germany from the Far East, over twelve days in February 1923. For it involved both his fellow Jews – German and otherwise – and the British colonial servants running the political affairs of the Mandate founded in 1920. Although Einstein had formed a positive impression of what he saw as British 'enlightened colonialism' and its 'civilising mission' in the places he visited on his way to and from Japan, such as Ceylon and Hong Kong, their application to Palestine was clearly a more sensitive matter, about which Einstein would express neither a positive nor a negative view in 1923.

On arrival by train in Jerusalem, the Einsteins were met by a British army officer, who took them by car up the Mount of Olives to Government House on the summit, the official residence of Sir Herbert Samuel, a British Jew who was the first High Commissioner of Palestine, where they were to be his guests for a few days. Einstein thought the building enormously pretentious and dubbed it 'Samuel's Castle'. Originally conceived as a hospice for German pilgrims in Jerusalem by Kaiser Wilhelm II on his visit to Jerusalem in 1899, its chapel boasted a mosaic mural depicting the Kaiser, accompanied by his wife, holding a replica of the building: 'very Wilhelminian', noted Einstein laconically in his diary.

But he got on well with Samuel and his small family, and formed a friendship that would last for many years; when Einstein visited London in 1930 to speak at a Jewish fundraising dinner, he again stayed with Samuel. He appreciated Samuel's 'English formality', his 'superior, multifaceted education' and his 'lofty view of life tempered by humour'. Samuel, for his part, described Einstein in his memoirs as 'a man of kindly disposition and simple ways. Recognised everywhere as the greatest scientist of our age, he carries his immense fame without the smallest self-consciousness, without either pride or diffidence. . . . His sense of humour is keen, and laughter comes readily.'

On the first day, which happened to be the Sabbath, Einstein and Samuel walked together on a footpath past the city walls to an ancient gate into the old city of Jerusalem, where they were joined by a Zionist thinker, Asher Ginsberg. According to Einstein's diary:

> Continue on into the city with Ginsberg. Through bazaar alleyways and other narrow streets to the large mosque on a splendid wide raised square, where Solomon's temple stood. Similar to Byzantine church, polygonal with central dome supported by pillars [the Dome of the Rock]. On the other side of the square, a basilica-like mosque of mediocre taste [the Al-Aqsa Mosque]. Then downward to the temple wall (Wailing Wall), where obtuse ethnic brethren [*Stammesbrüder*] pray loudly, with their faces turned to the wall, bend their bodies to and fro in a swaying motion. Pitiful sight of people with a past but without a present. Then diagonally through the (very dirty) city swarming with the most disparate assortment of holy men and races, noisy and Oriental-exotic.

After this distinctly mixed introduction to Jerusalem, most of Einstein's visit was chiefly concerned with introducing the world's most celebrated Jew to a wide range of local Jews (very few Arabs) in various places, including Tel Aviv, at the behest of the Palestinian Zionist organisation, which was determined to give him as favourable an impression as possible of Jewish Palestine. For example, three days after his arrival, Einstein spent the morning at two Jewish settlements west of Jerusalem with a workers' cooperative dedicated to training newly arrived settlers without any experience of the construction trades. In the afternoon, he met another philosopher, Hugo Bergmann from Prague, who was trying to establish the Hebrew University's library, followed by a local Jewish high-school teacher of mathematics, who showed him some interesting investigations in matrix algebra. The evening was then free for Einstein to accept the invitation of an English couple and their guests, where he made music for a long time, because he had become starved of western music in the Far East.

Norman Bentwich was an army officer stationed in Palestine who was attorney general in the British administration. His wife, Helen, left a lively account of their Einsteinian evening in a letter to her mother in England, mentioning her musical husband and his two musical sisters, Margery and Thelma. 'The great event has been Einstein,' she wrote.

> He is very simple and rather bored by the people but very interested in the music provided for him. Mrs Einstein is a mixture between a Hausfrau and a Madonna. Tuesday evening they came to dine, and there was music. Margery, Thelma, Norman, a man Feingold and Einstein played a Mozart quintet. Norman on the viola and Einstein on Norman's violin. He looked very happy whilst he was playing, and played extraordinarily well. He told some interesting things about Japan and his visit there, and talked of music, but not of his theories. He said of some man – 'he is not worth reading, he writes just like a professor' – which was rather nice. He only talks French and German, but his wife talks English. She said they got so tired of continual receptions and lectures, and longed to see the interesting places they visit alone and simply.

The general truth of this picture, especially the last comment, is borne out by Einstein's none-too-enthusiastic reaction in his

Einstein and his wife Elsa at Government House, Jerusalem, February 1923, during his first, and only, visit to Palestine, which was then under British administration. Between the Einsteins in the front row stand the high commissioner, Sir Herbert Samuel, and his wife Beatrice. Behind Sir Herbert is the attorney general, Norman Bentwich, who invited Einstein to his house, where he relished playing his violin after a long gap in the Far East.

diary to perhaps his most important formal engagement in Palestine: the first lecture of the nascent Hebrew University on 7 February. It took place in a hall of the British police academy on Mount Scopus, which had been hung with Zionist flags for the occasion, alongside the Union Jack, a portrait of the high commissioner, Samuel, and a portrait of Theodor Herzl, the father of modern Zionism. The audience of about 250 people consisted of government officials (including Samuel and the Bentwiches), Dominican Fathers, missionaries and of course many Jews. Einstein was introduced by the local president of the Zionist organisation, Menachem Ussishkin, with this concluding flourish: 'Mount the platform which has been waiting for you for 2,000 years.' Einstein then began lecturing on relativity with a single sentence in Hebrew, a language that was 'evidently unfamiliar', noted Samuel (Einstein never learned Hebrew as a child), immediately switched to French and concluded in German. After he had finished, he was formally thanked, quite wittily, by Samuel, who then strolled back and forth with Einstein on the hill road, engaging in philosophical conversation. Later, there was a banquet in his honour at Government House, attended by a range of British Mandate officials including the chief justice and the head of education, the Arab mayor of Jerusalem and a well-known American archaeologist, William F. Albright, and his wife. 'That evening, well and truly satisfied with all these comedies!' noted Einstein.

On the last day of his visit, the diary included Einstein's most insightful comment on his attitude to Palestine, at the end of a busy day with yet another lecture:

> Drive from terraced, very scenic Nazareth across the Jezreel Valley, Nablus, to Jerusalem. Quite hot at departure, then severe cold with pelting rain. En route, road blocked by a truck sunk in the mud. People and car take separate detours

> over ditch and field. Cars get heavily battered about in this country. In the evening, lecture in German in Jerusalem in a packed hall with inevitable speeches and presentation of diploma by Jewish medical doctors, the speaker scared stiff and froze. Thank heavens that there are also some with less self-assurance among us Jews. I am wanted in Jerusalem at all costs and am being assailed on all fronts in this regard. My heart says yes but my mind says no.

Einstein left Jerusalem on 14 February 1923. He would never return to Palestine. In 1952, he declined the presidency of Israel offered to him on the death of Weizmann. Instead, he worked assiduously for Jewish causes internationally from the 1920s through the Nazi period and the post-war impact of the Holocaust right up to his death. Indeed, his very last piece of writing is an unfinished draft of his proposed address for Israel's Independence Day in 1955, petering out with these cautionary words: 'Political passions, once they have been fanned into flame, exact their victims . . .'.

PACIFISM AND THE LEAGUE OF NATIONS

No doubt from the beginning of his involvement with the Jewish cause Einstein had sensed that Zionism – like all forms of nationalism – carried within it the seeds of armed conflict. He had lived through the German nationalism that led to the First World War, Germany's military defeat and the fierce international sanctions that followed it, which nourished the nationalist myth that Germany's collapse was the result of being 'stabbed in the back' by internal enemies, represented by Jews such as the soon-to-be-murdered Rathenau. From 1921 onwards, therefore, along with his support for a Jewish national home in Palestine, Einstein was simultaneously active in trying to promote world peace.

To begin with, his efforts focused on encouraging international understanding between scientists divided by war. In late 1921, he wrote a statement on 'The International Character of Science', intended for publication in German in a pacifist handbook. He commented that during the recent war, when nationalist delusions were at their zenith, Emil Fischer (the Nobel laureate in chemistry for 1902) had made an emphatic statement to a Prussian Academy meeting: 'You can do nothing, gentlemen, science is – and shall remain – international!' Then Einstein noted that scientific conferences were still being organised with the deliberate exclusion of professional scientists from former enemy countries. 'Solemnly argued political considerations stand in the way of the supremacy of purely factual considerations so essential in fostering the great causes.' What could well-intentioned people do to counteract this policy of exclusion? The most effective policy for them would be to maintain close contacts with 'like-minded fellows' from all the other countries and to advocate persistently the cause of internationalism within their own national spheres of influence. No doubt the success of such efforts would take time, but they were sure to bear fruit. 'I would not like to let this opportunity pass without pointing out with admiration that, particularly among a large number of our English fellow professionals, the effort to uphold the intellectual community has remained alive throughout all these difficult years.'

Soon after this, the League of Nations – founded in 1920 – decided to establish an advisory International Committee on Intellectual Cooperation, to promote international exchange between scientists, researchers, teachers, artists and intellectuals. The committee would formally exist until 1946, when it was dissolved and succeeded by the United Nations Educational, Scientific and Cultural Organisation (UNESCO).

Einstein, along with Marie Curie, the Dutch physicist Lorentz, the French philosopher Henri Bergson, the British classical scholar Gilbert Murray and other thinkers of international renown, were mooted as potential committee members. Since this was four years before Germany's admission to the League of Nations, when German scientists were still boycotted by scientific conferences organised by the former Allies (as noted above by Einstein), his name inevitably provoked some controversy. Murray – who was chairman of the committee from 1928 to 1939, following Bergson and Lorentz – recalled these early arguments at the end of his life in the 1950s, as follows:

> I was naturally eager to get Doctor Einstein made a member of the Committee on Intellectual Cooperation, partly because he would, in a sense, count as a German, and partly for his eminence, but there were two or three obstacles – some of my French colleagues objected to having a German so soon while some Germans argued that he was not a German at all but a Swiss Jew. Another difficulty was Einstein's own mistrust of the Committee on Intellectual Cooperation as merely a committee formed by the victors. A conversation with some leading members of the committee very soon satisfied him as to our real international and peaceful spirit. The German objection was not one that could be maintained; if he was a Swiss, the Germans had no ground for objecting to him.

In mid-May 1922, Sir Eric Drummond, the British secretary general of the League, formally invited Einstein to join the committee. He promptly accepted, if with a note of doubt: 'Although I am not clear at all as to the character of the work to be done by the committee, I consider it my duty to accept your invitation. In my opinion, no one, in times such as these, should refuse to take part in any effort made to bring about international cooperation.'

But soon he had second thoughts and decided to withdraw. The principal reason was probably Rathenau's assassination on 24 June and Einstein's wish to withdraw from German public life. He advised a French League of Nations official whom he knew personally: 'the situation here is such that a Jew would do well to exercise restraint as regards his participation in political affairs. In addition, I must say that I have no desire to represent people who certainly would not choose me as their representative, and with whom I find myself in disagreement on the questions to be dealt with.'

Murray pleaded with Einstein not to withdraw. So did Curie. She wrote to him:

> I have received your letter, which has caused me a great deal of disappointment. It seems to me that the reason you give for your abstention is not convincing. It is precisely because dangerous and prejudicial currents of opinion do exist that it is necessary to fight them and you are able to exercise, to this extent, an excellent influence, if only by your personal reputation which enables you to fight for toleration. I think that your friend Rathenau, whom I judge to have been an honest man, would have encouraged you to make at least an effort at peaceful, intellectual international collaboration. Surely you can change your mind. Your friends here have kind memories of you.

For whatever reason, Einstein did again change his mind and accept membership of the committee. However, he still felt unable to attend its first meeting in Geneva in August 1922. Instead he sent a telegram of support, before departing for the Far East in early October.

It turned out that a pattern had been set. Einstein truly believed in fostering internationalism among thinkers, yet he was uncomfortable to be seen as a representative of Germany; and by nature he disliked committees.

In March 1923, soon after returning from his Far Eastern trip, and without having attended any meeting of the International Committee on Intellectual Cooperation, Einstein once again resigned from it. This time he was provoked by the French government's unilateral decision to send occupation troops into the Ruhr district of Germany in January 1923, as a reprisal against Germany's failure to fulfil its obligations to pay war reparations, agreed at the post-war Versailles peace conference. For once, Einstein found himself on the side of German nationalists. But his reasons were different from theirs, as he explained to the League: 'I have become convinced that the League possesses neither the strength nor the sincere desire which it needs to accomplish its aims. As a convinced pacifist, I feel obliged to sever all relations with the League.' He therefore requested that his name be removed from the roster of committee members.

Once again, he heard from Murray. 'I fully understand your action, and even feel the strongest sympathy with it, but I hope and believe that you are wrong,' Murray wrote.

> I believe that the right line would have been for a number of us to say that it was impossible for the Committee on Intellectual Cooperation to function while the French were refusing to submit their case to arbitration and were creating practically a state of war in Europe. I believe that some other members of the committee would have been willing to take that line. The committee itself consists largely of people who have nothing particular to do with the League and are not, I fear, permeated with the League spirit.

Einstein stuck to his guns, so to speak, with reluctance. He told Murray in his reply: 'the League functions as a tool of those nations which, at this stage of history, happen to be the dominant powers. Thus, the League not only fails to uphold justice but actually undermines the faith of men of goodwill who believe in the possibility of creating a supranational organisation.'

But when Murray, with the unanimous support of the committee, tried to lure Einstein back a year or so after his 1923 resignation, he was again open to discussion. He assured Murray: 'I do not hesitate to tell you that my closest and most enlightened friends were the ones who expressed the deepest regret over my resignation. I myself have slowly come to feel that I was influenced more by a passing mood of disillusionment than by clear thinking.' Certainly, thus far the League had often failed; yet in such challenging times as these he recognised that the League was the institution that offered the greatest likelihood of effective action if its members were to strive honestly for international reconciliation.

Einstein re-joined the committee in June 1924 and remained a member, formally speaking, until 1932. But it has to be said that he was never an assiduous attender of its discussions, or an enthusiast for them, because he found the committee to be trapped between France's desire for political domination and Germany's desire to restore its political respectability.

Perhaps the only committee project that really caught Einstein's imagination was its commitment to encouraging and publishing 'an exchange of letters between leaders of thought, on the lines of those which have always taken place at the great epochs of European history'. From this emerged a pamphlet, *Why War?*, based on Einstein's own exchange with Sigmund Freud in 1932. It attempted to answer his opening question to Freud, 'Is there any way of delivering mankind from the menace of war?', and his concluding question, 'Is it possible to control man's mental evolution so as to make him proof against the psychosis of hate and destructiveness?' On which Einstein commented provocatively, bearing in mind his own exposure to the behaviour of German academics during the First World War: 'Here I am thinking by no means only of the so-called uncultured masses. Experience proves that it is rather the so-called "intelligentsia" that is most apt to yield to these disastrous collective suggestions,' because, he said, 'the intellectual has no direct contact with life in the raw but encounters it in its easiest, synthetic form – upon the printed page.'

Why War? was published by the League of Nations International Institute of Intellectual Cooperation in 1933 – ironically the year in which the Nazis seized power in Germany – with the active help of some German intellectuals, including physicists such as Lenard, and the silent cooperation of others, such as Planck.

Probably, Einstein's growing disillusionment with the League of Nations was what kindled his belief in militant pacifism. Dislike of war had been implicit in his childhood in Germany; hatred of it explicit in some of his statements during and after the First World War, including his participation in the 'Manifesto to the Europeans' published in 1917. However, he did not actually ally himself with war resistance movements until the later years of the 1920s.

In early 1928, he told the Women's International League for Peace and Freedom, which had arranged a conference on gas warfare to be held in Geneva simultaneously with a meeting of the League of Nations Disarmament Commission:

> It seems to me an utterly futile task to prescribe rules and limitations for the conduct of war. War is not a game; hence, one cannot wage war by rules as one would in playing games. Our fight must be directed against war itself. The masses of people can most effectively fight the institution of war by

> establishing, in time of peace, an organisation for absolute refusal of military service. The efforts made in this direction in England and Germany appear rather promising.

That same month, Einstein accepted election to the board of directors of the German League for Human Rights, which was then the leading pacifist movement in Germany.

Later in 1928, he sent a message to the No More War Movement in London, the British section of War Resisters' International, which was more emphatic than his earlier message:

> I am convinced that the international movement to refuse participation in any kind of war service is one of the most encouraging developments of our time. Every thoughtful, well-meaning and conscientious human being should assume, in time of peace, the solemn and unconditional obligation not to participate in any war, for any reason, or to lend support of any kind, whether direct or indirect.

Finally, in 1930, he made his most pungent statement about militarism in an article, 'The World as I See It', which soon became a key text on Einstein the humanitarian:

> I feel only contempt for those who can take pleasure marching in rank and file to the strains of a band. Surely, such men were given their great brain by mistake; the spinal cord would have amply sufficed. This shameful stain on civilisation should be wiped out as soon as possible. Heroism on command, senseless violence and all the loathsome nonsense that goes by the name of patriotism – how passionately I despise them! How vile and contemptible war seems to me! I would rather be torn limb from limb than take part in such an ugly business.

Einstein speaks at a Jewish fundraising dinner at the Savoy Hotel, London, October 1930, along with George Bernard Shaw (on the right). Between them sits Lord Lionel Rothschild, a leading British Jew. In his speech, Shaw counted Einstein among the 'makers of universes', in the company of Pythagoras, Ptolemy, Aristotle, Copernicus, Kepler, Galileo and Newton.

And that same year, at a meeting in New York, he declared himself a militant pacifist in a speech – the so-called 'Two-per-cent speech' – which quickly became a symbol for the international pacifist movement, both figuratively and literally, in the form of pacifist lapel buttons with the legend '2%'. He said: 'Even if only two per cent of those assigned to perform military service should announce their refusal to fight, as well as urge means other than war of settling international disputes, governments would be powerless, they would not dare send such a large number of people to jail.'

Soon afterwards, Bertrand Russell publicly welcomed this speech. But in a private letter to the secretary of War Resisters'

International, Russell warned: 'The next war will, I think be more fierce than the war which as yet is still called "Great", and I think governments would have no hesitation in shooting the pacifist two per cent.'

The rise to political power of Nazism in Germany in 1933 put Einstein the militant pacifist in an extremely awkward position, in which he would feel forced to change his mind about military service. But before coming to that turbulent period of his life, let us revisit his science. In the late 1920s, at the same time as he embraced militant pacifism, Einstein became a militant critic of the theory of quantum mechanics, developed from work done by his scientific friends and colleagues in Britain, Germany and several other countries inspired by Einstein's original quantum theory of 1905.

CHAPTER FOUR

God Does Not Play Dice with the Universe

Quantum mechanics is certainly imposing. But an inner voice tells me that it is not yet the real thing. The theory says a lot, but does not really bring us any closer to the secret of the 'old one'. I, at any rate, am convinced He is not playing at dice.

Letter from Einstein to Max Born, December 1926

From his original paper on the photoelectric effect in 1905 until his death in 1955, Einstein thought about the physical significance of quantisation in physics without coming to any firm conclusions – as vividly demonstrated in his many exchanges with one of the founders of quantum mechanics, Born, which began in Germany around 1925 and continued between the United States and Britain after Einstein and Born emigrated in 1933. As early as 1911, Einstein told Besso (who had crucially helped him with special relativity in 1905): 'I no longer ask whether these quanta really exist. Nor do I try to construct them any longer, for I now know that my brain cannot get through in this way. But I rummage through the consequences as carefully as possible so as to learn about the range of applicability of this conception.' In 1922, he told Ehrenfest: 'I suppose it's a good thing that I have so much to distract me, else the quantum problem would have long got me into a lunatic asylum. . . . How miserable the theoretical physicist is in the face of nature, and in the face of his students.' And in later life, he told another physicist, Otto Stern, a fellow Nobel laureate like Born: 'I have thought a hundred times as much about the quantum problem as I have about general relativity theory.'

Some of the issues it threw up are still very much with us more than a century after Einstein's first paper. Unlike relativity, quantum theory still provokes fierce debate. Indeed, physicists are fond of quoting provocative comments about the mysteriousness of quantum theory from its pioneers, such as this one from Richard Feynman, a founder of the powerful theory of quantum electrodynamics in the 1940s and 1950s, who wrote in 1967: 'I think I can safely say that nobody understands quantum mechanics.' In 2018, Carlo Rovelli, a founder of the (as yet unproven) theory of loop quantum gravity, admitted: 'The strange landscape of the physics of relativity . . . becomes even more alien when we consider quanta and the quantum properties of space and of time.'

EVOLUTION OF THE QUANTUM CONCEPT

There were two main phases of Einstein's role in the quantum story. The first ran from 1905, the date of his paper assuming the existence of light quanta (later called photons), to the mid-1920s, when his assumption was unequivocally validated by the experiments of Arthur Compton showing that X-rays were waves scattered by the free electrons in metal foil according to quantum rules. During this first phase, now known as the period of the 'old' quantum theory, Einstein maintained – almost alone – that light itself was quantised, while making major contributions to physics by employing this hypothesis. This is not to say that quantum concepts were not seriously discussed by others then; they certainly were, as in Planck's 1900 theory of the absorption and emission of black-body radiation and Niels Bohr's 1913 solar-system model of the atom, based on the nuclear model of Rutherford. But Einstein's light quanta were considered too radical for polite scientific society. In 1922, they were evaded in Einstein's Nobel prize citation, which referred instead to his 'services to theoretical physics and especially for his discovery of the law of the photoelectric effect'; and the same happened the following year when the Nobel prize was given to Robert Millikan partly for his experimental confirmation of the same law. During this first phase 'it was the *law* that was accepted, *not* the photon', the physicist Andrew Whitaker stressed in his historical study, *Einstein, Bohr and the Quantum Dilemma*. 'Einstein's initial conception of the photon was no less than an act of genius, and his perseverance with it, despite the negative response and his own misgivings over the relation between the wave and particle concepts, showed great determination and courage.'

Then in 1925–26, the beginning of the second phase of quantum theory, along came quantum mechanics, originated by Werner Heisenberg (from Germany) and Erwin Schrödinger (from Austria), together with Bohr (from Denmark), Born (from Germany), Louis de Broglie (from France), Paul Dirac (from England) and others – but not Einstein. Once again he stood almost alone. In this phase of the quantum revolution, from 1926 until his death, Einstein was profoundly sceptical about his colleagues' new interpretation of physical reality in terms of probability, indeterminacy and uncertainty – which did not prevent it from quickly becoming the orthodoxy it remains today, not only in physics and chemistry but throughout science. In Einstein's view, however successful quantum theory might be in describing natural phenomena, it remained incomplete, like gravitational theory before the invention of general relativity. As Einstein wrote of Newton in 1933, 'the tremendous practical success of his doctrines may well have prevented him and the physicists of the eighteenth and nineteenth centuries from recognising the fictitious character of the foundation of the system'. He believed that the same would eventually prove true of the quantum theory.

Three comments from pivotal figures in twentieth-century science, each of them close to Einstein, give a fair picture of the deep resistance to his 1905 theory of quantised light in the days of the old quantum theory. In 1910, the physical chemist Nernst called Einstein's quantum hypothesis 'probably the strangest thing ever thought up. If correct, it opens entirely new roads for so-called ether physics and for all molecular theories. If false, it will remain "a beautiful memory" for all times.' To Nernst, the hypothesis apparently looked alluring but illicit. Hence his decision to convene the first Solvay Congress in Brussels in 1911 in order to discuss the implications of the quantum hypothesis, at which Einstein gave the concluding address. Less sympathetic was Planck, who was of course a theoretical physicist like Einstein. Planck had greeted special relativity in 1905 as the work of a new Copernicus, but he was embarrassed by the intellectual offspring of his own quantum theory of black-body radiation. In 1913, when fulsomely recommending Einstein for membership of the Prussian Academy in Berlin, Planck nonetheless felt obliged to add a gentle apology for his distinguished protégé's subversive quantum notion: 'That sometimes, as for instance in his hypothesis of light quanta, he may have gone overboard in his speculations should not be held against him too much, for without occasional venture or risk no genuine innovation can be accomplished even in the most exact sciences.' Least sympathetic of all was the American experimental physicist Millikan, who in 1909 had first measured the charge on the electron in his classic oil-drop experiment. In 1916, Millikan bluntly called Einstein's quantum theory 'wholly untenable', a 'bold, not to say reckless, hypothesis', in two published scientific papers. What is particularly pointed about this criticism is that Millikan had just spent ten years in his laboratory testing the predictions of Einstein's 1905 equation for the photoelectric effect and reluctantly confirmed its striking accuracy. Even so, Millikan refused to accept Einstein's theoretical explanation of his own laboratory results, because to have allowed the existence of light quanta would have appeared an absolute contradiction to the ruling wave concept of light.

The earliest of Einstein's applications of the quantum hypothesis (after the photoelectric effect), which he published in 1907, was not directly to do with light quanta. It concerned the solid state.

In the 1820s, two physicists, Pierre Dulong and Alexis Petit, had experimented with heating various metallic elements such as copper, nickel and gold, and had discovered an interesting and useful rule, the so-called Dulong and Petit law. It states that the amount of energy required to increase the temperature of 1 kilogram of a substance by 1 degree Centigrade – known as its specific heat capacity – is inversely proportional to its atomic weight (more accurately, its relative atomic mass). The greater the atomic weight of an element, the smaller its specific heat capacity; multiplied together, the atomic weight and the specific heat equalled a constant value across a number of different substances, as measured by Dulong and Petit. Their law was thus good evidence for the atomic structure of matter and also suggested the surprising fact that the atoms of a range of different elements had exactly the same capacity for heat regardless of their atomic weight.

But as Einstein had been aware since his student days, Dulong and Petit's law worked well only at high temperatures and only with certain elements, not with others. At low temperatures the specific heat capacity fell and the law was not obeyed; and for diamond (carbon), boron and silicon, the specific heat was found to be much too low even at room temperature.

Einstein sought a quantum explanation of these specific heat anomalies. According to the kinetic theory, which explains Brownian movement in liquids and gases (as noted by Einstein in 1905), the atoms in solids must absorb heat by vibrating more vigorously on their crystal lattices, in the same way that atoms in liquids and gases zip around with higher velocities at higher temperatures. But suppose the fixed atoms in a solid oscillated not in a continuous manner but in a quantised way, such that they could increase their energy of vibration only in steps, not continuously? In other words, suppose the vibrations could take only discrete energy values. Einstein further assumed that the magnitude of the quantised energies could be calculated from Planck's simple quantum equation linking energy and frequency (here the frequency of atomic vibration). On this basis his calculation gave a remarkably accurate account of the general behaviour of simple solids. As Einstein predicted in his 1907 paper: 'If Planck's theory of radiation goes to the heart of the matter, then we must also expect to find contradictions between the present kinetic theory and experiment in other areas of the theory of heat – contradictions that can be resolved by following this new path.'

WAVE/PARTICLE DUALITY AND ATOMIC STRUCTURE

Two years later, after further reflection and publication on the subject, at the Salzburg meeting of German scientists in 1909, Einstein – instead of speaking on relativity as everyone had expected – gave his keynote address on 'The nature and constitution of radiation'. It included this astonishingly prescient statement:

> It cannot be denied that there exists a large group of radiation-related facts which show that light possesses certain fundamental properties which can much more easily be understood from the standpoint of Newtonian emission theory [i.e. light corpuscles/quanta] than from the standpoint of the wave theory. . . .
>
> It is my opinion that the next phase in the development of theoretical physics will bring us a theory of light that can be interpreted as a kind of fusion of the wave and the [particle] theory. . . . [The] wave structure and [the] quantum structure . . . are not to be considered incompatible.

The Salzburg speech was 'one of the landmarks in the development of theoretical physics', said Wolfgang Pauli, another pioneer of quantum mechanics, on Einstein's seventieth birthday in 1949. It was the first announcement of the disturbing idea of wave/particle duality.

Soon after this, Einstein shifted his attention to general relativity for the next five years, though of course he continued to think about quantum theory. He had no role at all in the next important quantum development, which came from Bohr, who was working in Rutherford's University of Manchester laboratory on the structure of the atom.

In 1911, Rutherford had discovered the atomic nucleus and conceived the solar-system model of the atom, in which an electron was thought to orbit the nucleus like a planet around the Sun, held in place not by gravity but by an electrostatic force acting between the positively charged nucleus and the negatively charged electron. This was a familiar enough concept from nineteenth-century physics. But, appealing though Rutherford's picture was, it did not explain atomic spectra, which had been documented over many decades. The colours of fireworks illustrate the visible emission spectra of different chemical elements and compounds, as does a sodium or neon street light. Yet, Rutherford's model did not account for why atoms of different elements emit and absorb electromagnetic radiation at specific frequencies/wavelengths, creating sharp bright and dark lines in the electromagnetic spectrum as characteristic of a given element as a fingerprint is of a human individual.

According to the Rutherford–Bohr proposal of 1913, the existence of spectra implied that the electrons in an atom could occupy only particular orbits, *not* continuously varying orbits. Then emission of light – a bright spectral line – would occur when an electron fell from one fixed orbit to another lower-energy orbit nearer the nucleus, thus decreasing its energy and emitting the balance of its initial energy as radiation of a characteristic frequency. Absorption of light – a dark spectral line – would entail the reverse of this process, with an electron jumping to a higher-energy orbit further away from the nucleus.

In order to explain these fixed orbits, Bohr, like Planck before him in 1900, was obliged to add a crucial postulate of his own: that the electron orbits of Rutherford's atom were quantised. The angular momentum (and hence the velocity and energy) of an orbiting electron could take only certain values, Bohr speculated. These values were whole-number multiples of a constant based on Planck's constant, which appears in Planck's equation connecting energy and frequency. On this basis Bohr successfully constructed a model of a one-electron hydrogen atom with orbital energy levels that accounted for the experimentally observable spectrum of hydrogen. In 1916, Einstein called this Bohr model a 'revelation'.

However, the Rutherford–Bohr model had two major weaknesses. First, it offered no convincing explanation for the stability of atoms. According to Maxwell's equations, electrons, being accelerated charged objects, must radiate energy and quickly spiral into the nucleus. Bohr's quantum postulate forbade such an atomic collapse by simple theoretical fiat. Second, although the electron orbits themselves were quantised, the radiation emitted and absorbed by the electrons was observed in the form of (continuous) *waves*. Even if one accepted this discrete/continuous contradiction, how could an electron 'know' when it left one orbit at what frequency it should immediately begin radiating before it had 'arrived' at its next orbit? How did it 'know' to which orbit it was going? What really occurred during the electron's transition? At this early stage of the quantum theory Bohr had no confidence in quantised *light* (he was one of the last physicists to take Einstein's photons seriously in the 1920s) – only in quantised electron orbits. In the end, Bohr's model of the atom blended nineteenth-century and quantum physics imaginatively, even brilliantly (as a Nobel prize for Bohr soon confirmed), but without fully satisfying anyone.

Einstein saw this, and saw he could connect Planck's radiation law of 1900 with Bohr's atomic energy levels of 1913 using his light quanta. In 1916–17, having completed general relativity, he published three papers using the quantum concept. His new idea was that atoms, in addition to emitting light spontaneously, could be forced or *stimulated* by light to emit light, in the process moving from a high-energy state to a lower-energy state. The effect would be that one light quantum would stimulate an atom and two quanta would emerge, resulting in light amplification. The laser – the word is an acronym standing for 'light amplification by stimulated emission of radiation' – eventually grew from this idea. 'Einstein was the first to recognise clearly, from basic thermodynamics, that if photons can be absorbed by atoms and lift them to higher energy states, then it is necessary that light can also force an atom to give up its energy and drop to a lower level. One photon hits the atom, and two come out,' wrote Charles Townes, one of the inventors of the laser in the 1950s. Einstein himself told his old friend Besso in 1916: 'With this, the light quanta are as good as certain.' But in his published paper he noted that his theory of stimulated emission had a failing: that it 'leaves the time and direction of the elementary process to "chance"'. Here was a hint of Einstein's coming dislike of quantum mechanics because of its random, probability-based foundation.

However, before we finally reach that great debate, there was still another prescient proposal from Einstein arising from light quanta. In 1924, he received a paper from an unknown physicist in India, Satyendra Nath Bose, entitled 'Planck's Law and the Light Quantum Hypothesis'. It derived Planck's radiation law not from classical electrodynamics but by regarding radiation as a gas composed of light quanta and then applying a statistical approach based on the fact that large numbers of photons – unlike, say, electrons – are permitted by nature to occupy exactly the same quantum state. Bose asked Einstein for help in getting his article published. Einstein immediately read it, translated it into German and recommended it to a journal – and then himself wrote two papers inspired by it, in which he applied Bose's approach to *atoms*. The results were called Bose–Einstein statistics and gave rise to a concept of a class of elementary particles now known as bosons. In 1925, Einstein predicted that bosons, given the right conditions at very low temperature, could condense into a new state of matter. In 1995, Bose–Einstein condensates were at last produced in the laboratory, fully seventy years after Einstein's prediction.

With Bose–Einstein statistics we come to the end of the 'old' quantum theory and the beginning of quantum mechanics. It was also the end of Einstein's central role in quantum theory; after 1926 he became a critic of, rather than a contributor to, quantum physics.

DEBATING QUANTUM MECHANICS

His criticisms turned out to be fundamental and fascinating. 'Were it not for Einstein's challenge, the development of quantum physics would have been much slower,' admitted Bohr in 1962. Bohr and Einstein were the most persistent protagonists in this debate for some ten years, but at various times Einstein challenged just about every pioneering contributor to quantum mechanics. For example, in 1924 he told Born humorously: 'I find the idea quite intolerable that an electron exposed to radiation should choose *of its own free will*, not only its moment to jump off, but also its direction. In that case, I would rather be a cobbler, or even an employee in a gaming-house, than a physicist.' And in 1948, he remarked bluntly to Born: 'if one abandons the assumption that what exists in different parts of space has its own, independent, real existence, then I simply cannot see what it is that physics is meant to describe'.

Modern quantum theory abandons exactly this assumption. In answer to Einstein's well-known poser, 'Does the moon really exist only when you look at it?', the physicist David Peat answered: 'Einstein's moon really exists. It is linked to us through non-local correlations but does not depend upon us for its actual being in the world. On the other hand, what we call the moon's reality, or the electron's existence, depends to some extent upon the contexts we create in thought, theories, language and experiments.'

Let us now attempt to summarise in just one paragraph the development of quantum mechanics, a very complex and mathematically sophisticated subject, before returning to Einstein's critique. In 1924, de Broglie proposed that all matter has a wave associated with it, and this was quickly confirmed for electrons by electron diffraction experiments. In 1926, Schrödinger, in his classic wave equation – aided importantly by Born – replaced the picture of an electron as a particle having a precise position and momentum as it orbits a nucleus with a *wave function* that predicted stationary waves of electron probability around the nucleus. Schrödinger's equation enabled physicists to calculate not the location of an electron at any given moment but rather its probability of being at any particular point in space. Hence the atom was no longer at risk of collapse, as in Bohr's original model, because no electric charge was being accelerated; the electron became a probability wave in the Schrödinger/Born model. Then in 1927, Heisenberg, in his far-reaching uncertainty principle, proved that the position and momentum of any elementary particle such as an electron could never be measured simultaneously with unlimited accuracy. The more an experimenter tries to pin down the position in space, the greater will be the uncertainty in the momentum, and vice versa, because the very act of observing the particle (say, by firing a photon at it) will inevitably disturb its position and momentum. The Heisenberg uncertainty principle states that the uncertainty in the position multiplied by the uncertainty in the momentum will always exceed a constant based on Planck's constant. Other kinds of uncertainty principle may also be derived, such as one which relates the uncertainty in the energy of a particle to the time interval in which one measures its energy.

At the Solvay Congress in 1927 and again in 1930, and after, Einstein tried to counter some of these ideas and their profound implications for physical reality with his own 'thought' experiments. Here is one of the best known.

Imagine, said Einstein, a box containing radiation. There is a hole in its side and a shutter to open and close the hole. The box is weighed. Then the shutter is opened for a short time T and one photon is allowed to escape. The box is weighed again. The loss in mass, which must equal the mass of the escaped photon, can be converted to a loss in energy (using $E = mc^2$). And this mass or energy can in principle be determined as accurately as one wishes, hence the uncertainty in the energy of the photon may be zero. The uncertainty in the time for the escape of the photon is finite, just T. This means that the two uncertainties multiplied together may be zero – in contradiction of Heisenberg's uncertainty principle.

'It was quite a shock for Bohr,' remembered one of the other physicists at the 1930 Solvay Congress, Léon Rosenfeld. 'During the whole evening he was extremely unhappy, going from one to the other, and trying to persuade them that it couldn't be true, that it would be the end of physics if Einstein were right; but he couldn't produce any refutation.' Einstein left the meeting, 'a tall

Solvay Congress in Brussels, Belgium, 1927, at which Einstein keenly questioned recent developments in quantum theory by Niels Bohr, Max Born, Louis de Broglie, Werner Heisenberg and Erwin Schrödinger. Einstein sits in the front row (fifth from right), along with Max Planck (second from left), Marie Curie (third from left) and Hendrik Lorentz (fourth from left). In the second row appear Peter Debye (first from left), Paul Dirac (fifth from right), Arthur Compton (fourth from right), de Broglie (third from right), Born (second from right) and Bohr (far right), and in the back row are Paul Ehrenfest (third from left), Schrödinger (sixth from right), Wolfgang Pauli (fourth from right) and Heisenberg (third from right). Surprisingly, this is the only photograph of Einstein with his great friend Born.

majestic figure, walking quietly, with a somewhat ironical smile, and Bohr trotting near him, very excited'.

But by the following morning, Bohr had a riposte ready. And it depended on general relativity! He had carefully considered, as Einstein had not, how the measurements of the loss in mass of the box and of the time interval for the shutter's opening and closing might actually be made by an observer. Bohr imagined hanging the box from a delicate spring balance and attaching the shutter to a clock inside the box. Then he realised that general relativity dictated that the clock must change its rate as it moved very slightly upwards with the escape of the photon – since the clock was being decelerated in a gravitational field. This must introduce an uncertainty into the time interval *T*. As a consequence, Bohr's calculations showed, the time-energy uncertainty principle would be obeyed after all.

On this occasion Einstein was vanquished, and it appears that after 1930 he accepted that quantum mechanics was internally consistent. In 1931, he nominated Schrödinger and Heisenberg to the Swedish Academy for a joint Nobel prize as the founders of 'wave, or quantum, mechanics' (note the uncertainty in the name). 'In my opinion, this theory contains without doubt a piece of the ultimate truth,' Einstein explained. In 1932 Heisenberg received the prize, and in 1933 so did Schrödinger, along with Dirac.

Yet we know that Einstein was far from satisfied with quantum mechanics, as he made abundantly clear for the rest of his life. This was his ultimate summary verdict:

> The conviction prevails that the experimentally assured duality of nature (corpuscular and wave structure) can be realised only by . . . a weakening of the concept of reality. I think that such a far-reaching theoretical renunciation is not for the present justified by our actual knowledge, and that

one should not desist from pursuing to the end the path of the relativistic field theory.

Einstein's comment was written in 1952. During the previous three and a half decades, since the publication of general relativity in 1916, Einstein had been relentlessly pursuing, in an increasingly solitary search, his own path towards such a field theory based on relativity, hopefully more fundamental than the new quantum mechanics.

UNIFIED FIELD THEORY

In 1925, Einstein explicitly employed a new term, 'unified field theory', in the title of one of his publications. 'Ten more papers appeared in which the term is used in the title, but Einstein had dealt with the topic already in half a dozen publications before 1925,' according to *The Cambridge Companion to Einstein*. 'In total he wrote more than 40 technical papers on the subject. This work represents roughly a fourth of his overall oeuvre of original research articles, and about half of his scientific production published after 1920.'

One of these papers, 'On the Unified Field Theory', produced a sensational flurry of world attention in 1929. 'Einstein on verge of great discovery; resents intrusion' ran a headline in the *New York Times* on 4 November 1928. Ten days later, the newspaper declared: 'Einstein reticent on new work; will not "count unlaid eggs".' Soon, to escape all the attention and concentrate on his work, Einstein left Berlin and went into hiding; he stayed alone in a friend's house throughout the winter, cooking for himself, 'like the hermits of old' as he wrote to Besso. On 10 January 1929, when Planck at last delivered Einstein's new paper to the Prussian Academy in Berlin on Einstein's behalf, there was feverish interest from the world's press. Einstein was said to have solved the 'riddle of the universe'. Telegrams came from all over the world requesting information and 100 journalists were held at bay by the academy until the publication of the six-page paper on 30 January. A delay of three weeks between delivery and publication was routine for a scientific paper, but given the unheard-of public speculation about its content the academy decided to up the usual print run to 1,000 copies. This instantly sold out and three further printings of 1,000 copies each were hastily arranged – a record for the academy's proceedings.

On 3 and 4 February, the *New York Times* and *The Times* in London carried a full-page article by Einstein, 'The New Field Theory', which discussed mainly relativity but then attempted to explain his latest idea of 'distant parallelism' (which he would soon quietly abandon). The *New York Herald Tribune* went one better and printed a translation of Einstein's entire scientific paper, including all the mathematics. But the most extraordinary response, surely, came when the six pages of Einstein's paper were pasted up side by side in the windows of Selfridges department store in London for the benefit of shoppers and passers-by. 'Large crowds gather around to read it!' an amazed and amused Eddington wrote to Einstein in a letter on 11 February.

Maybe the crowds had some dim inkling of Einstein's ambition, even if very few among them could comprehend his mathematics. As he apparently once told a former student (the astronomer Fritz Zwicky), the aim of his search was 'to obtain a formula that will account in one breath for Newton's falling apple, the transmission of light and radio waves, the stars, and the composition of matter'. The key concept, he thought, had to be the field, which had proved so fruitful in both Maxwell's equations, which had unified electricity, magnetism and radiation, and in general relativity.

Instead of particles of matter, Einstein imagined regions of very intense field – rather like knots in the even grain of a piece of wood. In *The Evolution of Physics*, he and his collaborator, Leopold Infeld, wrote in 1938:

> Could we not reject the concept of matter and build a pure field physics? What impresses our senses as matter is really a great concentration of energy into a comparatively small space. We could regard matter as the regions in space where the field is extremely strong. . . . A stone thrown is, from this point of view, a changing field. . . . There would be no place, in our new physics, for both field and matter, field being the only reality. This new view is suggested by the great achievements of field physics, by our success in expressing the laws of electricity, magnetism, gravitation in the form of structure laws and finally by the equivalence of mass and energy. Our ultimate problem would be to modify our field laws in such a way that they would not break down for regions in which the energy is enormously concentrated.

With each successive attempt, Einstein's unified field theory became more purely mathematical and less based on the real world. He had started his scientific life in the 1890s by imagining himself chasing a light ray, and had invented general relativity by wondering how gravity would feel if he jumped off a rooftop, but now he progressively lost interest in such physical ideas. Perhaps his flawed thinking in the 1930 'thought' experiment on quantum mechanics with the photon and the box was suggestive, in that the flaw lay in his failure to consider the physical method of measurement; by idealising the experiment too much, he overlooked a key element (as spotted by a triumphant Bohr).

During the 1930s, Einstein seems to have lost interest in the fundamental advances that were being made in physics. The discovery of the positron, the first known 'anti-matter' particle, in 1932/33 made little impact on his work – which was ironic given that Dirac had predicted its existence in 1928 by applying special relativity to the quantum mechanics of the electron (though Einstein did admire Dirac's mathematics). And the same happened with the discovery of the neutron in 1932 and the muon in 1936, which heralded the discovery of many other nuclear particles. The richness of the newly discovered subatomic world – each particle with its mass, spin, charge, quantum number and other features – did not emerge from Einstein's new field equations. Despite the importance of his 1905 equation $E = mc^2$ in understanding nuclear fission (discovered in 1938), he showed no serious interest in the emerging new model of the nuclear forces.

According to the physicist Steven Weinberg, a Nobel laureate who played a key part in the 'electroweak' theory of the 1960s and 1970s that unified electromagnetism with the weak interactions of the nucleus, one of Einstein's approaches to a unified field theory lives on, in much-modified form, in today's string theory. But of the other approach, the extension of general relativity to a non-symmetric metric, 'no trace remains in current research'. Einstein's three decades of endless calculation after 1925 have left little behind except manuscripts. Although physicists may honour his final search for its sheer faith in the possibility of unification – as is evident in the continuing search for a 'theory of everything' – his specific ideas were first ignored and then forgotten, in signal contrast with his work on relativity and quantum theory.

So why did Einstein stick with his search, one may well ask? Part of the reason may have been the stubbornness of an ageing physicist past his intellectual prime: a widely held criticism that Einstein himself joked about to Born and others. In addition, there was his sense of duty to physics. Einstein told a physicist who expressed regret at his efforts that although he knew the chance of success was very slight, he felt obliged to try. 'He himself had established his name; his position was assured, and so he could afford to take the risk of failure. A young man with his way to make in the world could not afford to take a risk by which he might lose a great career.' Yet, the main reason Einstein persisted was probably the one that fired his exchanges with Born. Not only had Einstein always been drawn to the deepest questions in physics, he was also philosophically convinced that reality was determined by laws, not by chance, and that these laws made physical reality independent of the human mind. God does not play dice – he was certain.

Perhaps the clearest expression of this conviction came in Einstein's meeting with Rabindranath Tagore in Germany in 1930 not long before the Solvay Congress. Tagore, though best known as a poet (for which he won the Nobel prize in 1913), a song composer, a philosopher, and as a spiritual leader and fighter for India's freedom beside Mahatma Gandhi, was also interested in science. But Tagore's philosophical position was quite opposed to Einstein's. Their 1930 conversation, soon published in the *New York Times*, shines a bright light on Einstein's philosophical position and throws it into sharp relief.

'There are two different conceptions about the nature of the universe – the world as a unity dependent on humanity, and the world as reality independent of the human factor,' said Einstein. Tagore responded: 'This world is a human world – the scientific view of it is also that of the scientific man. Therefore, the world apart from us does not exist; it is a relative world, depending for its reality upon our consciousness.'

'Truth, then, or beauty, is not independent of man?' asked Einstein. 'No,' replied Tagore. 'If there were no human beings any more, the Apollo Belvedere no longer would be beautiful?' queried Einstein. 'No,' said Tagore. 'I agree with regard to this conception of beauty, but not with regard to truth,' said Einstein. 'Why not? Truth is realised through men,' asked Tagore. 'I cannot prove that my conception is right, but that is my religion,' said Einstein firmly.

Then he became concrete: 'The mind acknowledges realities outside of it, independent of it. For instance, nobody may be in this house, yet that table remains where it is.' 'Yes,' said Tagore, 'it remains outside the individual mind, but not the universal mind. The table is that which is perceptible by some kind of consciousness we possess.'

'If nobody were in the house the table would exist all the same, but this is already illegitimate from your point of view, because we cannot explain what it means, that the table is there, independently of us. . . . We attribute to truth a superhuman objectivity,' said Einstein. 'In any case, if there be any truth absolutely unrelated to humanity, then for us it is absolutely non-existing,' replied Tagore.

'Then I am more religious than you are!' exclaimed Einstein.

Bohr's view of reality – and the views of some other quantum physicists – had more in common here with Tagore's view than with Einstein's. For quantum mechanics maintains, like Tagore, that reality is dependent on the observer. In science, said Einstein, 'we ought to be concerned solely with what nature does'. Bohr, however, insisted that it was 'wrong to think that the task of physics is to find out how nature *is*. Physics concerns what we can say about nature.'

Soon after his conversation with Tagore, in a seventieth birthday message for him, Einstein wrote: 'Man defends himself from being regarded as an impotent object in the course of the Universe. But should the lawfuless of events, such as unveils itself more or less clearly in inorganic nature, cease to function in front of the activities in our brain?' From an early age Einstein had believed human free will to be an illusion. He had a gut belief in the existence of a supreme law-giver – called God, if you will (as Einstein often did). Somehow this belief in determinism coexisted with his extreme individualism and exceptionally strong ethical values. 'I have never been able to understand Einstein in this matter,' wrote Born.

COSMOLOGY AND THE EXPANDING UNIVERSE

Interestingly, Einstein's resistance to the new discoveries in quantum mechanics at the subatomic level was not paralleled by a comparable resistance to equally revolutionary new discoveries in cosmology in the far reaches of the universe during the same period. In fact, Einstein would apply general relativity, following the theory's confirmation by English astronomers in 1919, to a spate of radical new American astronomical observations made in the late 1920s.

In the history of cosmology, the fifteen years from 1917 to 1932 are reminiscent of the early seventeenth century, when Galileo's telescope provided astronomical evidence for the Copernican solar system and Kepler reformulated the planetary orbits as ellipses. 'Theory fed on observation, observation fed on theory, and in the end science ended up much grander and more powerful than before. This time around, astronomers recognised the Milky Way as one of countless galaxies strewn through a vast and dynamic universe, each one composed of many billions of stars,' wrote a former NASA space scientist, Corey Powell, in his study of Einstein, cosmology and religion. 'And the cosmologists were ready to make sense of it all, to demonstrate they could explain our place among the fleeting galaxies as readily as their ancestors had put the Earth in motion among the planets.'

At the beginning of this period, in 1917, Einstein set about applying general relativity to the universe as a whole. Comparatively uninformed about the latest empirical work in astronomy, his primary interest was not to construct a cosmological model from observations, but rather to build 'a spacious castle in the air' (as he told the astronomer Willem de Sitter), in order to test his theory. Much to his surprise, and even dismay, general relativity predicted the cosmos to be dynamic, not static: either expanding or contracting over time. Since Einstein knew of no astronomical evidence for such movement, he added a term to his existing field equations of relativity, intended to counteract the attractive influence of gravity and thereby stabilise the universe, making it static and therefore eternal, as he thought it should be. Known as the 'cosmological constant', it allowed Einstein to predict a cosmos that was both static and finite, with a radius and average density of matter that could be calculated from first principles rather than from astronomical observations. But he admitted in his published paper that the new term was 'not justified by our actual knowledge of gravitation' and was 'necessary only for the purpose of making possible a quasi-static distribution of matter, as required by the fact of the small velocities of the stars'. In other words, the cosmological constant was something of a fudge factor.

Now, however, other theoreticians entered the picture by exploring different relativistic models of the cosmos. A physicist and mathematician, Alexander Friedmann, proposed that non-static models of the universe should be considered. In 1922–24, Friedmann, using Einstein's field equations, derived a whole class of dynamic cosmic models. Soon after, a theoretical physicist and Catholic priest, Georges Lemaître, treated emerging astronomical observations of a systematic recession of distant galaxies as evidence of an expansion of space on the largest scales. He postulated an origin of the universe in a 'primeval atom': the first conception of what would become the Big Bang model that dominates cosmology today. Unaware of Friedmann's work, Lemaître demonstrated how such a cosmic expansion could be derived from Einstein's field equations. But when Einstein was made aware of the work of both Friedmann and Lemaître, he could not accept their cosmic models. In a discussion with Lemaître in 1927, Einstein said he regarded theoretical models of an expanding universe as 'totally abominable'.

In 1929, new observations compelled him to change this view. The American astronomer Edwin Hubble with his assistant Milton Humason, working with the advanced telescope at the Mount Wilson Observatory in California, observed a linear relation between the recession velocity of distant galaxies and their radial distance. 'Many theorists saw the phenomenon as possible evidence for an expansion of space, and set about constructing relativistic models of an expanding universe similar to those of Friedmann and Lemaître,' according to physicist Cormac O'Raifeartaigh. 'In all these theories, it was assumed that the average density of matter in the universe would decrease as space expanded – what is known as an "evolving" universe.'

After Einstein had seen the astronomical evidence for expansion with his own eyes on a visit to the Mount Wilson Observatory in 1931, he too published papers with 'evolving' universes: one on his own in 1931, and another with de Sitter in 1932. In both cases, Einstein abandoned his 1917 cosmological constant on the grounds that the constant was now redundant. In later years, he even supposedly referred to the cosmological constant as the 'biggest blunder' of his life (according to the cosmologist

George Gamow). But, ironically, evidence from the late twentieth century restored the need for the cosmological constant. It now appears to be connected with the fact that the expansion of the universe is accelerating. The possibility of a cosmological constant 'did not go away so easily', wrote Weinberg in 1993.

> Einstein in 1915 operated under the assumption that the field equations should be chosen to be as simple as possible. The experience of the past three quarters of a century has taught us to distrust such assumptions; we generally find that any complication in our theories that is not forbidden by some symmetry or other fundamental principle actually occurs. It is thus not enough to say that a cosmological constant is an unnecessary complication. Simplicity, like everything else, must be explained.

As Einstein disarmingly remarked the year before his death, while commenting on the life and work of Eddington and the many conflicting theories of the origin of the universe, 'Every man has his own cosmology and who can say that his own theory is right!'

His own 'evolving universe' paper was published in Berlin in April 1931. A week or two later, he set off for Oxford to give three public lectures about relativity, including current references to cosmology and the unified field theory. Being Einstein, he would not shy away from presenting his latest scientific thinking. How much of this theorising even his physicist host, Professor Lindemann, would be capable of understanding was highly questionable. Without doubt, however, Einstein's second major visit to England would expand both his own universe and that of an ancient university.

CHAPTER FIVE

A Barbarian among the Holy Brotherhood in Tails

Doctoral ceremony in large hall. Serious, but not wholly accurate speech in Latin. Then my last lecture at Rhodes House on the mathematical methods of field theory. The dean slept wonderfully in the first row. Frightfully well-behaved and friendly audience. Afternoon nap at Lindemann's. Meal in college and finally pacifist students in cute old private house. Great political maturity among the Englishmen. How pitiful are our students by comparison!

Comment by Einstein about a day in Oxford in his travel diary, May 1931

In the 1920s, England had taken Einstein to its heart, following his initial burst of scientific fame in 1919 and his first personal visit to Manchester and London in 1921. In 1924, George Bernard Shaw – who had met Einstein (a decided fan of Shaw's work) at the house of Lord Haldane – privately informed him that 'You are the only sort of man in whose existence I see much hope for this deplorable world', while frankly admitting his own inability to understand Einstein's theory. In 1925, Bertrand Russell (for whose book *Political Ideals* Einstein had written an enthusiastic introduction to its German edition in 1922) published an introductory book, *The ABC of Relativity*. Russell kicked off with this come-on: 'Everybody knows that Einstein did something astonishing, but very few people know exactly what it was that he did.' At the same time the poet Sir John Squire remarked epigrammatically, in extending two classic lines about Newton written by Alexander Pope in 1730:

> Nature, and Nature's laws lay hid in night.
> God said, *Let Newton be!* and all was light.
> It did not last: the Devil howling 'Ho!
> Let Einstein be!' restored the status quo.

In 1925, the Royal Society awarded Einstein its highest honour, the Copley Medal, which had been given to Faraday in 1838. The Society's secretary, Sir James Jeans, while officially informing Einstein, added a personal touch: 'I think you are the youngest recipient in the two hundred years or so since it has been awarded; in any case if you are not, I think you ought to be.'

By 1930, according to Shaw, Einstein belonged to the pantheon of the immortals. Speaking at a public dinner in London for a Jewish cause where Einstein was the guest of honour, Shaw counted him among the 'makers of universes', in the company of

Einstein near the Sheldonian Theatre, Oxford, during his doctoral ceremony, May 1931. The public oration about Einstein, given in Latin, failed to translate 'relativity' or to mention Isaac Newton.

Pythagoras, Ptolemy, Aristotle, Copernicus, Kepler, Galileo and Newton – 'not makers of empires'. He added: 'and when they have made those universes their hands are unstained by the blood of any human being on earth'. (A humble Einstein responded: 'I, personally, thank you for the unforgettable words which you have addressed to my mythical namesake, who has made my life so burdensome, who, in spite of his awkwardness and respectable dimension, is, after all, a very harmless fellow.')

INTRODUCING FREDERICK LINDEMANN

On 1 May 1931, Lindemann's chauffeured Rolls Royce collected Einstein from the docks at Southampton when his passenger liner arrived from Hamburg. But instead of heading straight for Oxford in the car, Lindemann broke the journey at Winchester so that Einstein could see the town's wonderful Gothic cathedral and also pay a surprise visit to the cloistered seclusion of its notably intellectual boys' public school, Winchester College, founded in 1382, which has the longest unbroken history of any school in England.

Here, however, Professor Lindemann encountered a problem: the school porter refused to admit him and his guest on the grounds that the school was closed because the boys were at work. Attempts to persuade the porter to make an exception for Albert Einstein failed – no matter how many names of Lindemann's eminent friends, including the prime minister's, he dropped. Finally, Lindemann said he had a message to give to a boy, John Griffiths, from his mathematician–physicist father in Oxford, who worked with Lindemann at the Clarendon Laboratory. This recommendation worked the necessary magic, and a passing junior boy was sent to find Griffiths, who now takes up the story (as he recalled in the school's magazine, *The Trusty Servant*, half a century later).

'I looked out from the window of Second Chamber, and saw the immaculately attired Lindemann standing about half-way along Middle Sands, attended by a short figure, dressed in a Middle-European style cape with frizzy hair escaping from a kind of skull cap.' But when young Griffiths, who was shortly due in class, hurried out to be introduced to Professor Einstein, he knew that his school German was utterly inadequate for communication. Fortunately, Lindemann – a fluent speaker of German – proved to be a 'masterly' interpreter. The three of them went on a quick tour of some of the school buildings. Since Einstein wanted to see where the boys worked, they visited one of the classrooms. Here, on the ancient walls, marble plaques commemorating past members of the school 'intrigued Einstein beyond measure'. A little later, on the way out, they saw another room, used as a changing-room for football, cricket and other sports. It too contained marble plaques on its walls and beneath them were pegs with sweaty games-clothes hanging from the hooks. Einstein, despite a total lack of interest in team sports, stopped to ponder. 'But the Great Mind remained perplexed: the seconds ticked by as its owner stood plunged in thought.' Then at last the connection dawned: '*Ach! Ich verstehe: der Geist der Gestorbenen geht in die Beinkleider der Lebenden hinüber*,' Einstein remarked. 'The sense eluded me then,' remembered Griffiths, but 'well do I remember Lindemann's smile as he translated for my benefit: "The spirit of the departed passes into the trousers of the living."'

And indeed the unique encounter with Einstein and Lindemann had an inspiring coda. For after Einstein reached Oxford, he heard through Griffiths' father of a successful textbook, *Readable Relativity*, by a Winchester schoolmaster, C. V. Durrell, which Griffiths junior had been studying in class. Einstein naturally wanted to see a copy. So the schoolboy copy was sent to Oxford, including its doodles, marginalia and all. Not long afterwards, 'my Dad wrote to say that Einstein had hugely enjoyed it' and commented that: 'No German schoolmaster would ever have thought of doing it like that, or if he had, have done it so well.' Soon after, Griffiths senior sent the book back, now with Einstein's signature on its inside cover. Later, the heirloom passed into the hands of John Griffiths' younger son, Robin, who became a mathematician.

Apart from its charm, the story of this flying visit to Winchester captures some of the key elements in Einstein's Anglophilia: not least his admiration for the English belief in tradition. 'More than any other people, you Englishmen have carefully cultivated the bond of tradition and preserved the living and conscious continuity of successive generations. You have in this way endowed with vitality and reality the distinctive soul of your people and the soaring soul of humanity,' Einstein told the Royal Society in a message celebrating the bicentenary of Newton's death in 1927.

It also reveals something of Einstein's talented and worldly English host, Lindemann. On closer acquaintance he turns out to be an intriguing character, if diametrically opposite to Einstein in intellect, interests, politics and personality, not to mention dress sense. Even so, their relationship was one of both mutual respect and considerable warmth, which undoubtedly enhanced Einstein's already favourable opinion of England.

Though born in Germany (in 1886, seven years after Einstein), the son of a decidedly wealthy German father and an American mother, Lindemann had been brought up and educated as a British citizen. Indeed, all his life he resented the accident of his birthplace and came to regard himself as more English than the English, with an accompanying distrust for certain aspects of Germany. In his mid-teens, however, he returned to Germany for further schooling and then attended the University of Berlin. After graduating, he earned a doctorate in physics working under Walther Nernst who, as we know, sent him to the Solvay Congress in 1911, where he first encountered and befriended Einstein. Just before the outbreak of war in August 1914, however, Lindemann left Germany, to avoid being interned, and settled for good in England. In 1915, after failing to obtain a military commission because of his German background (a rejection which rattled him), he joined the Royal Aircraft Factory at Farnborough, learned to fly the following year and soon became semi-legendary for having extricated himself from a potentially lethal aircraft spin through rapid mental calculation, navigational skill and sheer courage, while empirically testing his own theory to explain the nature of the spin. A few months after the end of the war in 1918, he was appointed to the professorship in physics at Oxford's Clarendon Laboratory which he would hold for the rest of his scientific career. He was also a fellow of Wadham College – at the time of Einstein's first visit to Oxford in 1921 – and in 1922 he joined Christ Church. There he would reside in a suite of fine rooms until his death in 1957, and be known as 'The Prof', and, after 1941, as Lord Cherwell, the scientific adviser and confidant of Sir Winston Churchill.

As a physicist, Lindemann was highly rated, but never placed in the top rank. 'If your father were not such a rich man, you would become a great physicist,' Nernst once told him. Lindemann 'was a man of intuition and flair in widely diverse fields, but he never pursued any one subject long enough to become its complete master. Much of his brilliance was shown in discussion at scientific conferences, and has not survived in published form,' commented historian Lord Robert Blake, a Christ Church colleague, in the *Oxford Dictionary of National Biography*. 'For this reason later generations have not found it easy to understand the high esteem in which he was held by such persons as Albert Einstein, Max Planck, Max Born, Ernest Rutherford, and Henri Poincaré.' This assessment is confirmed by Einstein's own private summary of Lindemann, as reported by Harrod: 'The Prof., so it went, was essentially an amateur; he had ideas, which he never worked out properly; but he had a thorough comprehension of physics. If something new came up, he could rapidly assess its significance for physics as a whole, and there were very few people in the world who could do that.'

Lindemann's political views explain his appeal to Churchill. They were well to the right (though never sympathetic to Nazism). 'He was an out-and-out inequalitarian who believed in hierarchy, order, a ruling class, inherited wealth, hereditary titles, and white supremacy (the passing of which he regarded as the most significant change in the twentieth century),' wrote Blake. When a guest in Christ Church's Senior Common Room happened to remark 'One shouldn't kick a man when he's down,' a cynical Lindemann replied, 'Why not? It's the best time to do it because then he can't kick you back.' He himself became the butt of spiteful jokes because he spent so much time in the 1920s and 1930s moving in British aristocratic circles. Why is Lindemann like a Channel steamer? Answer: Because he runs from pier/peer to pier/peer. Yet in private he was kind-hearted and most generous to those in need, drawing on his wide contacts and personal wealth. Such attitudes – both public and private – underscored his obituary of Einstein for the *Daily Telegraph* in 1955. Overflowing with respect for Einstein's science, it was not surprisingly somewhat critical of his liberal and pacifist politics: 'Like many scientists Einstein was politically rather naïve. He hated violence and war and could not understand why his own natural sweet reasonableness was not universal. Absolutely truthful himself, he tended to be credulous in political questions and was easily and often imposed on by unscrupulous individuals and groups.' Yet, Lindemann concluded: 'As a man his simplicity and kindliness, his unpretentious interest in others and his sense of humour charmed all who knew him.'

Undoubtedly, Lindemann's difficult personality polarised his contemporaries (as it does even today). 'It has often been asked how a prickly, eccentric, arrogant, sarcastic and uncooperative man – to use some of the adjectives from time to time levelled against Lindemann – could have developed and sustained such a warm friendship with Churchill,' according to Adrian Fort, Lindemann's most recent biographer. 'The answer is of course that he did not display those characteristics to Churchill.' Presumably the same was true in Lindemann's somewhat less warm, and certainly less intense, friendship with Einstein.

OXFORD AND THE RHODES MEMORIAL LECTURES

It was in 1927 that Lindemann began to court Einstein for a second visit to Oxford. He had the support of the Rhodes Trust, which wished to launch the Rhodes Memorial Lectures in Oxford in memory of Cecil Rhodes, the British-born Victorian businessman, mining magnate and politician in southern Africa, whose strong support for imperialism would presumably have appealed to Lindemann – if rather less to Einstein (and not at all to most Oxford dons today). The trustees' aim was to attract to Oxford leading figures in public life, the arts, letters, business or science from around the world, whose presence would counteract the prevailing insularity of the university (such as had been exposed in the inadequate 1919 Oxford debate on relativity between Lindemann and the philosophers Smith and Joseph). To cite the devastating words of a British government commission of inquiry into the universities at Oxford and Cambridge, reporting in 1922: 'It is a disaster that, at a moment when we have become far more deeply involved than ever before in the affairs of countries overseas, our highest academical class is condemned through poverty to knowing little or nothing of life or learning outside this island.'

Although the Rhodes trustees were conscious of the recondite nature of relativity, and wary of the fact that Einstein would need to speak in German, they pressed ahead with an invitation to him, given his worldwide renown. One of them, the Oxford historian and Liberal politician H. A. L. Fisher, recruited Einstein's 1921 English host, Lord Haldane, to make the introductory approach. Haldane wrote to Einstein in Berlin in June 1927 introducing the unfamiliar Rhodes lectures: 'The university and the trustees desire that the lectures should next year be delivered by the foremost man of science in the world, and they are unanimous in their choice of your name.' Haldane hoped Einstein would accept, not least because this would be 'very good for Anglo-German relations that the choice should be proclaimed to the world'. As for the subject, it should be 'just what you select. Not too technical in detail, but extending to anything you please, mathematico-physical or otherwise.' As for the Oxford audience, it would include 'learned men as well as the public'. At the end of his letter Haldane mentioned that Lindemann would soon get in touch with the details of the invitation.

Einstein was interested, but he refused, for a mixture of reasons. He frankly explained to Lindemann in July: 'How gladly would I accept, particularly as I value highly the milieu of English intellectuals, as being the finest circle of men which I have ever come to know.' Unfortunately, however, scientific commitments to people in Germany would prevent him from being away for such a long time. Secondly, his poor health would make 'a long stay in foreign and unfamiliar surroundings . . . too great a burden for me, particularly bearing in mind the language difficulty'. Lastly, he modestly confessed that his current work was not at the forefront of physics, as compared with that of some other physicists who would appeal more to an Oxford audience.

But in August he changed his mind, and gave Lindemann encouragement: 'During the holidays I have often reproached myself because I haven't accepted your kind invitation to Oxford.' Perhaps he could come to the university for just four weeks during the next summer term? 'It is very important to me that in England, where my work has received greater recognition than anywhere else in the world, I should not give the impression of ingratitude.' However, he realised that following his earlier refusal someone else had probably been invited in his place. In which case, he trusted that Lindemann would make clear to the Rhodes trustees the warmth and gratitude he felt for their proposal.

By now, the American educationist Abraham Flexner had been approached to give the 1928 Rhodes lectures, which he duly delivered at Rhodes House on 'The idea of a modern university'. (In 1932–33, Flexner would persuade Einstein to join his newly founded Institute for Advanced Study at Princeton.) Einstein was therefore invited to speak in the following year, 1929, and apparently accepted; but again negotiations broke down for reasons of health. In the meantime, the Rhodes lectures began to establish themselves after a well-attended series on world politics given in 1929, not at Rhodes House but at the nearby larger Sheldonian Theatre, by Jan Christiaan Smuts, the South African soldier and statesman. This success renewed the determination of both the trustees and Lindemann to secure agreement from Einstein. At last, following a personal visit to Einstein in Berlin by Lindemann in October 1930, arrangements were finalised. Einstein agreed to visit Oxford for some weeks in May 1931, give the Rhodes lectures, and live in Lindemann's college, Christ Church.

After his acceptance was publicly announced, there was an ominous comment from the *Jewish Telegraph Agency* in December 1930: 'The movement to induce Prof. Einstein to settle permanently in England after his summer stay in England has gained momentum here as a result of a recent report from Berlin to the effect that Einstein may not return to Germany in case the Hitlerites obtain control of that country.' It was perhaps the first clear portent of political events that would overshadow Einstein's relationship with England during 1933.

The opening lecture by Einstein took place in the Milner Hall at Rhodes House on 9 May 1931. Given in German (like his other two lectures) without notes but with a blackboard, its English title was simply 'The theory of relativity'. The second lecture, in the same place on 16 May, dealt with relativity and the expanding universe: a subject then of course in a state of great flux (following Einstein's abandonment of the cosmological constant a few months before). It required 'two blackboards, plentifully sprinkled beforehand in the international language of mathematical symbol' (as *The Times* reported). The last lecture, also in Rhodes House, on 23 May, immediately after the university had awarded Einstein an honorary doctorate in the Sheldonian Theatre, tackled Einstein's constantly evolving unified field theory: 'an account of his attempt to derive both the gravitational and electromagnetic fields by the introduction of a directional spatial structure', as *Nature* chose to announce it.

The scientific content of the lectures was of no lasting significance, since it either repeated Einstein's existing published work on relativity or would quickly be rendered redundant by his (and others') subsequent ideas. More interesting is the reaction of the very mixed Oxford audience, which included some 500 selected students, to such an unparalleled educational-cum-social occasion.

The *Oxford Times* captured the atmosphere in two reports on the opening and final Einstein lectures. The first of these, headlined 'Women and relativity', remarked on 15 May:

> Women in large numbers flocked to hear Prof. Einstein speak on relativity at Rhodes House on Saturday morning. The front of the hall was filled with heads of houses and the back of the hall and the gallery with younger members of the university. It was unfortunate that no interpreter was provided, but Oxford seems to fight shy of interpreters. One wonders how many of those who were present thoroughly understood German, or if they could understand the language in which Prof. Einstein spoke, how many of them could follow the complexities of relativity. Prof. Einstein is a man of medium height with a wealth of black curly hair, already greying. Entirely unaffected, he had charm as well as simplicity of manner, which appealed to his audience.

The second report on 29 May began with a reference to the just-completed doctoral ceremony at the Sheldonian:

> Prof. Einstein, wearing his new doctor's robes, acknowledged the applause which greeted his appearance by smiling and bowing. His manner in beginning his lecture suggested that he was dealing with a difficult part of the subject, and at first he spoke earnestly from the desk, with his hands clasped in front of him, only leaving it occasionally for the blackboard. As the lecture proceeded, not only equations but a singular diagram appeared on the blackboard, and Prof. Einstein gesticulated helpfully in curves with the chalk to explain it. At this point he turned repeatedly from his audience to the board and back. Later, the diagrams were rubbed off in favour of more

formulae, and the better informed members of the audience were kept busy taking them down.

By now, at least one less-informed member had fallen asleep, however. The dean of Christ Church, Henry Julian White, a biblical scholar in his seventies, slept soundly during the lecture in the front row, opposite the speaker. Einstein was amused to see this, and perhaps also learned a lesson. For after one of the lectures, he apparently remarked in his curious English that the next time he had to lecture in Oxford, 'the discourse should be in English delivered'. Hearing this, one of his Oxford don companions, the physiologist John Scott Haldane (brother of Lord Haldane) was heard to murmur in German '*Bewahre!*' However, Einstein did follow his advice to himself: when he gave his most important lecture in Oxford, the Herbert Spencer lecture in 1933, he had it translated into fluent English and then read it aloud.

Not too surprisingly, given the fluid state of cosmology and of his unified field theory in 1931, Einstein showed almost no interest in preparing his Rhodes lectures for publication – unlike Smuts in 1929, whose lectures were published by the Oxford University Press in 1930. The secretary of the delegates of the press, R. W. Chapman, regarded Einstein's lectures – however demanding their subject matter might be – as a potential ornament to the publisher's list, and strongly pursued the possibility of their publication. But Chapman received no reply from Einstein to his follow-up letters and cables. After a final proposal (apparently suggested by Lindemann) – that Einstein might produce a reduced text of about fifty pages – went nowhere, an exasperated Chapman gave up on what he now called 'l'affaire Einstein'.

Two years later, at a social gathering in Oxford in 1933, Einstein intimated to the warden of Rhodes House, Sir Carleton Allen, that publication was impossible because 'he had since discovered that everything he had put forward in the lectures was untrue'. He explained, with 'rather comic contrition', that 'in my subject ideas change very rapidly'. 'I had not the hardihood to say that that was true of most subjects,' commented Allen, when reporting his conversation with Einstein in a letter to the secretary of the trustees, Lord Lothian. Instead, 'I suggested that he might publish the lecture with a short note at the end – "I do not believe any of the above", or words to the effect. He felt, however, that others might take up his ideas and convince him that what he knew to be untrue was true.' As for Einstein's vague suggestion that he might write an alternative book, Allen told Lothian ironically that perhaps an Einstein book on 'My view of Hitler' or 'Hitler in time and space' might help to recoup the large amount that the Rhodes Trust had spent on Einstein. In the end, his Rhodes lectures went entirely unrecorded, apart from an eight-page pamphlet printed in early May 1931, compiled probably with Lindemann's help, and three non-technical summary reports published in *The Times*, apparently based on this pamphlet. But the Oxford University Press did at least get to publish Einstein's 1933 Herbert Spencer lecture.

BLACKBOARD MATTERS

A more immediate source of friction between Einstein and the university was his blackboards. On 16 May, after the second lecture, Einstein told his diary with singular annoyance: 'The lecture was indeed well-attended and nice. [But] the blackboards were picked up. (Personality cult, with adverse effect on others. One could easily see the jealousy of distinguished English scholars. So I protested; but this was perceived as false modesty.) On arrival [at Christ Church] I felt shattered. Not even a cart-horse could endure so much!'

The idea of rescuing and preserving Einstein's blackboards seems to have come from some Oxford dons who attended his first lecture on 9 May. A memo from the then warden of Rhodes House, Sir Francis Wylie, to one of the trustees, Fisher, dated 13 May, states plainly that 'Some of the scientists seem to be anxious to secure for preservation in the Museum the blackboard upon which Einstein draws. I was first approached about it by de Beer, who is a fellow of Merton, and now Gunther has written to me, asking whether, if it is desired, the blackboard with Einstein's figures on it may be given to the university.'

Gavin de Beer was an embryologist, who became a fellow of the Royal Society and director of the Natural History Museum in London. Robert Gunther was a historian of science, who founded

One of the blackboards used by Einstein at Rhodes House, Oxford, May 1931, now kept at the Museum of the History of Science, Oxford. His calculations describe the density, size and age of the expanding cosmos, and contain a mathematical error. The blackboard was preserved by Oxford dons against the wishes of Einstein and is today the most famous object in the museum.

THE LEWIS EVANS COLLECTION OF SCIENTIFIC INSTRUMENTS

The Old Ashmolean
Broad Street
Oxford

19 May 1931

Dear Sir,

Your Present of 2 black boards used by Professor Einstein in his lecture *has been duly received, and I beg you to accept my sincere Thanks for your kindness in thus contributing to promote the objects for which the Lewis Evans Collection of Scientific Instruments has been founded in the University.*

I am,

Yours faithfully,

R. T. Gunther *Curator.*

To the Secretary
The Rhodes Trustees.

Letter to the Rhodes trustees from historian Robert Gunther, May 1931, thanking them for the donation of two Einstein blackboards used in his second Rhodes House lecture. Gunther was the founder of the Museum of the History of Science at Oxford. (The second blackboard was later cleaned by mistake.)

the Museum of the History of Science in Oxford in 1926–30. Yet another Oxford academic involved in the rescue was Edmund Bowen, also a fellow of the Royal Society, whose laboratory work in photochemistry had confirmed some of Einstein's theoretical work. Presumably, they were among the audience on 16 May for the second Rhodes House lecture. Certainly, on 19 May, Gunther formally thanked the secretary of the Rhodes trustees for 'your present' to the newly established museum 'of two blackboards used by Professor Einstein in his lecture'. There was even a subsequent note dated 25 May from Rhodes House to Gunther, written after the third Einstein lecture: 'I should be glad if you could come round and see the two blackboards which Einstein used on Saturday. They would normally be used again here tomorrow morning.' But by then, it appears that Gunther felt that he had acquired sufficient written evidence of Einstein's evanescent lectures.

Today – whether Einstein would approve or not – one of his Rhodes House blackboards is the most famous object in Oxford's museum, notwithstanding the museum's collection of some 18,000 objects dating from antiquity to the twentieth century. (The second blackboard was accidentally wiped clean of Einstein's fragile symbols in the museum's storeroom!) It intrigues uncomprehending visitors from around the world, many of whom come specially to see it and no other object. Its mathematical symbols neatly summarise Einstein's cosmology paper of April 1931, based on Friedmann's relativistic model of an expanding cosmos, with the cosmological constant set at zero and Hubble's measurements of the expanding universe used to estimate three quantities: the density of matter, the radius of the cosmos and the timespan of the cosmic expansion (given as 10,000 million years). However, its arithmetic was not totally accurate. 'It appears that Einstein stumbled in his use of the Hubble constant,' according to Cormac O'Raifeartaigh, 'resulting in a density of matter that was too high by a factor of a hundred, a cosmic radius that was too low by a factor of ten, and a timespan for the expansion that was too high by a factor of ten.' No doubt this mistake was just one of the many 'untrue' elements that Einstein had in mind by the time he returned to Oxford in 1933.

HONORARY DOCTORATE FROM OXFORD

By contrast with the lectures and their aftermath, the award of Einstein's honorary doctorate was free from friction, though not without its own comedy. The ceremony took place before his third lecture on 23 May 1931 in the grandeur of the Sheldonian Theatre designed by Sir Christopher Wren, in the presence of Oxford's vice-chancellor, Frederick Homes Dudden, a theological scholar and chaplain to King George V, and naturally in front of a packed house, at least some of whose members were by now personally known to Einstein.

Oxford's public orator, who presented the academically attired Einstein in Latin, had perhaps the most difficult role. He was a classical scholar, A. B. Poynton, later master of University College in Oxford. 'In so far as he understood what Relativity was about, [he] grappled manfully and ingeniously with the task of rendering it into Ancient Tongue,' noted the Winchester College schoolboy Griffiths.

Poynton's speech opened with a reference to the solar eclipse in late May 1919, almost exactly twelve years before, and the fact that 'Mercurius' (the planet Mercury) had on that occasion been observed in the position predicted by Professor Einstein. '*Atque utinam Mercurius hodie adesset, ut, cuius est eloquentiae, vatem suum laudaret!*' ('If Mercury were present today, he would of course praise his poet with his own eloquence!') At the end, the public orator attempted to relate relativity to classical philosophy. According to a translation of the Latin published a few days later in the *Oxford Times*:

> The doctrine which he interprets to us is, by its name and subject, interpreter of a relation between heaven and earth. It bids us view, under the aspect of our own velocity, all things

> that go on in space; to right and left, upward and downward, backward and forward. This doctrine does not in any way supersede the laws of physicists, but adds only the 'momentous' factor which they most desired. But it directly affects the highest philosophy, and it is not unwelcome to Oxford men, who have not the Euclidean temper of mind, but have learnt from Heraclitus that no man can step twice into the same river – nay, not even once; who are glad to believe that the Epicurean 'swerve' is not a puerile fiction; who, finally, in reading the *Timaeus* of Plato, have felt the want of a mathematical explanation of the universe more self-consistent and more in agreement with realities. This explanation has now been brought down to men by Prof. Albert Einstein, a brilliant ornament of our century.

Laudatory as it was, the speech contained no attempt to translate the term 'relativity' into Latin, no reference to gravity or electromagnetism, and not even a name check for the immortal – if Cambridge-based – Newton. (Contrast *The Times* in its lengthy editorial on 25 May, 'Professor Einstein at Oxford', which noted that 'Like Newton, Professor Einstein is not primarily an experimental physicist, but a mathematician.') Moreover, contrary to the speech, general relativity does 'supersede the laws of physicists', in the sense that it is more fundamental than Newton's laws of motion. No wonder Einstein noted in his diary in the evening that the speech was 'serious, but not wholly accurate'. He must have based this remark on a translation given him during the day (perhaps by Lindemann), since Einstein did not understand Latin. Yet, even when the public orator was speaking, Einstein had recognised his mention of Mercurius. 'I had noticed his face lit up when "Mercury" was named,' according to a friend in the audience at the Sheldonian.

She was Margaret Deneke, who had got to know Einstein soon after his arrival in Oxford. She would provide the most vivid vignettes of him among all of his contacts at the university during his visit in 1931, and subsequent visits in April–May 1932 and May–June 1933, recorded at length in her diary in translation from her frank conversations with Einstein. Not only was Deneke fluent in German, she was also intensely musical: two characteristics that immediately endeared her to Einstein.

MUSIC AND ART WITH MARGARET DENEKE

The younger of two surviving daughters of a wealthy London merchant banker born in Germany and his German-born wife who was a close friend of the celebrated pianist Clara Schumann, Margaret and her elder sister, Helena, were born in London and later moved to Oxford. In 1913, Helena was appointed bursar and tutor in German at Lady Margaret Hall, the university's first women's college, while Margaret became a musician/musicologist. Originally trained in the work of the great German romantic composers – Ludwig van Beethoven, Johannes Brahms, Franz Schubert and Robert Schumann – she then studied modern English music under the influence of Oxford musical scholars, especially Ernest Walker and Sir Donald Tovey, and was soon interpreting English music to many school-children. Together the sisters lived in a Gothic villa named Gunfield, very close to Lady Margaret Hall, where they staged frequent performances in their music room by both famous professionals, such as Adolf Busch and Marie Soldat-Roeger, and gifted amateurs. 'Generations of Oxford undergraduates, colleagues and friends enjoyed the Denekes' hospitality at the many Gunfield concerts,' according to the *Oxford Dictionary of National Biography*'s entry on Helena Deneke. 'Marga Deneke, herself a talented pianist, was choirmaster at Lady Margaret Hall and, raising considerable sums of money through concerts and lecture recitals, became one of the college's benefactors.' The Oxford Chamber Music Society met at Gunfield free of charge for some twenty-seven years, with Margaret Deneke making up any deficits; especially during the Second World War, the Society owed its survival to the Deneke sisters' generosity. In May 1931, inevitably, they would be joined by a visiting amateur violinist: Einstein.

'In he came with short quick steps. He had a big head and a very lofty forehead, a pale face, a shock of grey, untidy hair,' Margaret Deneke recalled of her first meeting with Einstein on 11 May. She introduced him to Marie Soldat, who was a violin virtuoso originally discovered by Brahms and a pupil of Joseph Joachim. After dinner

> he turned to Mother with an engaging smile: 'You have provided a delightful meal; now the enjoyable part of our evening is over and we must get down to work on our instruments. Shall we play Mozart? Mozart is my first love – the supremest of the supreme – for playing the great Beethoven I must make something of an effort, but playing Mozart is the most marvellous experience in the world.'
>
> The players started with Mozart; under Marie Soldat's rich tone on her Guarnerius del Gesu [a famous 1742 violin], the professor's borrowed violin sounded starved and raucous, but his rhythm was impeccable. Before passing on to Haydn there was an interval for a chat. Marie Soldat commented on the professor's long violin fingers, tapering usefully at the tips. The professor said, 'Yes I never have practised and my playing is that sort of playing, but physical build cannot be altogether divorced from mental gifts, an unusually sensitive temperament will make its mark on a body.'

> I said Adolf Busch [an intimate friend of Einstein] had got short fat fingers.
>
> 'Well I must admit without any fingers at all no one can play a fiddle.'

Before they left, the guests signed the visitors' book. 'In his small clear handwriting,' Deneke observed, Einstein wrote: 'Albert Einstein *peccavit.*'

A few days later, he 'sinned' again. The occasion was a somewhat strained formal dinner at Rhodes House given in his honour by its warden, Wylie, the evening before Einstein's second lecture. (Pre-dinner, poor Einstein had had to grab a needle and thread in the bachelor sleeping quarters and sew up his ill-fitting dress shirt, so that his hairy chest did not peer out during dinner.) 'Lady Wylie thought he would enjoy himself more if music could be introduced,' noted Deneke. 'Professor Einstein's English was rather halting in those days and to converse in French or German might not be too easy for the trustees.' When the meal was finished, he, Soldat and Deneke formed a trio. According to her diary:

> we were established around the piano; the trustees saw their lion disporting himself with Bach's Double Concerto and Handel and Purcell Sonatas. He tucked the violin under his chin with a will and tuned long and loud. Then he chose the piece he wanted and made suggestions: 'No repeats in the Adagio please and the Allegro not too fast, there are tricky bits for me.' We started obediently and he threw himself whole-heartedly into the music. He made no effort at all to discover what the trustees might like to hear. Unashamedly we played for our own enjoyment, without the slightest pretence about performing. The trustees smoked in silence,

witnessing their guest of honour having a happy evening. I doubt if they listened.

Indeed, according to Einstein's somewhat franker diary, when their music started up, 'The guests hastily left the room'!

How good a musician was Einstein? Opinions have varied over the decades, in both Germany and beyond (not helped by the occasional confusion of Einstein with a distinguished musicologist, Alfred Einstein, his contemporary in both Germany and the United States). Clearly Deneke had some reservations about his playing, yet she was well aware that Einstein always had to use a borrowed violin during his time in Oxford in 1931. When he returned in 1932, she recorded his advice about an instrument she was thinking of buying. 'He scrutinised the violin with great interest, and after he had played on it he advised me not to buy it as the tone was uneven.' Instead, he recommended, she should acquire a cheap instrument and give it to the man who had treated his own violin by adding varnish and cutting away little bits to improve the tone. 'He had had no other violin than this treated cheap fiddle, thin in its wood, but clear in voice.' As for the opinion of professional musicians on Einstein, it is probably summarised by the comment, 'relatively good', given by the pianist Artur Balsam who once played with him. Undoubtedly, Einstein was an intellectual match for professional musicians in the speed of mind essential for ensemble playing, even if he lacked their tone. At the same time, as a dedicated amateur quartet player, he was (to quote an American musicologist), 'the denizen of dimly lit music rooms of the world where enthusiastic friends and fiddlers bend together over their instruments and sleepy children yawn, and towards the end of a long evening someone says "Let's play some Haydn and then call it a night."'

By no means all of Deneke's Einstein diary for 1931–33 concerns music. She met him not only at Gunfield, but also in his rooms at Christ Church and elsewhere around Oxford, including Lady Margaret Hall, where he had agreed (somewhat reluctantly) to give a Deneke lecture named after her late father, on atomic theory. She also persuaded him to sit for a portrait by a little-known Tyrolese peasant artist, F. Rizzi, who had come to Oxford not long before Einstein's arrival in May 1933 to do a portrait of Deneke's mother at the family's request. When Mrs Deneke unexpectedly died, Rizzi was left at a loose end, deprived of his main commission.

Rizzi had never heard of Einstein, but both he and his subject got on genially when Deneke brought Rizzi to Einstein's rooms in Christ Church. On 31 May, she returned with two big bunches of flowers supplied by Lady Margaret Hall's gardens (which were designed and looked after for decades by her sister, Helena). She noted:

> Professor Einstein was still at his breakfast table and was delighted with the flowers. He had no coat on, no stockings but sandals on his bare feet. He pointed to the pile of letters and complained that correspondence was a great burden. I confirmed June 13 for the Deneke lecture and at his request made this entry in his diary. Then I asked if he would let Rizzi sketch him – we wanted work for the painter. He consented: 'he can draw my portrait whilst I am at work; then I sit still anyhow.' I promised Rizzi would be silent.

The following morning, she brought the artist again, installed him on some curious steps leading to the room's main window overlooking the college's famous cathedral, and left him alone with Einstein. Around noon, the Christ Church porter – who had

Drawing of Einstein by F. Rizzi, a little-known Tyrolese peasant artist, produced in Einstein's rooms at Christ Church during his third visit to Oxford, in 1933. It is now on display in the college's Senior Common Room.

been instructed to protect Professor Einstein from unscheduled visitors – phoned Gunfield to say that 'Miss Deneke's little man was waiting in the porch'. Immediately bicycling to Christ Church, she found Rizzi in the porch surrounded by a group of people who were admiring his profile portrait of Einstein looking down at a book. (Today it hangs in Christ Church's Senior Common Room.) The two of them then carried it off to a photographer, but all of a sudden Rizzi remembered that 'Professor Eisenstein', as he habitually called Einstein, had not signed the portrait. They returned to Christ Church, and found that their quarry had gone for a walk in Christ Church's meadows. The two of them set off in hot pursuit, but Einstein had got too far ahead, and so the signature had to wait until the artist returned the next day. When Einstein finally signed the portrait in his college rooms, Rizzi told Deneke that he laughed heartily over the artist's German aphorism: '*Nichts koennen ist noch lange keine Moderne Kunst*.' ('To be a Modern artist, it is not enough to lack any skills.') Einstein's taste in drawing, like his taste in music, was firmly in favour of the classical.

VISITOR AT CHRIST CHURCH

Christ Church's relationship with Einstein proved amiable but eccentric from beginning to end. The dinner-jacketed and gowned Christ Church dons were 'the holy brotherhood in tails' ('*der heiligen Brüderschaar im Frack*'), noted a wryly amused Einstein in his diary. He always disliked having to wear formal dress – and even, famously, socks – whether he was in Germany, England, the United States or any other country. 'He was by nature a rebel who enjoyed being unconventional,' wrote his Oxford-educated scientific collaborator in Princeton, Banesh Hoffmann. 'Whenever possible he dressed for comfort, not for looks.' Einstein regarded such formalities as part of the German *Zwang* ('compulsion' or 'coercion') that he resisted throughout his life, from childhood onwards. One of the Christ Church dons, the economist Sir Roy Harrod (whom we encountered in 1919 as an undergraduate interested in relativity), later remarked of their famous visitor: 'In our governing body I sat next to him; we had a green baize table-cloth; under cover of this he held a wad of paper on his knee, and I observed that all through our meetings his pencil was in incessant progress, covering sheet after sheet with equations.' Another don, Gilbert Murray (who had befriended Einstein while serving on the League of Nations Committee on Intellectual Cooperation in the 1920s), remembered coming across the political refugee Einstein in 1933 sitting alone in the college's grand Tom Quad with a smiling, faraway look on his face. 'Dr. Einstein, do tell me what you are thinking.' Einstein replied: 'We must remember that this is a very small star, and probably some of the larger and more important stars may be very virtuous and happy.'

Appropriately enough, Einstein's first set of Christ Church rooms, overlooking Tom Quad, had been occupied in the later nineteenth century by the mathematician (and clergyman) Charles Lutwidge Dodgson – better known as Lewis Carroll, the author of *Alice's Adventures in Wonderland* and, of course, the poem which inspired 'The Einstein and the Eddington' quoted earlier. By 1931, the rooms were home to a war veteran and classical scholar, Robert Hamilton Dundas, who was away from England on a world tour in 1930–31, luckily for Einstein. When Dundas returned, he was charmed to find that Einstein had written a poem of his own in the visitors' book. More doggerel than Carroll, it is nonetheless quite thoughtful and witty, in this free translation from Einstein's rhymed German by an Oxford literary scholar, J. B. Leishman:

Dundas lets his rooms decay
While he lingers far away,
Drinking wisdom at the source
Where the sun begins its course.
That his walls may not grow cold
He's installed a hermit old,
One who undeterredly preaches
What the art of Numbers teaches.
Shelves of towering folios
Meditate in solemn rows;
Find it strange that one can dwell
Here without their aid so well.
Grumble: Why's this creature staying
With his pipe and piano playing?
Why should this barbarian roam?
Could he not have stopped at home?
Often, though, his thoughts will stray
To the owner far away,
Hoping one day face to face
To behold him in this place.

A year later, Einstein and Dundas – the 'barbarian' and his bibliophile host – did meet, when Einstein returned to Christ Church in 1932. The poem was published in *The Times* soon after Einstein's death, and in due course the visitors' book was donated to the Bodleian Library in Oxford.

Einstein's joke against himself refers to perhaps his only serious reservation about Christ Church (and in fact the university as a whole): its penchant for formality, symbolised by the dreaded dinner-jacket. His two earliest diary entries after arrival in the college with Lindemann catch the flavour well. 'Evening club meal in dinner-jacket. The apartment is reminiscent of a small fortress and belongs to a philologist who is currently in India. Young servant; communication droll,' he noted on 1 May. 'The dinner takes place with about 500 professors and students, the former all in dinner-jackets and black gowns, a bizarre as well as boring affair. Of course the service is men only. One gets a slight idea of how horrible life would be without women. All in a kind of art basilica!' (Today Christ Church's dining-hall displays Einstein in a stained-glass window.) And in his next, briefer entry on 2/3 May he wrote: 'Silent existence in the hermitage in bitter cold. In the evening the solemn Communion Supper of the holy brotherhood in tails. On 3 May with deans (clergymen), who introduce me as a quasi-guest, taciturn and solemn but benevolent with delicate jokes on the tips of their tongues.' Among them was of course Dean White, who would later fall asleep at Einstein's third, and toughest, Rhodes lecture.

Lindemann, and some other Christ Church colleagues, notably Harrod and Murray, compensated for the overall atmosphere of formality. Einstein 'was a charming person, and we entered into relations of easy intimacy with him,' Harrod recalled. 'He divided his time between his mathematics and playing his violin; as one crossed the quad, one was privileged to hear the strains coming from his rooms.' (Like Lindemann, however, Harrod thought Einstein 'naïve' in human affairs.) Furthermore, over time Einstein himself came to appreciate somewhat better the college's English reserve, if not so much its clerical aura. On the whole, though, Einstein's most fruitful contacts in Oxford took place less in Christ Church than in other settings, ranging from other colleges and university societies to private houses and more informal meetings – including, of course, the dinner-concerts at Gunfield organised by Deneke.

Einstein in conversation, possibly in German, somewhere in Oxford, probably in 1931. The man on the right might be Hermann Fiedler, professor of the German language and literature at Oxford, who according to Einstein's diary went for walks in the city with him. The man in the middle might be Frederick Lindemann, professor of experimental philosophy (physics) at Oxford, Einstein's host at the university, who was later the chief scientific adviser to Winston Churchill. If so, this 'mystery' picture is the only British photograph of Einstein with Lindemann, who disliked being photographed.

PHYSICS, PACIFISM, SPORTS AND WANDERING IN OXFORD

Some of these encounters naturally concerned physics and mathematics. Einstein 'threw himself into all the activities of Oxford science, attended the colloquiums and meetings for discussions and proved so stimulating and thought provoking that I am sure his visit will leave a permanent mark on the progress of our subject', Lindemann wrote in June 1931, after Einstein's departure. 'Combined with his attractive personality, his kindness and sympathy have endeared him to all of us and I have hopes that his period as Rhodes lecturer may initiate more permanent connections with this university which can only prove fertile and advantageous in every respect.'

Admittedly, Lindemann addressed this encomium of Einstein to Lothian at the Rhodes Trust, probably with an eye on future funding for him in Oxford. Nevertheless, Lindemann's comments were essentially true concerning Einstein's attitude. What they overlooked, however, was the fundamentally experimental orientation of Oxford science in 1931, which included hardly any theoreticians capable of discussing physics and mathematics at Einstein's level. There was to be no Oxford equivalent for Einstein of Cambridge's Sir Arthur Eddington.

Thus, Einstein's dinner at New College with John Sealy Townsend, Wykeham Professor of Physics, led nowhere, other than a visit to the college chapel for a fine performance of Mozart's Requiem and a tour of Townsend's laboratory. And a lunch at Wadham College with the eminent pure mathematician G. H. (Godfrey Harold) Hardy, author of *A Mathematician's Apology*, was noteworthy only for Hardy's showing Einstein an interesting game with matches. The most promising candidate for a serious discussion was a cosmologist, Edward Arthur Milne, who had been appointed the first Rouse Ball Professor of Mathematics at Oxford in 1929. On 5 May 1931, Einstein attended a meeting with Milne at Trinity College, during which Milne gave a speech on novae (new stars) to a small group. He is a 'very clever man', Einstein noted in his diary. The following day Milne had further discussions with Einstein in the company of Lindemann, and another meeting with Einstein the day after that. But when Milne went on during 1932 to develop a theory of 'kinematical relativity' based on his conviction that general relativity was unsound, which aimed to derive cosmological models by extending the kinematical principles of *special* relativity, Einstein regarded this approach as unsound. Einstein's doubts were confirmed by two independent analyses in 1935 and 1936, which 'showed that Milne's distinctive approach led, ironically, to the same set of basic models already studied in relativistic cosmology', noted *The Cambridge Companion to Einstein.*

Next to physics and music, Einstein's other preoccupation in Oxford was political, on each of his three visits. For example, on 22 May he visited Ruskin College, an independent institution set up as Ruskin Hall in 1899 with the support of the trades union movement to offer courses for working-class students unable to gain access to the University of Oxford. Ruskin students were permitted to attend the university's lectures, however. Having met its forty or so young men and women, Einstein pronounced Ruskin an 'excellent institution', and noted that nineteen British Members of Parliament were former members of Ruskin.

He also had meetings with political activists from both inside and outside the university. On 20 May, for example, he attended the League of Nations Society, and answered questions for two hours on internal German and Russian affairs. And on 23 May, on the evening of the day of his doctoral ceremony, he met pacifist university students at a private house, and was impressed by their political maturity – especially as compared with their 'pitiful' German equivalents in Berlin.

Another meeting on 26 May, with some members of War Resisters' International under its chairman, the British member of parliament A. Fenner Brockway – who had served time in prison during the First World War for his anti-conscription activities – brought forth a categorical response from Einstein, recorded by Brockway. He exclaimed: 'There are so many fictitious peace societies. They are prepared to speak of peace in time of peace, but they are not dependable in time of war. Advocates of peace who are not prepared to stand for peace in time of war are useless. To advocate peace and then to flinch when the test comes means nothing – absolutely nothing.' Surely this was a statement Einstein would come to regret in 1933.

A final meeting, with the Quaker-run Friends' Peace Committee on 27 May 1931, was probably the most revealing of all about Einstein's pacifist views. A report of it in *The Friend* opened with a reference to his recent controversial 'Two-per-cent speech' in the United States, and discussed his views of how to organise war resistance in countries without conscription (such as post-war Britain), and also how to promote peace internationally. 'For example, he suggested that it is very important to organise the churches and get declarations from them against participation in war', in particular the Roman Catholic Church, 'as this would have so much influence in France and Italy.' As for diminishing Germany's rising militancy, Einstein advised that pacifist endeavours to denounce the war guilt clause in the Versailles peace treaty were less likely to work than international efforts to relieve Germany's 'terrible economic depression' by finding a solution to its war reparations problem. But he was not optimistic when asked about the prevention of war by international diplomacy, no doubt because of his experiences with the International Committee on Intellectual Cooperation. 'He pointed out that the machinery is there in the League of Nations, but that unfortunately in his view it is too weak. He believes, however, that the machinery is capable of being made strong and effective. "That depends," he said, "on what the people *will*."' Apropos, Einstein paid this unexpected tribute to religion:

> To Friends, perhaps the most interesting part of the interview was Professor Einstein's statement that his attitude to war was held because he can 'do no other.' He agreed that the strongest anti-war convictions are those with a religious basis. People may be convinced intellectually that war is futile, but that is not enough. This greatest of thinkers does not trust to the intellect alone. 'Reason,' he says, 'is a factor of secondary importance.'

Yet it would be untrue to leave the impression that all of Einstein's time in Oxford during May 1931 was taken up with scientific, musical and political activities. As his diary made plain, albeit often laconically, he had a varied range of other experiences.

For example, a physics research student at Christ Church, Douglas Roaf, hearing of Einstein's love of sailing, took him out on the River Thames in a skiff down to the Abingdon Cut. Seeing that Roaf was properly attired for the occasion and wearing plimsolls, Einstein offered to take off his brown boots. He also saw at first hand the sporty side of Lindemann, who had been a championship tennis player in both Germany and England in his younger days. While Lindemann played squash on a private squash court, Einstein watched from the spectators' gallery, as the mysteries of the game were explained to him by one of his undergraduate friends at Christ Church, Alfred Ubbelohde (later professor of thermodynamics at Imperial College in London). On another occasion, having attended a university regatta by the river in the afternoon, Einstein went to an extraordinary lecture in the university church about old Coptic music. He noted that the (unnamed) lecturer – 'a fat giant with a red face', standing in a blue habit on a blue podium – was 'a picturesque swindler'. More productively, he visited the Ashmolean Museum with Lindemann to see the famous objects excavated from the Minoan civilisation in Crete by Sir Arthur Evans. They struck Einstein as 'more Egyptian than Greek in character'.

In addition, he enjoyed plenty of informally dressed walking in Oxford, either with others – including Hermann Fiedler, the professor of the German language and literature – or, quite frequently, wandering on his own in the streets and parks. As he told Deneke: 'The types of humanity in the streets here are interesting to me – they are quite unlike those seen at home.' And he was taken out of Oxford by car into the Cotswold countryside, the beauty of which he much appreciated. Lindemann introduced him to his eighty-five-year-old father at his country house in the Thames Valley, who impressed Einstein with his liveliness. Adolph Lindemann, besides being an amateur astronomer keenly interested in relativity, had been an engineer and businessman making ships for the Russian navy under the tsars. He spoke of corruption in Russia. Having delivered ten ships, he was paid for nine of them. When he asked the government official in charge of the purchase about payment for the tenth ship, the official replied: 'Make sure you get home as soon as possible.' At another country house, belonging to a friend of Lindemann, old Lady Fitzgerald, Einstein was tickled to see a strange, new, technological advance: drinking fountains for cows. When a cow pressed her muzzle against a metal plate, a valve opened and the water flowed into a drinking bowl. 'Soon there will be water-closets for cows,' mused Einstein, the former patent clerk, in his diary. 'Long live civilisation!'

Not recorded in the diary was his brief flirtation with a woman who had followed him from Germany to Oxford. In total contrast to the musical Margaret Deneke, Ethel Michanowski was a Berlin socialite. Einstein composed a brief poem for her on a notecard from Christ Church, which began: 'Long-branched and delicately strung, / Nothing that will escape her gaze'. Michanowski then sent him an expensive present, which he did not welcome. 'The small package really angered me,' he wrote. 'You have to stop sending me presents incessantly. . . . And to send something like that to an English college where we are surrounded by senseless affluence anyway!'

But probably the most evocative memory of Einstein in Oxford concerned simply his charisma. It was recalled in an account of a chance encounter by William Golding, the future author of *Lord of the Flies* and Nobel laureate, who started as an undergraduate in science and then changed to literature. Sometime in 1931, Golding happened to be standing on a small bridge in Magdalen Deer Park looking at the river when a 'tiny moustached and hatted figure' joined him. 'Professor Einstein knew no English at that time, and I knew only two words of German. I beamed at him, trying wordlessly to convey by my bearing all the affection and respect that the English felt for him.' For about five minutes the two of them stood side by side. At last, said Golding, 'With true greatness, Professor Einstein realised that any contact was better than none.' He pointed to a trout wavering in midstream. '*Fisch*,' he said. 'Desperately I sought for some sign by which I might convey that I, too, revered pure reason. I nodded vehemently. In a brilliant flash I used up half my German vocabulary: '*Fisch. Ja. Ja.*' I would have given my Greek and Latin and French and a good slice of my English for

Einstein in Oxford during one of his three visits in 1931, 1932 and 1933. He liked to stroll around the city on his own, comparing its life with that of Berlin. The precise location is unknown.

enough German to communicate. But we were divided; he was as inscrutable as my headmaster.' For another five minutes, the unknown undergraduate Englishman and the world-famous German scientist stood together. 'Then Professor Einstein, his whole figure still conveying goodwill and amiability, drifted away out of sight.'

ELECTED 'STUDENT' OF CHRIST CHURCH

Even before Einstein left Oxford on 28 May 1931, Lindemann appears to have begun negotiations within Christ Church to lure him back. His idea was that Einstein should be elected a 'research student' (i.e. a fellow) of the college and be offered a bursary from college funds so that he could spend relatively brief periods of time in Oxford each year at his own convenience. By late June, Dean White of Christ Church informed Lindemann that the college was in a position to offer a 'studentship' to Einstein for five years, with an annual stipend of £400, a dining allowance and accommodation during his periods of residence, which it was hoped would last for about a month each year during Oxford term time. Lindemann promptly intimated this possibility to Einstein in a letter.

Einstein was immediately tempted – not least because of the disastrous economic and political situation in Germany, with banks at risk of collapse, escalating unemployment and the rising popular appeal of the Nazi Party. 'Your kind letter has filled me with great pleasure and brought back to me the memory of the wonderful weeks in Oxford,' he wrote to Lindemann on 6 July. However, he went on to advise Lindemann of a difficulty that had put him 'on the horns of a dilemma': whether to accept Christ Church's offer or a parallel offer from the California Institute of Technology in Pasadena, since he was unable to fulfil both obligations given his commitments in Berlin. He therefore proposed the following course of action: that Lindemann write immediately to the dean of Christ Church asking him not to send his invitation to Einstein yet. 'I should not like either to delay replying to him or to have to answer in the negative.' Better, he said, first to await the answer from Pasadena and then he would take a decision on what he should do.

By mid-July, it became clear that Einstein was ready to accept Christ Church's offer. But in a letter to the dean he did not clarify whether he accepted all of the terms of the studentship, in particular its annual residence requirement. Lindemann persuaded the college to give Einstein the benefit of the doubt: although he might spend less than a month at Christ Church in any one year, he would make up for this during another year. On 21 October, the governing body elected Einstein unanimously to a research studentship. Einstein accepted the offer on 29 October with a warm letter to the dean referring to the college's 'harmonious community life'.

In the interval, however, Dean White received a stern letter of protest at the college's decision. Dated 24 October, it came from a former tutor and student of Christ Church who had taught classical history there from 1900 to 1927, before migrating to Brasenose College when he became Camden Professor of Ancient History: John George Clark Anderson. He began:

> Dear Dean, I was amazed to read the announcement of your latest election to a research studentship, and I hope that, in view of my long connection with Christ Church, to which I gave the best years of my life, and my part in framing the new statutes, particularly those relating to research, you will not resent my writing a line to you about it. My only concern is that Christ Church should always appear to do the right thing.

According to Anderson, 'I am sure it never occurred to the mind of anyone concerned with the new statutes that there was any possibility of emoluments being bestowed on people of non-British nationality. The old statutes were, I think, explicit about British nationality as a qualification for election to studentships . . .'. He continued: 'I cannot help thinking that it is unfortunate that an Oxford college should send money out of the country in the present financial situation and at a time when the university is receiving a large government grant at the expense of the taxpayers for educational purposes. The more I think of it, the more strange does this new development appear to me . . .'. And he concluded: 'Forgive me if I intrude: I have no wish to do that. I have written only as a loyal member of the House [Christ Church], who has its welfare at heart.'

At no point in Anderson's letter did he mention Einstein by name or give even the merest hint that he was aware of Einstein's eminence. The dean took up this point in his reply:

> I think that in electing Einstein we are securing for our society perhaps the greatest authority in the world on physical science; his attainments and reputation are so high that they transcend national boundaries, and any university in the world ought to be proud of having him. Then in spite of his scientific position he is a poor man, and this quite moderate pecuniary help will enable him to carry on his work better.

In answer to Anderson's other points, the dean wrote:

> I do not quite follow your argument about our statutes, and persons of non-British nationality; and of course I was never here under the old statutes. But it seems to me that the only possible reason for deleting the restriction must have been the wish to widen the area of selection. If the college wished to exclude foreigners, why did it not say so?
>
> It is quite true that we are paying money *out* of England; but I think we are getting more than our money's worth.

A further letter from Anderson expanded at length on his arguments about funding, some of which were reasonable, especially in a time of serious economic depression. Yet, the emotions underlying the arguments were clear from two comments: that a research studentship should not go to 'a German who has no connection with the university (beyond being the recipient of an honorary degree)'; and that 'it does not seem to me to be patriotic, especially in such times as the present, to use college revenues to endow foreigners. Charity should always begin at home.' Anti-German feeling and Oxford academic parochialism were still, sadly, alive and well in 1931. To the credit of Christ Church, its governing body rose above such attitudes with Einstein, well before he became a target of Nazi attacks in 1933.

Amusingly, even though the British tax authorities agreed with Anderson's argument about money going out of England, they did not accept the negative conclusion he drew from it. In 1932, a zealous Oxford tax inspector suggested that Einstein's Christ Church stipend should be liable for income tax. A concerned Lindemann discussed the matter with the chairman of the board of the Inland Revenue, Sir James Grigg, and the Revenue's special expert on the subject, a certain W. G. E. Burnett. According to Burnett, Einstein's annual stipend from Christ Church should be exempt from British tax. Einstein did not live or work in Oxford, he wrote, and thus 'The world at large, and not Christ Church in particular, gets the benefit of his work.' Although England would get its money's worth from Einstein's visits to Oxford, his true value would have no national boundaries.

CHAPTER SIX

The Reality of Nature and the Nature of Reality

Experience can of course guide us in our choice of serviceable mathematical concepts; it cannot possibly be the source from which they are derived; experience of course remains the sole criterion of the serviceability of a mathematical construction for physics, but the truly creative principle resides in mathematics.

Lecture by Einstein, 'On the Method of Theoretical Physics', in Oxford, June 1933

Einstein's second stay in Oxford, from late April to late May 1932, was less eventful as compared with his busy and much-publicised visit exactly a year earlier. This time he avoided giving lectures in England, except for the Rouse Ball lecture on mathematics on 5 May in Cambridge, which provided him with a welcome opportunity to meet Eddington. (But he did agree at this time to give the Herbert Spencer lecture during Oxford's Trinity term in mid-1933.) He also kept largely clear of politics, giving only one press interview, to the *Jewish Chronicle*. Asked by its reporter in his college rooms at Christ Church whether or not 'Jews as a race make good scientists' and 'possess peculiar gifts in the sphere of music', Einstein replied that while Jews had always taken an interest in intellectual problems, they had excelled more in science. But, he said, 'I do not believe in any special gifts among the Jews. It is more an *inclination* towards a particular occupation.' Pressed on his view of Palestine and Jewish–Arab relations, he added that the Jewish situation there would remain a problem. 'The coexistence of human beings with different traditions always constitutes a problem.' Most of his time in Oxford seems to have been spent quietly working on physics and mathematics in his new college, taking walks about the city and playing music with amateurs and professionals, including Marie Soldat, at the Denekes' house, Gunfield. On one occasion, they finished the last note of the Brahms Piano Quintet at 11.20 p.m. Einstein called out: 'The gate at Christ Church is locked at eleven – what am I to do now?' Having rushed to the telephone and called the porters' lodge, they discovered the college would remain open until midnight (perhaps in Einstein's honour?). Before hurrying into the Denekes' car, Einstein scribbled a postcard to Sir Donald Tovey thanking their musicologist friend for the gift of his book on the art of the fugue. 'Marie Soldat felt our evening had been merrier than any were last year,' noted Margaret Deneke happily. 'The professor was more sans gêne and we others had overcome the shyness of having him as our guest.'

THE COMING TO POWER OF THE NAZIS

In Germany, however, May 1932 had been an eventful month. When Einstein returned to Berlin, he found a city that was ominously different from the one he had left a month earlier. Political events in his absence had involved a secret deal on 8 May between an influential military leader, General Kurt von Schleicher, and Adolf Hitler, head of the Nazi Party. This was followed on 30 May by the official removal of the chancellor, Heinrich Brüning, and the appointment of a new, ultra-right-wing chancellor, Franz von Papen, with Schleicher as his minister of defence – all at the behest of the aged president, Field Marshal Paul von Hindenburg. On 2 June, a German Christian leader and Nazi deputy, Wilhelm Kube, announced to the Prussian Diet that 'when we clean house the exodus of the Children of Israel will be a child's game in comparison', adding that 'a people that possesses a Kant will not permit an Einstein to be tacked onto it'. Thus began the slide towards the Nazi seizure of power less than a year later and the subsequent exile of Einstein from his native country, which would propel him back to Oxford for his final stay in May–June 1933.

During that summer of 1932, when a professor visiting Einstein at his lakeside villa at Caputh near Berlin expressed the hope that the army might curb the Nazis, Einstein responded firmly: 'I am convinced that a military regime will not prevent the imminent National Socialist revolution. The military dictatorship will suppress the popular will and the people will seek protection against the rule of the Junkers [the Prussian landed nobility] and the officers in a right-radical revolution.' When he and his wife Elsa locked up their Caputh house in early December 1932, to board a ship in Antwerp heading for California, he told her: 'Before you leave our villa this time, take a good look at it.' 'Why?' she asked. 'You will never see it again,' Einstein quietly replied. His wife thought he was being rather foolish, because they had made plans to return to Berlin in March. Yet it turned out that he was being prescient.

On 10 March 1933, Einstein made his first public statement about the newly arrived power of Nazi Germany, as a major earthquake shook him at the California Institute of Technology. 'As long as I have any choice in the matter, I shall live only in a country where civil liberty, tolerance and equality of all citizens before the law prevail,' he told a New York newspaper reporter. 'Civil liberty implies freedom to express one's political convictions, in speech and in writing; tolerance implies respect for the convictions of others whatever they may be. These conditions do not exist in Germany at the present time.' The truth of this analysis was soon forthcoming: Einstein's house at Caputh was reported to have been broken into, allegedly in search of concealed arms. 'The raid,' said Einstein in a statement issued from on board ship to Europe, 'is but one example of the arbitrary acts of violence now taking place throughout Germany. These acts are the result of the government's overnight transfer of police powers to a raw and rabid mob of the Nazi militia.'

On arrival in Antwerp on 28 March, the Einsteins decided to stay in Belgium, where Einstein had friends, including the royal family. (He and Elisabeth, the unconventional and artistic Queen of Belgium, enjoyed playing violin together.) That very day, he resigned by letter from the Prussian Academy of Sciences, just before the Nazis held their first national day boycotting German Jews on 1 April.

In response, a German newspaper published an anti-Semitic cartoon on 1 April. It showed a sharp-nosed Einstein on his hands and knees being kicked out of a German consulate by a large boot. According to its satirical caption: 'The concierge of the German embassy in Brussels is authorised to cure an Asiatic [i.e. an East European Jew] of the delusion that he is a Prussian.' After Einstein formally applied for release from German citizenship on 4 April, the irritated Nazi regime took almost a year to enact his expatriation.

A Nazi view of Einstein. This anti-Semitic cartoon published in the *Deutsche Tageszeitung*, 1 April 1933, the day of Germany's first national day boycotting its Jews, shows Einstein being booted out of the German embassy in Brussels. (See text above the cartoon for a translation of the German caption.) Shortly after the cartoon's publication, Einstein applied for release from German citizenship, having relocated his residence from Germany to Belgium.

As for the Prussian Academy, it immediately bowed cravenly to what the majority of its members assumed their furious government expected from them – by publicly accusing Einstein of 'atrocity propaganda' against Germany. A horrified Max Planck informed the acting secretary of the academy on 31 March: 'Even though in political matters a deep gulf divides me from him, I am, on the other hand, absolutely certain that in the history of centuries to come Einstein's name will be celebrated as one of the brightest stars that ever shone in our Academy.' In a personal response to Planck, Einstein, while denying the allegation of 'atrocity propaganda', added prophetically: 'But now the war of extermination against my Jewish brethren has compelled me to throw the influence I have in the world into the balance of their favour.' Planck, ever the social conservative, replied equating such persecution of the Jews with Einstein's pacifism and refusal of military service: 'Two ideologies, which cannot coexist, have clashed here. I have no sympathy with the one or the other.' It was a sad and very bitter way to end the long and loyal friendship between these two great physicists. When Planck died in 1947, Einstein wrote to his widow: 'The hours which I was permitted to spend at your house, and the many conversations which I conducted face to face with that wonderful man, will remain among my most beautiful memories for the rest of my life. This cannot be altered by the fact that a tragic fate tore us apart.'

During 1933–35, the German government officially seized all of the Einsteins' assets in Germany. First to go were their bank deposits, 'in order to maintain public security and order and also to prevent future anticipated subversive Communist activities', according to an official letter sent to Einstein by the Office of the Secret State Police on 10 May. Then it was the turn of their villa in Caputh and Einstein's beloved sailboat, *Tümmler* (Porpoise).

Happily, the boat was sold in error not to a Nazi Party member, as intended by the Prussian prime minister, but to a man who forbade his son from joining the Hitler Youth and would support five orphans of an anti-Fascist executed by the People's Court in Berlin in 1944. But attempts by Einstein, as a long-time Swiss citizen, his relatives and their lawyers, to enlist the help of the Swiss government in rescuing his German assets during 1933, failed completely, because the Swiss did not want to upset the Nazis.

Some Belgian colleagues had offered the Einsteins temporary accommodation in an old country house near Antwerp. Since they were likely to be staying in Belgium for some time, they decided to rent a holiday house, the Villa Savoyard, in Le Coq sur Mer, a small seaside resort near Ostend, without servants and without a telephone. Though less spacious than their house in Caputh, its magnificent situation among coastal sand dunes appealed to Einstein. Not only was it isolated enough to discourage unwanted callers, it was also fine for solitary walking and reflection – both on science and on politics. In due course, it would also prove practical for the protection of Einstein by an armed contingent of Belgian police.

INTRODUCING OLIVER LOCKER-LAMPSON

Around the time he moved to Le Coq, Einstein received a surprising letter in German from an Englishman, a complete stranger based in London. Dated 28 March 1933, it was sent from the House of Commons. Prompted by the press coverage of Einstein's homeless predicament, Commander Oliver Stillingfleet Locker-Lampson, a Conservative member of parliament since 1910, wished to offer Einstein his private residence in London as a refuge from the Nazis for a year, at any time that suited his guest. He put it like this:

> Highly Esteemed Professor,
>
> It was at the time of your presence in Oxford – when Lord Haldane was still with us – that I had the honour to make your acquaintance – and that is what I would like to refer to now.
>
> My letter today is, above all, inspired by the wish to assure you, dear Professor, how sincerely a large number of my countrymen take part in the suffering that your fellow-believers in Germany have to endure.
>
> The fact that 'Einstein is without a home' has deeply moved me, and perhaps this may serve as a justification for daring to approach you with a suggestion that, as a modest member of the public, would otherwise not be appropriate to the greatest scholar of our time. And I hope, therefore, that you, dear Professor, will see in my little offer nothing but a genuine sign of my unreserved respect and desire to serve you in my own way.

Coming down to brass tacks, Locker-Lampson explained that his London house consisted of a hallway, dining-room, living-room and lounge, two or three bedrooms, three bedrooms for employees and well-equipped kitchen facilities. Both running costs and servants would naturally be included in his offer. Then he concluded: 'My house may not be as comfortable as yours, of course, but who knows, whether the "Ether-Atmosphere" of our English love of "Fair Play" might not help you to penetrate even deeper into the "Relativity-Mysteries".' ('Ether-Atmosphere', 'Fair Play' and 'Relativity-Mysteries' appear in English in the German original.)

Locker-Lampson, though largely forgotten today, was a well-known politician in Britain in 1933. The antithesis of Einstein in almost every respect, he was the son of a Victorian man of letters and poet who had been friendly with Alfred Lord Tennyson and

Oscar Wilde; a wealthy landowner with properties in London, Norfolk and Surrey; and a decorated war veteran, who had commanded a British armoured column on the Russian front fighting on behalf of Tsar Nicholas II, with the political backing of his family's friend, Churchill. Tall, lean, dashing, maverick, mercurial – and, when crossed, vindictive – the strongly anti-Bolshevist commander had previously praised the up-and-coming Nazis, in common with a wide variety of upper-class Englishmen during this pre-war decade. They 'despatched their children to Nazi Germany in droves' and 'many openly admired Hitler – for the way he had pulled his country up by its bootstraps and particularly for his determination to defeat Bolshevism', according to a recent historical study, *Travellers in the Third Reich*. But now that Hitler was actually in power, Einstein had apparently become Locker-Lampson's hero.

What were Locker-Lampson's real motives in making his undoubtedly generous offer? With someone of his dissembling contradictions it is difficult to be sure, as we shall constantly discover while his intriguing and crucial relationship with Einstein unfolds during the second half of 1933.

There is an unintentional clue in the letter's opening paragraph. Locker-Lampson claims vaguely to have met Einstein in person in Oxford 'when Lord Haldane was still with us'. That is, during Einstein's flying visit to Oxford in 1921 (not in 1931), given that Haldane died in 1928. But this supposed memory is extremely unlikely to be true, since Einstein met virtually no one in Oxford (not even the vice-chancellor), other than his host Lindemann, during the few hours he spent in Oxford on 14 June 1921. Perhaps Locker-Lampson misremembered and actually met Einstein in London in June 1921, maybe at Haldane's private reception or the official dinner after Einstein's speech at King's College? But if so, there is no record of his presence in the detailed contemporary newspaper and magazine reports listing distinguished guests and visitors at these events, despite the fact that Commander Locker-Lampson was by 1921 a fairly well-known political figure: a long-time friend of Winston Churchill, and the parliamentary private secretary of the chancellor of the exchequer, Austen Chamberlain, in 1919–21, with whom he had attended the 1919 Versailles peace conference. So it seems most probable that Locker-Lampson's claimed encounter with Einstein in England was simply a convenient fantasy.

Much stronger evidence of his tendency to embroider historical facts comes from Locker-Lampson's bizarre article, 'Adolf Hitler as I know him', published in late September 1930, shortly after the Nazi Party made its first major electoral gains in Germany, in the *Daily Mirror*, which was then a right-wing national newspaper. So bizarre, in fact, that the article is worth discussing at considerable length – given the importance of Locker-Lampson's coming role in Einstein's life in England during September 1933.

It began with a tantalising tale about Hitler, the war of 1914–18 and cricket. 'My first recollection of Herr Hitler is remote and casual.' Locker-Lampson was then supposedly in south Germany, talking to some British officers who had been prisoners of war in Germany. Hitler was much on their minds because of the latest news of his failure to grab power in the 1923 Munich Putsch. They recalled that he had been in hospital while they were in a prisoner-of-war camp on parole. One day Hitler had come to them and asked if he might watch a cricket eleven at play, so as to initiate himself into the mysteries of the British national game. They welcomed him, and wrote out the rules 'in the best British sport-loving spirit'. With these, Hitler vanished. However, he returned a few days later and announced that he was already training a German team and was looking for an early opportunity to challenge his British instructors. 'I believe they even played a friendly match.'

Even more significantly, Hitler returned again with the astonishing information that he had reflected over the rules of cricket, and wished to alter them radically to suit serious-minded Teutons rather than hedonistic British people. Among his essential improvements were the discontinuance of pads, which he dismissed as 'unmanly and un-German', and the introduction of a bigger and harder ball. In other words, Hitler saw cricket not as his 'innocent' British instructors did, but instead as 'a possible medium for the training of troops off duty and in times of peace'.

Then Locker-Lampson gave a laudatory analysis of Hitler the up-and-coming politician (though without lending any support to anti-Semitism), apparently based on personal knowledge. Before his current fame, 'he seemed just an ordinary German officer with . . . tooth-brush moustache in the latest military style, a soft collar always united with a pin shaped like a swastika, and eyes hidden behind loaded lids – suggestive of hidden fire and fury. Even when he spoke in his deep guttural voice, we were not necessarily thrilled.' However, 'after a few hours in his company any honest observer must admit that folk become electrified. The temperature of the room rises in his presence. He enhances the value of life. He makes his humblest follower feel twice the man.'

That said, the political difficulties in Hitler's way were still formidable, Locker-Lampson conceded, in a country with fifteen parties, in which his own party – the Nazi Party – comprised more than the usual ragbag of competing views and ambitions. How to unite these when his party got into power might prove even trickier for Hitler than how to reconcile them out of office. 'But he means to ride off on the patriotic ticket, and play for a tear-up of the treaties and a rip-up of reparations. That is his soul's consecration – that is what makes him a legendary hero already.'

Finally, the article reverted to cricket. Hitler's 'motto', suggested Locker-Lampson, might be the German motto he had suggested during the world war to his British cricketing friends when he was rewriting the old game's rules: '*Ohne Hast, ohne Rest*' (without haste, without rest). 'Only I doubt his ability to wait – or his country's wish that he should.'

No reliable evidence exists for the accuracy of Locker-Lampson's cricket story. Notwithstanding a claim made in *The Times* in 2010 that the story is 'true', it is very unlikely to be factual, according to current historians of early Nazism (such as Thomas Weber, author of *Becoming Hitler: The Making of a Nazi*), given the authoritative details of Hitler's war record and his probable lack of knowledge of conversational English in 1914–18. Nor is there any evidence, including the draft for Locker-Lampson's unwritten memoirs, that he ever met Hitler in person in Germany during the 1920s, although such a meeting is certainly conceivable, given his open sympathy at this time for both Germany and Fascism – in Italy, as well as Germany – if not for anti-Semitism. In 1931, Locker-Lampson founded a short-lived patriotic movement with semi-Fascist leanings, the Sentinels of Empire, also known as the Blue Shirts. It held mass rallies in London's Albert Hall, led by Locker-Lampson, who composed its anthem, 'March on!' (set to music from the British Gaumont film, *High Treason*), which he sent to Benito Mussolini on a 78-rpm phonographic record along with Blue Shirts silver and blue-enamelled cufflinks and a badge. And he himself received a gold cigarette case, a gift from an influential Nazi ideologue, Alfred Rosenberg, as a 'token of his esteem' (an item that Locker-Lampson, to his credit, did not accept). Yet, *Time* magazine joked, after attending a Blue Shirts Albert Hall rally, that few people expected Locker-Lampson to become 'in more than nickname "Britain's Hitler", much less "Britain's Mussolini"'. Nonetheless, there can be little doubt that he worshipped, and wanted for himself, some of the glamour of famous people. In 1930, his icon was apparently Hitler; by mid-1933, it had certainly become Einstein.

Had Einstein been aware of Locker-Lampson's *Daily Mirror* article, he would presumably have avoided any kind of association with him. Even the public letter Locker-Lampson now addressed to Hitler, printed in *The Times* on 1 April 1933 as a postscript to the newspaper's long report on the 'Nazi boycott of Jews', could hardly have appealed to Einstein. While sounding a new note of warning about Nazi anti-Semitism, Locker-Lampson's letter retained some of the commander's earlier praise for the German leader in its opening phrase: 'As a member of Parliament and former officer who has always and openly stood for Germany's claims to military equality and territorial revision and who has been for years your sincere admirer . . .'. But it continued less positively: 'I take the liberty of calling your attention to the fact that the decision to discriminate against the German Jews has had a most damaging effect upon the good feeling for Germany which was growing stronger and which culminated on your accession to power.' Then it reverted to praise: 'We hoped to see Germany strengthened under your leadership . . .'. But it concluded: 'This action against the Jews is making the work of myself and other friends of Germany almost impossible. Forgive me, Chancellor, for these frank words of an Englishman who has often cheered you in your meetings in Germany.' (When Locker-Lampson stepped up his public campaign in the mid-1930s, and became a noted sponsor of desperate German-Jewish refugees, Hitler eventually retorted by calling Locker-Lampson 'a Jew and a Communist'!)

Einstein in Tom Quad, the main quadrangle of Christ Church, Oxford, the college where he lived in June 1933. By now, Einstein was a refugee from Germany, his houses and bank account having recently been confiscated by the Nazi regime.

However, it seems that Einstein was ignorant of Locker-Lampson's politics at the time of the commander's invitation. At any rate, he had no wish to abandon his independent life by the sea in Belgium and move to metropolitan London. While thanking Locker-Lampson for his offer, he declined it. Yet, he and his wife would keep the possibility of such an English refuge in mind.

Instead, Einstein began to plan a further month in Oxford, as well as a visit to Glasgow in Scotland, where he had agreed to give a lecture on the history of general relativity at the University of Glasgow on 20 June. During early May, there was a revealing exchange of letters between Einstein in Le Coq and Lindemann in Oxford, mixing science with politics.

RETURN TO OXFORD

It started with a brief letter from Einstein on 1 May about returning to England. He began: 'I am sitting here in my very pleasant exile with Professor Mayer.' He would be in Glasgow on 20 June. Could he visit Oxford again that month? Might Christ Church be able to offer him a small room? It need not be so 'grand' as his previous lodgings in 1931 and 1932. Then Einstein abruptly switched subjects and alluded to politics: 'You have probably heard of my little duel with the Prussian Academy. I shall never see the land of my birth again.' Finally he mentioned physics: he had worked out with Professor Mayer 'a couple of wonderful new results of a mathematical-physical kind'.

Lindemann replied immediately on 4 May, saying that he would have written earlier but had had no address for Einstein, and that he gathered from the newspapers that 'there was not much prospect of a letter to Berlin being forwarded'. He naturally welcomed Einstein's visit, but suggested that, since Oxford's Trinity term would end on 16 June, Einstein should arrive at the end of May, so that his visit to Glasgow would fall 'at the end of your stay instead of in the middle of it'. A set of rooms would be available, but 'as we did not know your plans I am afraid they will be somewhat smaller than last year'.

Then he discussed his own recent visit to Berlin, for four or five days in mid-April over Easter, when he had seen many of Einstein's German colleagues. About the Prussian Academy's condemnation of Einstein and the wider political situation he commented:

> The general feeling was much against the action taken by the Academy, which was the responsibility of one of the secretaries without consultation with the members. I can tell you more about it when you come. Everybody sent you their kind regards, more especially Schrödinger, but it was felt that it would be damaging to all concerned to write to you, especially as the letter would almost certainly not be forwarded. Conditions there were extremely curious. It seems, however, that the Nazis have got their hands on the machine and they will probably be there for a long time.

Lindemann went on to consider what could be done to help some of the German-Jewish physicists, by trying to find them positions at Oxford. 'I need scarcely say that very little money is available and that it would cause a lot of feeling, even if it were possible to place them in positions normally occupied by Englishmen.' He specified two promising individuals, Hans Bethe and Fritz London (the first of whom would win a Nobel prize), recommended to him by Einstein's non-Jewish colleague, the theoretical physicist Arnold Sommerfeld. Lindemann asked whether Einstein would be willing to recommend Bethe and London too, while adding characteristically: 'Perhaps there are others whom you might consider better, but I have the impression that anyone trained by Sommerfeld is the sort of man who can work out a problem and get an answer, which is what we really need in Oxford rather than the more abstract type who would spend his time disputing with the philosophers.' This was the launch of Lindemann's historic campaign to obtain funding for notable refugee experimental physicists to come to Oxford in 1933–34. He would help a group of distinguished Jews, including the low-temperature physicist Franz (later Sir Francis) Simon, who became a professor at Oxford, worked on the atomic bomb project and eventually took over from Lindemann as head of the Clarendon Laboratory.

Einstein responded on 7 May, advising that he would try to reach England on 21 May. Lindemann should not go to any bother about his accommodation because he would need only 'one room' in order to be comfortable. About politics, he added ominously, 'I think that the Nazis have got the whip hand in Berlin.' He had been told on good authority that the Nazis were hurriedly collecting war materiel, notably aeroplanes. 'If they are given another year or two the world will have another fine experience at the hands of the Germans.' As for the two physicists mentioned by Lindemann, he recommended London as 'a great source of strength' but said he knew too little about Bethe to express an opinion. Regardless of which individuals might be chosen, he was very grateful to Lindemann for his efforts to relieve refugee physicists. He offered to give a third of his salary that year to help his threatened German-Jewish colleagues.

Then, on 9 May, Einstein wrote again very briefly, announcing that he would not be able to arrive in Oxford until about the 26th because his younger son had been taken seriously ill. If he were to have any mental peace in England, he could not wait six weeks before seeing him in Zurich. 'You are not a father yourself, but I know you will certainly understand.' Not long before heading for Oxford in late May, he would see his son, Eduard, a long-term psychiatric patient suffering from schizophrenia, who was being looked after by his ex-wife, Mileva, and by professional clinics, in Zurich. Einstein chose to stay with Mileva. 'There is no written evidence about Einstein's feelings when he visited his son,' noted Einstein's German biographer Albrecht Fölsing. 'No doubt he was profoundly shaken, and he certainly determined to make sure his son's future was financially secure.' Although Einstein would remain in touch with Eduard by letter, he would never see his son, or his ex-wife, again. (Eduard Einstein survived his father, dying in a Swiss psychiatric hospital in 1965.)

LANDING CARD FOR NON-BRITISH SUBJECTS.
Landingskaart voor niet Britsche onderdanen.
Carte de débarquement pour sujets non Britanniques.

From OOSTENDE

THIS CARD MUST BE FILLED IN BY EACH PASSENGER LANDING.
Deze kaart moet, bij landing, door ieder reiziger ingevuld worden.
Ce questionnaire doit être rempli par chaque voyageur au débarquement.

PORT OF EMBARKATION ABROAD. Haven van inscheping in het Buitenland. Port d'embarquement à l'étranger. OOSTENDE

SURNAME IN BLOCK LETTERS / Naam in hoofdletters / Nom en caractères gros: EINSTEIN
CHRISTIAN NAMES (Prénoms) Voornamen: albert
NAMES AND AGES OF DEPENDENTS UNDER 16 ACCOMPANYING. Namen en leeftijd van de meereizenden onder de 16 jaar. Noms et âges des dépendants qui ont moins de seize ans.
AGE (Leeftijd) 1879 SEX (Geslacht Sexe) M OCCUPATION (Beroep) Professor
NATIONALITY Nationaliteit Nationalité: Swiss
NATIONALITY AT BIRTH Nationaliteit bij geboorte Nationalité de naissance: German
PROPOSED ADDRESS IN UNITED KINGDOM Voorgenomen adres in het Vereenigde Koninkrijk Adresse proposée dans la Grande-Bretagne: Oxford
SIGNATURE Handteekening van den reiziger Signature du voyageur: A. Einstein

The landing card completed by Einstein on arrival in Britain at Dover, 26 May 1933. It notes his nationality at birth as German, but his current nationality as Swiss; and that his British residence will be in Oxford.

One decidedly puzzling omission from this May correspondence with Lindemann was the Herbert Spencer lecture in Oxford, which Einstein had agreed to give in Trinity term 1933, during his Oxford visit in May 1932. Neither Einstein nor Lindemann refers to the lecture at all. (Nor was it mentioned in a substantial report on 'Einstein as an Oxford don' published in the *Manchester Guardian* on 17 April 1933, which noted that Einstein was expected in Oxford during the summer term.) Although the lecture actually took place at Rhodes House on 10 June 1933, it would appear that this date must have been settled by Einstein at the very last minute, relatively speaking – either shortly before he left Le Coq in mid-May or perhaps soon after he arrived in Oxford on 26 May. Whichever was the case, the lecture must surely have been prepared under conditions of much personal and professional stress for Einstein, exacerbated by the Nazi announcement in mid-May of the seizure of his and his wife's German financial assets.

As he informed Max Born – who had just escaped from Germany to the Italian Alps and would soon settle in Britain – on 30 May, in a letter sent from the cloistered calm of Christ Church: 'You know, I think, that I have never had a particularly favourable opinion of the Germans (morally and politically speaking). But I must confess that the degree of their brutality and cowardice came as something of a surprise to me.' He concluded: 'I've been promoted to an "evil monster" in Germany, and all my money has been taken away from me. But I console myself with the thought that the latter would soon be gone anyway.'

Moreover, at a public event in Oxford's University Museum on 2 June Einstein appeared sorely in need of public reassurance. He had been invited to offer a vote of thanks for a lecture by Rutherford to the Junior Scientific Society on 'The Artificial Transmutation of the Elements'. Not only was Rutherford a

Nobel laureate, like Einstein, he was also a peer of the realm, the 1st Baron Rutherford, and, in addition to his honours, a big booming extrovert with a voice loud enough to disturb sensitive scientific experimental apparatus – according to a standing joke among his Cavendish Laboratory co-workers in Cambridge. Lord Rutherford made quite a contrast with the smaller figure of Einstein, a theoretician who typically worked alone at home or in an office, never in a laboratory, and was naturally unconfident at public speaking in English. According to one of the Oxford undergraduates at the lecture, C. H. Arnold, Einstein seemed 'a poor forlorn little figure' beside Rutherford. While Einstein was delivering his speech of thanks, somehow coping with English, 'it seemed to me that he was more than a little doubtful about the way in which he would be received in a British university'. However, the moment he sat down, he was greeted by a thunderous outburst of applause. As Arnold vividly recalled more than three decades later:

> Never in all my life shall I forget the wonderful change which took place in Einstein's face at that moment. The light came back into his eyes, and his whole face seemed transfigured with joy and delight when it came home to him in this way that, no matter how badly he had been treated by the Nazis, both he himself and his undoubted genius were at any rate greatly appreciated at Oxford.

HERBERT SPENCER LECTURE IN OXFORD

The psychological strain seems to have expressed itself in Einstein's scientific thinking as well as his personal behaviour. In his lecture on 10 June, 'On the method of theoretical physics' – the German manuscript of which lay on his Christ Church desk

Einstein (front row, second from left) as a guest at a political debate at the Oxford Union, June 1933. In the second row, third from left, is Michael Foot, then a student at the university, who later became leader of the Labour Party in Britain. Einstein did not speak in the debate, which was about British politics and did not refer to Germany. After a brief stay in Oxford, he left the city, never to return.

at the very time he was writing to Born – he tried to escape from the messy physical reality inherent in experimental physics, including quantum mechanics, and substitute for it the paradise of pure mathematics, which he had been pursuing for some years in his unified field theory, most recently with the help of his calculator, Walther Mayer, in Le Coq. 'The sanctuary from personal turmoil that Einstein sought in physics may also have coloured the extreme rationalist pronouncements in his Herbert Spencer lecture,' according to the editors of *The Cambridge Companion to Einstein*. Opinions consequently differ as to the lecture's value. One Einstein biographer, Fölsing (who originally trained as a physicist), condemned it as 'a reckless overestimation of the possibility of understanding nature through mathematics alone – a mistake he would not have been capable of in his most productive years' (while acknowledging that 'this faith, though ultimately unproductive, sustained him for decades in his search for the unified field theory'). By contrast, another Einstein biographer, Abraham Pais, a practising physicist who knew Einstein personally over a long period, hailed the lecture as 'perhaps the clearest and most revealing expression of his mode of thinking'.

Theoretical physics had always been Einstein's sanctuary, as he revealed on several occasions during his life, including his 'Autobiographical notes' written for his seventieth birthday in 1949, which called theoretical physics a liberation 'from the chains of the "merely personal"'. Back in 1897, when he was eighteen, while breaking up with his first girlfriend he wrote to her mother:

> Strenuous intellectual work and looking at God's Nature are the reconciling, fortifying, yet relentlessly strict angels that shall lead me through all of life's troubles. . . . One creates a small little world for oneself, and as lamentably insignificant as it may be in comparison with the perpetually changing size of real existence, one feels miraculously great and important, like a mole in his self-dug hole.

And as an adult in 1918, while struggling with wartime privations, divorce and illness that left him bedridden for several months, he made this powerful statement in a speech on the sixtieth birthday of Planck:

> I believe with Schopenhauer that one of the strongest motives that leads men to art and science is escape from everyday life with its painful crudity and hopeless dreariness, from the fetters of one's own ever shifting desires. A finely tempered nature longs to escape from personal life into the world of

> objective perception and thought. . . . With this negative motive goes a positive one. Man tries to make for himself in the fashion that suits him best a simplified and intelligible picture of the world; he then tries to some extent to substitute this cosmos of his for the world of experience, and thus to overcome it. This is what the painter, the poet, the speculative philosopher, and the natural scientist do, each in his own fashion. Each makes this cosmos and its construction the pivot of his emotional life, in order to find in this way the peace and security which he cannot find in the narrow whirlpool of personal experience.

Einstein's Oxford lecture opened with an uncharacteristically emotional introduction – at least by his unemotional standards – perhaps hinting at his mental state in early June 1933:

> I wish to preface what I have to say by expressing to you the great gratitude which I feel to the University of Oxford for having given me the honour and privilege of delivering the Herbert Spencer lecture. May I say that the invitation makes me feel that the links between this university and myself are becoming progressively stronger?

Then he thanked three colleagues at Christ Church – a philosopher, Gilbert Ryle, a classicist, Denys Page and a physicist, Claude Hurst – 'who have helped me – and perhaps a few of you – by translating into English the lecture which I wrote in German'. (Oddly, he did not mention a role for Lindemann.) This time at Rhodes House, unlike in May 1931, in Einstein's first-ever lecture solely in English, the audience did not have to struggle with an unfamiliar language – although Einstein's inimitably accented English, as he read from the dense translation, might sometimes have appeared to have been a foreign tongue. Nor were there any blackboards chalked with baffling mathematics, to be saved by eager science dons. That said, the lecture, as printed, was demanding enough to challenge any listening physicist or philosopher, not to mention the anonymous correspondent of *The Times* with the unenviable task of trying to summarise its content for a general readership. (The *Times* report on 12 June was safely, if unimaginatively, headlined 'Basic concepts in physics'.)

The physics started with some typically Einsteinian humour. He ironically reprimanded himself for claiming more authority for his remarks to come than perhaps he should:

> If you wish to learn from the theoretical physicist anything about the methods which he uses, I would give you the following piece of advice: don't listen to his words, examine his achievements. For to the discoverer in that field, the constructions of his imagination appear so necessary and so natural that he is apt to treat them not as the creations of his thoughts but as given realities.
>
> This statement may seem to be designed to drive my audience away without more ado. For you will say to yourselves, 'The lecturer is himself a constructive physicist; on his own showing therefore he should leave the consideration of the structure of theoretical science to the epistemologist.'

Having openly voiced this subtle objection, Einstein further warned his listeners that his personal view of the past and present of theoretical physics was bound to be coloured by what he was currently trying to achieve and hoped to achieve in the future – an implicit reference to his ongoing work on the unified field theory (which he would briefly mention later in the lecture). 'But this is the common fate of all who have adopted the world of ideas as their dwelling-place. He is in just the same plight as the historian, who also, even though unconsciously, disposes events of the past around ideals that he has formed about human society.'

Then Einstein got to grips with the relationship in physics between pure theory, that is the free inventions of the human mind, and the data of experience, that is our observations of physical reality. 'We honour ancient Greece as the cradle of western science,' he initially reassured his audience, many of whom were no doubt classically trained. 'She for the first time created the intellectual miracle of a logical system, the assertions of which followed one from another with such rigour that not one of the demonstrated propositions admitted of the slightest doubt – Euclid's geometry.' Thinking of his own boyhood, he added: 'The man who was not enthralled in youth by this work was not born to be a scientific theorist.'

Yet, for science to comprehend reality, more than Greek thought was required, he reminded his audience:

> Pure logical thinking can give us no knowledge of the world of experience; all knowledge about reality begins with experience and terminates in it. Conclusions reached by purely rational processes are, so far as reality is concerned, entirely empty. It was because he recognised this, and especially because he impressed it upon the scientific world, that Galileo became the father of modern physics and in fact of the whole of modern natural science.

Newton, 'the first creator of a comprehensive and workable system of theoretical physics', agreed with Galileo's view, Einstein continued.

> [He] still believed that the basic concepts and laws of his system could be derived from experience; his phrase '*hypotheses non fingo*' can only be interpreted in this sense. In fact, at the time it seemed that there was no problematical element in the concepts of space and time. The concepts of mass, acceleration and force, and the laws connecting them, appeared to be directly borrowed from experience. Once this basis is assumed, the expression for gravity seems to be derivable from experience; and the same derivability was to be anticipated for the other forces.
>
> However, Newton was aware of certain difficulties:
>
> One can see from the way he formulated his views that Newton felt by no means comfortable about the concept of absolute space, which embodied that of absolute rest; for he was alive to the fact that nothing in experience seemed to correspond to this latter concept. He also felt uneasy about the introduction of action at a distance. But the enormous practical success of his theory may well have prevented him and the physicists of the eighteenth and nineteenth centuries from recognising the fictitious character of the principles of his system.

In other words, they did not recognise that the principles were free inventions of the human mind.

> On the contrary, the scientists of those times were for the most part convinced that the basic concepts and laws of physics were not in a logical sense free inventions of the human mind, but rather that they were derivable by abstraction, i.e. by a logical process, from experiments.

Then Einstein mentioned his own contribution:

It was the general theory of relativity which showed in a convincing manner the incorrectness of this view. For this theory revealed that it was possible for us, using basic principles far removed from those of Newton, to do justice to the entire range of the data of experience in a manner even more complete and satisfactory than was possible with Newton's principles. But quite apart from the question of comparative merits, the fictitious character of the principles is made quite obvious by the fact that it is possible to point to two essentially different principles, both of which correspond to experience to a large extent. This indicates that any attempt logically to derive the basic concepts and laws of mechanics from the ultimate data of experience is doomed to failure.

However, said Einstein,

[i]f it is the case that the axiomatic basis of theoretical physics cannot be an inference from experience, but must be a free invention, have we any right to hope that we shall find the correct way? Still more – does this correct approach exist at all, save in our imagination? Have we any right to hope that experience will guide us aright, when there are theories (like classical [i.e. Newtonian] mechanics) which agree with experience to a very great extent, even without comprehending the subject in its depths?

He answered confidently, if controversially: 'in my opinion there is *the* correct path and, moreover, that it is in our power to find it'. Then followed the most quoted words in his Herbert Spencer lecture (given below in italics):

> Our experience up to date justifies us in feeling sure that in nature is actualised the ideal of mathematical simplicity. It is my conviction that pure mathematical construction enables us to discover the concepts and the laws connecting them which give us the key to the understanding of the phenomena of nature. Experience can of course guide us in our choice of serviceable mathematical concepts; it cannot possibly be the source from which they are derived; experience of course remains the sole criterion of the serviceability of a mathematical construction for physics, but *the truly creative principle resides in mathematics.*
>
> In a certain sense, therefore, I hold it to be true that pure thought is competent to comprehend the real, as the ancients dreamed.

The rest of the lecture was more technical, mentioning some of the mathematical concepts, such as Riemann's geometry and Dirac's spinors, that had proved fruitful in general relativity and quantum mechanics, and naming key theoretical contributors to the latter field, such as Born, de Broglie, Dirac, Heisenberg and Schrödinger, during the previous decade. (Bohr, strangely, went unmentioned.) But in his conclusion Einstein made no bones about his by now well-known view of quantum mechanics as being a theory of only transitory significance:

> I still believe in the possibility of giving a model of reality, a theory, that is to say, which shall represent events themselves and not merely the probability of their occurrence. On the other hand, it seems to me certain that we have to give up the notion of an absolute localisation of the particles in a theoretical model. This seems to me to be the correct theoretical interpretation of Heisenberg's uncertainty principle. And yet

> a theory may perfectly well exist, which though it is in a genuine sense an atomistic one (and not merely on the basis of a particular interpretation), nevertheless involves no localisation of the particles in a mathematical model. . . . Only if this sort of representation of the atomistic structure be obtained could I regard the quantum problem within the framework of a continuum theory as solved.

MATHEMATICS, PHYSICS AND REALITY

Thus, in his Herbert Spencer lecture, Einstein assured his Oxford audience, and by extension the international world of physics, that mathematics, on its own, could provide the basis for understanding nature. He apparently now rejected his own earlier position, as elegantly stated in 1921: 'As far as the laws of mathematics refer to reality, they are not certain; and as far as they are certain, they do not refer to reality.' As evidence of his new belief, he cited his own general theory of relativity, conceived in 1915–16, which he now claimed to have been essentially based on mathematical concepts rather than physical observations – for all its crucial confirmation by British astronomers in 1919. No doubt many theoretical and experimental physicists, especially those working in quantum mechanics, were taken aback and unconvinced by such a bold claim, even coming from Einstein, flying as it did in the face of so much of the history of physics, beginning with Galileo and Newton, that evidently arose from a combination of theory, observation and experiment. But which of them was in a position to contest its validity with general relativity's world-famous creator?

Perhaps they should have taken Einstein's initial humorous warning in Oxford more seriously. Was Einstein himself really the best authority on the origins of his own theory? Maybe not, as he himself had hinted. 'It was not until several decades later that a team of scholars scrutinised his notebooks and demonstrated that he had developed his theory. They saw clear evidence that he used a two-pronged strategy, involving both mathematics and physical reasoning, right up until he completed the theory, yet he subsequently downplayed the role of physical reasoning,' writes physicist, historian and Dirac's biographer Graham Farmelo. 'Einstein appears to have largely based his new philosophy of research on distorted recollections of his work in the final month of his search for the correct field equations of gravity.' According to an associate of the team, Jeroen van Dongen, 'Einstein overemphasised the part mathematics had played in his development of his theory of gravity, probably to try to persuade his critical colleagues of the value of his way of trying to find a unified theory of gravity and electromagnetism.'

Ironically, there was a clear indication of Einstein's tendency towards such distorted recollection a mere ten days after his Herbert Spencer lecture, in his lecture in Glasgow on 20 June. Speaking at the university in considerable technical detail, for the second time in English, on 'The Origin of the General Theory of Relativity', Einstein commented on the dark days of late 1915, after two years of excessively hard work, when he had felt lost. Finally, he recognised certain errors of thought, and 'after having ruefully returned to the Riemannian curvature, succeeded in linking the theory with the facts of astronomical experience'. In other words, general relativity rested not only on mathematical concepts but also on physical – in this case astronomical – observations. He closed the lecture with the following memorable statement:

> In the light of the knowledge attained, the happy achievement seems almost a matter of course, and any intelligent student

> can grasp it without too much trouble. But the years of anxious searching in the dark, with their intense longing, their alternations of confidence and exhaustion and the final emergence into the light – only those who have experienced it can understand that.

Little wonder, then, that the origins of general relativity should be an obscure and contentious subject – even to Einstein himself.

For the wider public, of course, even the basics of relativity remained as perplexing in 1933 as they had been on Einstein's first visit to England in 1921. Glasgow railway station appeared to supply yet another example of this truth. Einstein arrived there from London apparently a day earlier than was expected. He found himself standing on the platform alone, so to speak, in a large crowd – who were awaiting not Einstein but the Hollywood comedy star Thelma Todd (of Marx Brothers fame), who happened to be on the same train. Fortunately, a local newspaper reporter recognised the professor and telephoned the university authorities, who soon rescued him. According to the *Manchester Guardian*, however, relativity was at work: 'Professor Einstein is of all living philosophers the one whose name is most widely known to the multitude – but in the matter of railway station receptions even he could not hope to loom so large as a film star. There are "kinks in fame" as it is estimated by the multitude, even as there are "kinks in space" as it is measured by mathematicians.'

Having collected a by now customary honorary doctorate from the University of Glasgow along with a former prime minister of France, Édouard Herriot, near the end of June Einstein left London and returned to his home and his wife in Belgium. Although he could not have anticipated it, he was about to embark on perhaps the most anxious and exhausting period of his life: a direct clash between his personal vision of the world and the dark reality of Nazi Germany, in which England – in the person of the enigmatic Commander Locker-Lampson – would help to save Einstein from being assassinated.

CHAPTER SEVEN

On the Run

Through your well-organised work of relief you have done a great service not only to innocent scholars who have been persecuted, but also to humanity and science. You have shown that you and the British people have remained faithful to the traditions of tolerance and justice which for centuries you have upheld with pride.

Opening words of a speech by Einstein at the Albert Hall in London, October 1933

Hitler estimated that what he called the 'rebirth of Germany' in 1933, and after, cost 330 lives. A current scholar of Nazism, Daniel Siemens, offers a more realistic estimate in *Stormtroopers*, his history of Hitler's Brownshirts, bearing in mind that on 31 July 1933 the leader of the Brownshirts, Ernst Röhm, issued a secret decree that for every stormtrooper killed by political opponents, regional leaders should execute up to twelve members of the enemy organisation behind the attack. According to Siemens, during 1933, the Nazis interned more than 80,000 Germans, and killed more than 500 people, 'maybe even twice as many', either directly or through beatings and torture. Some of the dead were described by name in *The Brown Book of the Hitler Terror* – a book compiled by the World Committee for the Victims of German Fascism – which was published on 1 August in German and a month later in an English edition. It commented: 'Murder stalks through Germany. Mutilated corpses are carried out of Nazi barracks. The bodies of people disfigured beyond recognition are found in woods. Corpses drift down rivers. "Unknown" dead lie in the mortuaries.'

The educated German middle classes mostly condemned the Nazi excesses in private, but averted their eyes from them in public. Fear was obviously the main reason for their behaviour, but there was also an element of approval of the violence as a supposedly necessary transition from the economic and political chaos of recent years to a brighter and more stable future under Hitler.

In May, the viciously anti-Semitic illustrated brochure mentioned in the Prologue featured Einstein and some sixty prominent Jews and alleged Jews, alive and dead, including Charlie Chaplin. (Chaplin was described as 'a little sprawling Jew, as boring as he is repulsive'.) Entitled *Juden Sehen Dich An* (*Jews Are Watching You*), the brochure was written by Johann von Leers, a close collaborator of Josef Goebbels and a future officer in the armed wing of the SS, the elite corps of the Nazi Party. Beneath Einstein's photograph von Leers provided the caption: 'Discovered a much-contested theory of relativity. Was greatly honoured by the Jewish press and the unsuspecting German people. Showed his gratitude by lying atrocity propaganda against Adolf Hitler. (Not yet hanged.)' The brochure must have sold well in Germany, because it went into a second edition.

The German-Jewish reaction to the Nazi persecution was mostly one of paralysis, like 'a bird fascinated by a serpent', according to Elsa Einstein's close friend Antonina Vallentin, a biographer born in Poland, educated in Germany and by 1933 settled in France. In her 1954 biography of Einstein, Vallentin was highly critical of German Jews at this time. 'Had they become so totally absorbed in the German nation? Were they Germans more than they were Jews, in spite of being rejected by the new Germany?' Many of them openly blamed Einstein for provoking the persecution with his criticisms of the Nazis from the safety of exile. 'We get as many angry letters from the Jews as we do from the Nazis,' a distraught Elsa wrote to Vallentin from Le Coq in April 1933. 'My husband has not allowed himself to be silenced. Nothing could stop him from speaking out his mind. He has remained faithful to himself.' But, she added miserably, her daughters were still in Berlin: a source of huge anxiety both to themselves and to their mother in Belgium. Although Margot soon escaped, Ilse was in Berlin until May. (Ilse died in Paris in 1934, and Margot emigrated to the United States, like her mother.)

Along with the abuse of Einstein from Germany – some of it from Jews – came widespread support from other countries. For example, he received a moving letter from Murray, his friend from the ill-fated International Committee on Intellectual Cooperation. Writing from Oxford on 31 March, Murray remarked:

> I need hardly tell you with what feelings of indignation and almost despair your friends here have been watching the persecution both of Jews and Liberals in Germany, or with what great personal sympathy we have thought of you. Fortunately you are out of Germany, and if you choose to renounce your nationality all the world will be ready to welcome you. It is not for me to influence your choice. I know your friends in Oxford would love to have you here, but I know also that there will be competition among all civilised countries for the honour and pleasure of having you as a citizen.

OFFERS FROM UNIVERSITIES IN MANY COUNTRIES

Murray was right. During April, Einstein received offers of professorships from the Collège de France in Paris, the University of Madrid, the new Institute for Advanced Study in Princeton and the Hebrew University in Jerusalem, and from other countries, including Holland and Turkey. He agreed to the French and Spanish appointments on condition that he could devote to them only a little time; he accepted the offer from Princeton, with the proviso that he would not arrive until October 1933; and he turned down the Hebrew University. In the meantime, of course, during June he expected to visit Oxford, where Lindemann would certainly have been sympathetic to finding Einstein a professorship, had he wished for one. 'I now have more professorial chairs than reasonable ideas in my head,' Einstein joked in late April to his old friend from Olympia Academy days in Zurich, Maurice Solovine. 'The devil makes a fool of himself with their size!'

In each case, except in Oxford, his Jewishness proved to be an issue. In Paris, the editor of an influential royalist journal, *Action Française*, Léon Daudet, vigorously protested against the election of Einstein to the Collège de France. 'There is no need for us to provoke a *casus belli* with the Germany of Hitler out of love for Israel,' wrote Daudet. He explicitly linked the matter with the notorious Dreyfus Affair that had divided France on anti-Semitic lines between 1894 and 1906.

The Spanish appointment caused the *Jewish Chronicle* (in England) to rejoice:

> Spain's offer to Einstein of a chair at the Madrid University is an incident by which no Jew can fail to be moved profoundly. Four centuries and more ago she expelled the Jews from the peninsula. Today the German Reich has laid a bridge over that time gap and marched back to the medieval days. Thereupon modern Spain opens its doors, and grants a signal honour to the leading Jew among German exiles.

Einstein agreed to visit Spain during 1934. But when the Spanish Catholic press attacked his professorial appointment, he withdrew from it.

In the case of the Princeton professorship, Einstein himself objected to the fact that Princeton University practised a *numerus clausus* in the admission of Jewish students. Although the new Institute for Advanced Study was not part of Princeton University, it relied, according to its literature, 'on a fortunate symbiosis' with the university 'with which it enjoys close academic and intellectual relations', as Einstein noted in a letter to the institute's director, Abraham Flexner. He was therefore concerned that his name might be associated with this Princeton University admissions quota for Jews.

Regarding the Hebrew University, there had long been major differences between Einstein and its management, originating in his first visit to Palestine in 1923. By 1929, these had become so severe that he resigned from the university's governing body. But Chaim Weizmann, the Zionist leader based in Britain, was still resolutely determined to persuade the world's most famous Jewish intellectual to spend time in Jerusalem as a visiting professor. Einstein's exile from Germany in March 1933 seemed the perfect moment for yet another invitation from the Hebrew University. In Weizmann's view, as told to the *New York Times*, 'There is his place, and there he would cease to be a wanderer among the universities of the world. . . . Jerusalem, although it cannot offer him the same facilities, has certainly a claim on him – particularly since he does not need any special equipment but only a pencil and a piece of paper – and that we could afford him in Jerusalem.'

Einstein robustly – and very publicly – refused. A reporter from the *Jewish Chronicle* who interviewed him in Le Coq in April asked whether he was willing to cooperate with the university. Despite the crisis for Jews in Nazi Germany,

> [h]e answered emphatically in the negative. . . . He did not specify the exact nature of his complaint but, in view of his statements, I felt justified in enquiring whether he had had an opportunity of closely examining the work of the Hebrew University and upon what his opinions were based. The professor replied that his opinions had been formed at the time when he was a member of the curatorium of the university and on information which he had obtained from those in whom he had complete confidence. He had also formed his opinion when he saw who had been retained by the university and who had been estranged.

To Weizmann himself, Einstein wrote privately on 7 May, using a word more usually associated with anti-Semites: 'It is completely clear to me that tampering with the constitution will be of no use as long as downright vermin continue to play the leading role in the executive and faculty in Palestine.' His particular bugbear, as Weizmann well knew, was the university's founding chancellor, Judah Magnes, a prominent but academically undistinguished rabbi from New York who wanted to model the Hebrew University along American collegiate lines. Only when Magnes agreed to step down as chancellor after the report of an official committee of inquiry in 1933–34 chaired by the British scientist and educationist Sir Philip Hartog, so as to become the university's first president in 1935, was Einstein willing to rejoin the board of governors. Even then, he did not agree to leave Princeton and visit the Hebrew University as a professor.

Jewish affairs of various kinds – rather than academic or scientific matters – undoubtedly motivated Einstein's next visit to England in July, about a month after his return from giving lectures in Oxford and Glasgow. However, its chief goal remains something of a mystery.

On 20 July, a cryptically brief letter from Locker-Lampson in London to Lindemann in Oxford, mentioning their mutual friend Winston Churchill, abruptly and dramatically announced: 'Someone has seen Einstein and is bringing him to England and has asked me to put him up at my cottage this weekend. I have, therefore, arranged to do this and am taking him to Winston's on Saturday. I do hope you are likely to be there.' A second letter on 21 July from Locker-Lampson's secretary to another Einstein friend and zealous protector in England – the London-based, Palestinian-Jewish linguistic scholar Abraham Yahuda – referred more specifically to 'a friend' of the commander who 'has seen Professor Einstein abroad'. The secretary added: 'He may even arrive tonight, although I really cannot be certain of anything till he turns up.'

The identity of this unnamed Locker-Lampson/Einstein contact has not been established. Nor is it clear why Einstein decided to leave Belgium at short notice and arrive unaccompanied in London on the evening of 21 July. Although his mission was certainly political, connected with the Nazi threat to the German Jews, its precise purpose is unknown. Perhaps it had some connection with his personal affairs, such as the possibility of his becoming a naturalised British citizen and also of his fighting the confiscation of his money and property in Germany. But these seem to have been ancillary considerations for Einstein, judging by a letter he wrote from Le Coq on 20 July. This was in response to one sent to him from Paris, dated 18 July, written by a German-Jewish businessman and anti-Nazi activist, Lionel Ettlinger, then staying discreetly in a Paris hotel. Ettlinger proposed a plan for a central office in Geneva attached to the League of Nations dedicated to the political problems imposed on German Jews by Hitler's regime. Would Einstein agree to advocate such a plan? Einstein responded: 'I am going to England tomorrow to speak to the most respected English Conservatives.' He would submit the plan to them, and if they judged that his support would help its reception by the politicians, he would lend his name. By now, Einstein was becoming more circumspect in his public pronouncements against the Nazis. As he warned Ettlinger: 'When I appear in public as a prosecutor against the German government, this has the most terrible consequences for the German Jews.'

CONVERSATION WITH WINSTON CHURCHILL

On the day after Einstein's arrival in London, 22 July, Locker-Lampson took his guest to see Churchill at the latter's country

Einstein with Winston Churchill at the latter's country house, Chartwell, July 1933. They discussed the Nazi threat to world peace, which they recognised to be serious, ahead of most of their contemporaries, and agreed that an armed response would be necessary.

house, Chartwell, in Kent, not far from Locker-Lampson's cottage in Surrey. A photograph shows the two of them in Chartwell's garden, with Einstein in a white cotton suit and tie looking uncharacteristically smarter than a casually countrified Churchill. Lindemann was present, too, and presumably acted as an interpreter, since Churchill spoke little or no German – or perhaps Locker-Lampson did the translating. Later that day, Einstein reported to his wife in Belgium that he had been with Churchill around midday. 'He is an eminently wise man, and it became quite clear to me that these people have planned well ahead and will act soon.' Twenty Jewish researchers had already been found places in England. During the afternoon an important English cancer researcher had made interesting comments about his research. Einstein was glad to get to know these 'leading Englishmen'. Lindemann was 'untiring', Locker-Lampson 'touching'; he 'seems to have no egoistical motives for his undertaking – a black swan.' (Einstein's final German phrase translates literally as 'a white raven'.) Yahuda was scheduled to arrive from London that evening.

This, unfortunately, is all that is known about the sole personal encounter between two of the leading candidates for the title of 'Person of the Century' in *Time* magazine in 1999. Indeed, Einstein said almost nothing about Churchill post-1933, while Churchill maintained an absolute silence about Einstein until his death – as he did about many other world-leading figures whom he encountered. (When in 1946 Churchill was offered a large sum of money by a news agency for an article attacking a 1945 article by Einstein praising socialism, he ignored the invitation.) As for the star witnesses of the Chartwell meeting, Lindemann and Locker-Lampson, each kept his own counsel. Einstein's signature does not even appear in Churchill's visitors' book.

No doubt Einstein and Churchill were an unlikely couple – like Einstein and Locker-Lampson, for that matter – given Churchill's aristocratic background, intense patriotism, convinced militarism and ignorance of science (hence his need for Lindemann). And yet they were similar in their early distrust of Nazism, even if Einstein was – almost inevitably – the more prescient of the two about the Nazi military threat. 'As soon as Hitler took power, Einstein was quicker than any politician to judge what was going to happen,' wrote C. P. Snow, who met both Einstein and Churchill. 'He was much more rapid than Churchill in recognising that the Nazi Reich had to be put down by force.'

After the meeting with Churchill, Locker-Lampson introduced Einstein to two other senior British politicians, also out of office in 1933, during the next three days. The two of them took tea with Sir Austen Chamberlain, the former foreign secretary (and former boss of Locker-Lampson), who shared Churchill's attitude towards Nazism and in 1934 also became an early advocate of British rearmament. They also dined at the country house in Surrey of David Lloyd George, the former prime minister, who was less perceptive than Chamberlain about the Nazis. In neither case does a direct record of the meeting survive. However, Lloyd George's widow later noted of Einstein that: 'L. G. was no scientist, but the two fraternised very quickly, L. G. being naturally sympathetic to the sufferings of the Jews under Hitler.' In a telling detail observed by Locker-Lampson, Einstein, while signing Lloyd George's visitors' book, paused for a moment at the 'Address' column, and then wrote '*Ohne*' – 'Without any'.

DISTINGUISHED VISITOR AT THE HOUSE OF COMMONS

On 26 July, this detail was highlighted by Locker-Lampson in a speech before his fellow Members of Parliament sitting in the

House of Commons in London, while Einstein himself sat listening in the Distinguished Visitors' gallery. The occasion was a motion introduced by Locker-Lampson under the ten-minutes rule: 'That leave be given to bring in a bill to promote and extend opportunities of citizenship for Jews resident outside the British Empire.'

He opened his short, and even now quite stirring, argument on an individual note:

> I am not personally a Jew. I do not happen to possess one drop, so far as I know, of Jewish blood in my veins, but I hope that I do not require to be a Jew to hate tyranny anywhere in the world. I hope I only require English birth and breeding to loathe the oppression of a minority anywhere. It is un-English, it is caddish to bully a minority, and it is the duty of this House to consider the circumstances of people who are no longer citizens of a state which we recognise. I am not anti-German, and many of us in this House are almost pro-German. But I was one of the few people on this side of the House who, after the war, pleaded for fair play for Germany. I felt that the great German people had been misled by their leaders.

Then he spoke of the Nazis' current treatment of German Jews, in particular Einstein:

> And who altered me towards Germany? It was the German Jews who pleaded best for Germany, who day in and day out, tried to get England to be fair to Germany. And those citizens of Germany, the most eloquent and the most patriotic, are now being driven out. Germany is not driving out her cut-throats or her blackguards; she has selected the cream of her culture and suppressed it. She has admitted – and this is the

> point – that the Jews stand higher in the realms of art and of affairs, and for their superiority they must be punished. She has even turned upon her most glorious citizen – Einstein. It is impertinent for me to praise a man of that eminence. The most eminent men in the world admit that he is the most eminent. But there was something beyond mere eminence in the case of Professor Einstein. He was beyond any achievements in the realm of science. He stood out as the supreme example of the selfless intellectual. And today Einstein is without a home. He had to write his name in a visitors' book in England, and when he came to write his address, he put 'Without any'. The Huns have stolen his savings. The road-hog and racketeer of Europe have plundered his place. They have even taken away his violin. A man who more than any other approximated to a citizen of the world without a house! How proud we must be that we have afforded him a shelter temporarily at Oxford to work, and long may the tides of tyranny beat in vain against these shores.

Then he came to practicalities, including the League of Nations:

> And now how are we to help the Jews in Germany? They have been made outlaws and aliens of the German state. I wish the League of Nations could send a commission of inquiry to Germany or supply passports. Because if there ever were a time when the League ought to relax the rigid interpretation of narrow laws, and adjust these to the true spirit of its purposes, it is today. But if that League does not act, there is another league of nations which should – the British Empire. We are a real league of nations, and we should stand by Jewry in its trouble. We have been granted the Mandate of Palestine, and to help to fulfil the Messianic miracle there.

Finally, Locker-Lampson reminded the House of Commons why England owed a debt to its Jews as a result of the 1914–18 war, in which he himself had fought:

> The Jews in the British Empire stood by England in the war in her fight for freedom. We must stand by their side in their fight for freedom, too. I think the only Member of this House who became, or was subsequently, a V.C. [Victoria Cross] was a Jew. In the village where I live there is only one Jewish family, and in the entire district where I live there is only one mother who lost three sons fighting in the war. They were the sons of that Jewish mother. She lost three fighting in the battles of the British Empire, and when I was asked whether or not I would subscribe to a Cross in the district, I said, 'Only if we put up a tribute to those Jewish fallen, too.'

The House of Commons voted to support Locker-Lampson's bill on its first reading. A second reading was scheduled for 7 November 1933. This was a relatively rare accomplishment for any bill introduced under the ten-minutes rule. 'Commander Locker-Lampson showed himself something of an artist to achieve it on Wednesday,' remarked the parliamentary correspondent of *The Sunday Times*.

Part of the credit must surely go to Einstein's personal attendance in Parliament, as arranged by his ever-alert English host. Members of the House found themselves constantly glancing upwards towards their almost-legendary visitor during the business of 'questions', as diffused lighting from above threw into relief the white-suited Einstein's aureole of grey hair; while the attendants in the Distinguished Visitors' gallery kept busy showing Einstein off to arriving journalists with an awe they normally reserved for visiting sports stars. According to the *Manchester Guardian*, 'As a people we are not supposed to bother ourselves about general ideas – unless body-line bowling be a general idea – but there was no mistaking the universal interest which the propounder of the theory of relativity attracted.' Afterwards, as Einstein stood with Locker-Lampson in the lobby, 'Members eagerly came forward to be introduced to the greatest scientist of the age,' wrote the *Jewish Chronicle*. 'As the professor walked out of the lobby, it was clear that his appearance in the House had intensified the Members' appreciation of the grim reality of the plight of the Jews of Germany.' Certainly the Nazi newspaper, *Völkischer Beobachter*, took note in its 29 July report headlined 'Einsteinish Jewish Theatre in British Parliament', which accused Locker-Lampson of having staged the performance for the purposes of self-publicity in the foreign press. The combative references in his speech to the predatory 'Hun' naturally provoked a bitter Nazi denunciation of the British parliamentarian.

For all the parliamentary theatre, Einstein himself – frequently astute about political realities – was unconvinced that action would follow the vote. On 28 July, after returning to Le Coq, he wrote to Ettlinger that he had pursued the League of Nations plan with British politicians at length – hence the reference to the League in Locker-Lampson's speech – but that the plan had become entangled in the particular political situation of England with reference to the Jews, that is, the British Mandate in Palestine. Locker-Lampson's advocacy of the idea of giving Jewish refugees fleeing the Nazis a Palestinian passport and thus English protection, while no doubt morally admirable, would not prove feasible, in Einstein's view. 'I cannot believe that such a thing can really be done, because the English absolutely must avoid the danger of an influx into Palestine and I do not see what legal formality could avert this danger.' Yet, Einstein added to Ettlinger, he had felt obliged to

Einstein with Commander Oliver Locker-Lampson MP, his host in Britain, July 1933. The photograph may have been taken near the Houses of Parliament in London, where Locker-Lampson gave a rousing speech about the Jewish refugee predicament, watched from the visitors' gallery by Einstein, who was the centre of attention from the assembled MPs.

support the parliamentary motion, given Locker-Lampson's 'truly touching' commitment to the Jewish cause.

Events proved Einstein correct. The parliamentary bill never received a second reading. Nor did Locker-Lampson's appeal to the home secretary to grant British citizenship to Einstein himself come to fruition, as had been feared by his friend Yahuda, who sternly admonished Locker-Lampson for going public with the idea to the press on 27 July, before the government had had a chance to consider his proposal. In this case, however, the reason was not so much political as personal. First, Einstein desired to avoid upsetting his ongoing negotiations with the Swiss government about his confiscated money and property in Germany. Second, he was entirely unsure whether his future lay in England, the United States or perhaps some other country. Just before leaving London on 27 July, still aglow with his personal welcome in Parliament on the previous day, he told the *Daily Telegraph*: 'I love this country. Your family life always astonishes and pleases me. Englishmen know the right way to treat assistants and servants. As for the spirit of personal freedom here, I drink it in at every pore.' But what about his undoubted first love – physics and mathematics? Would England undoubtedly provide the best place to settle for his scientific research?

RENUNCIATION OF PACIFISM

During August, which he spent in Belgium, Einstein's clash with the Nazis hotted up. On 20 July, responding to a letter from a French anti-militarist in Belgium who had requested him to intervene with the Belgian government on behalf of two Belgian conscientious objectors in prison, Einstein had delivered a rebuff. 'In the heart of Europe lies a power, Germany, that is obviously pushing towards war with all available means,' he declared. In his view, there was now no choice but to renounce his ardent pacifism and recommend open European military preparations, including conscription, against Germany's secret rearmament. The publication of Einstein's letter in the French press on 18 August produced international repercussions in the pacifist movement.

Lord Arthur Ponsonby of War Resisters' International wrote to Einstein from London with chagrin on 21 August:

> I am sure you will not take it amiss if I express deep disappointment over the change in your attitude on war resistance. I understand only too well your distress and despair at the events in Germany. However, no matter how provocative a government may be, this fact is not, in my view, a sufficient justification for denying the reasonableness and effectiveness of refusing military service. Hitler's methods may be insane and criminal, but I am firmly convinced he is not such a fool as to think he could gain anything for Germany by waging war against another country. He would have all of Europe arrayed against him, and utter defeat would be inevitable. Besides, he has neither money nor arms and is much too concerned with his own security to become involved in such stupid ventures. Belgium's security, now and in the future, hinges solely on a policy of disarmament. All who work towards that goal, by refusing any kind of participation in war, deserve our unswerving respect and encouragement. Refusal of military service is not only a desirable policy in time of peace; it should enlist our full support at all times, particularly in time of crisis. My belief in the necessity of war resistance remains firm and unshaken. I venture to express the hope that, although the present cruel and oppressive measures adopted in Germany may have shaken your faith, you will not allow

> your change in viewpoint – a temporary change, I feel sure – to become public knowledge, at least not until you have given the matter mature reconsideration. Should your views be made known, you can be sure that every chauvinist, militarist and arms merchant would delight in ridiculing our pacifist position.

But Einstein was unpersuaded. He replied firmly and pointedly to Ponsonby on 28 August:

> Under circumstances such as prevailed in Europe until late last year, refusal of military service was, in my opinion, an effective weapon in the struggle for reason and dignity. Now, however, the situation has changed; I hope it will not remain so for long.
>
> Can you possibly be unaware of the fact that Germany is feverishly rearming and that the whole population is being indoctrinated with nationalism and drilled for war? Do you believe for a moment that Germany's overlords will be any easier on the French than they have been on their own fellow citizens who are not willing tools? What protection, other than organised power, would you suggest?
>
> I loathe all armies and any kind of violence; yet I am firmly convinced that, in the present world situation, these hateful weapons offer the only effective protection. I am certain that, if you yourself held today a responsible office in the French Government, you would feel obligated to change your views in the face of the prevailing danger.

At the same time as his militant rejection of pacifism, throughout August and early September Einstein further infuriated the Nazis by his public support for *The Brown Book of the*

'Einstein takes up the sword'. This cartoon by Charles Raymond Macauley appeared in the *Brooklyn Eagle* during 1933. It expresses Einstein's radical change of mind about pacifism after the coming to power of the Nazis.

Hitler Terror. Part of this book, concerning the violence wreaked on the victims, was quoted earlier. Another part dealt with the responsibility of the Nazi leadership:

> It is the National Socialist leaders who have organised the pogroms and lynchings, the burnings and the pillories, the

> tortures of the first, second and third degrees. The methods of the Middle Ages have been employed publicly in so far as they were effective as propaganda. But the tortures have been carried out in private, in the darkness of the night. Even now millions of Germans are ignorant of them.

Earlier in the summer, during May, Einstein had agreed to become the official chairman of the international committee responsible for *The Brown Book*. He was then apparently unaware that it was being edited by a Stalinist secret agent, Otto Katz (unnamed in the book), and that most of the information – including harrowing photographs of Nazi victims intended for reproduction in the book – was being collected by Communists in Germany and surrounding countries, often at considerable personal risk. Even its publisher – a London-born, Oxford-educated Jew, Victor Gollancz – was well known in England for his Communist sympathies. However, Einstein certainly had nothing directly to do with the book's preparation. His name did not appear on its spine or in its prelims, or in its introduction written by the Labour Party politician Lord Dudley Marley. The name 'Einstein' occurred chiefly in the section dealing with the Nazi impact on German science, which described his world-wide distinction and noted that his current mistreatment 'is enough to make Hitler's Germany a laughing-stock in the world of modern science'. He came to be prominently associated with the book only because of its London publisher. In search of a celebrity endorsement, Gollancz was 'anxious that the book should be published "By an International Committee under the Chairmanship of Albert Einstein"' – as one of the committee's members, the British left-wing activist and former Labour member of parliament 'Red' Ellen Wilkinson, informed her friend Katz in late June. After Einstein, perhaps naïvely, agreed to this endorsement, Gollancz in due course splashed his name across the English edition's dust-jacket.

Even so, Einstein refused to dissociate himself from the book as a work of Communist-inspired propaganda following its international publication on 1 September, notwithstanding the embarrassed encouragement of Wilkinson and Gollancz, who were appalled that Einstein's association with it was now endangering his life. Instead, he told Wilkinson quietly in an interview with her for the *Daily Express*: 'They shall not force me to do that. The work your committee has done is good.' He also stated mildly to *The Times*: 'I was not responsible for the *Brown Book* which has angered them. I was on the committee which authorised the publication of the book, but I did not write anything in it, although I agreed with its contents.' Inevitably, though, the Nazis regarded Einstein as one of the key suspects behind *The Brown Book*. Indeed, in late 1933, the *Völkischer Beobachter* went so far as to claim that Einstein had been 'proved to be the author of the book'. It continued: 'In this book, in the foulest way, he incites people against Germany, appeals for a preventive war and demands that this country, from whom the whole world has received only benefits, be manured with the blood of its people.'

Equally inevitably, Einstein was also sought out in Le Coq by disgruntled Nazis – or at least unknown persons posing as such. 'Belgium was dangerously near Germany,' recalled Vallentin after a visit to the Einstein house in August. 'There was a rumour that [Hermann] Göring's brother had come to Le Coq. Men with foreign accents asked too many questions about Einstein. Suspicious individuals roamed around the house.' One such approach started with a letter from an unknown man urgently requesting an interview with Einstein. Elsa Einstein refused him for fear of trouble, but when the man repeatedly insisted, she agreed to see him alone without her husband. The man informed her that he was a former Nazi stormtrooper who had fallen out with the Brown Shirts and was now opposed to them. He was willing to sell Einstein all the secrets of the paramilitary organisation for 50,000 francs. 'Why do you assume that Professor Einstein is interested in the secrets of your former party?' asked Mrs Einstein. 'Oh, we all know very well that Professor Einstein is the leader of the opposing party throughout the entire world, and that such a purchase would therefore be very important to him,' the stranger ingenuously replied. Absurd as this was, the encounter was very disturbing for the Einsteins. For if it were now definitely the case that the Nazis regarded Einstein as the head of the official opposition, '[a]ll sorts of unpleasant surprises had to be expected', wrote his friend and biographer Philipp Frank, who personally heard this story from a near-desperate Elsa while on a visit to Le Coq.

DEATH THREATS FROM NAZI EXTREMISTS

How serious was the risk to Einstein's life from Nazi assassins in August? There is no written evidence one way or the other, not too surprisingly. Serious enough, according to the Belgian royal family, to require armed police to guard Einstein's house. Two plainclothes policemen shadowed the solitary Einstein's every moment, which he found extremely irksome – especially when he wanted to take a walk on the dunes. 'At the very moment of my arrival at Le Coq I saw one of them rush into the room,' recalled Vallentin.

> He was wiping his purple face and pulling at his long whiskers. His eyes were popping out of his head and the heavy pocket of his coat was flapping. 'Where is the professor?' he shouted in despair. 'He is resting upstairs,' Elsa replied calmly. 'He isn't

> there – my friend has just been to see – he's gone . . . .' His despair was so comical that Elsa, in spite of her fears, could not help laughing. 'We'll try to find him. . . . Never have I had so hard a task. He slips out of our fingers like an eel . . . . His Majesty's orders were so very strict,' he grumbled. He crunched the gravel angrily under his feet. 'You shouldn't have behaved like that, Albert,' Elsa said to him an hour later. 'Hm . . . didn't I give them the slip . . . ?' Einstein looked at us, shaking with laughter, his eyes shining with triumph.

Then, around 1 September, there seemed to be a quantum jump in the danger level. Just as *The Brown Book of the Hitler Terror* was published in London with Einstein's dust-jacket endorsement came the news that Theodor Lessing had been shot on 30 August by three Nazi agents through the window of his

The Nazi threat to Einstein's life. He and his wife Elsa were extensively protected at their exiled home in Le Coq, Belgium, by the Belgian police force, one of whose officers is shown here with the Einsteins in mid-1933. In September, Einstein escaped from Belgium to rural England.

study at his exiled home in Marienbad in Czechoslovakia. The agents escaped into neighbouring Germany, and their victim died in hospital on 31 August. Lessing, like Einstein, had long been a target for abuse by the Nazis because of his international reputation as a philosopher. They liked to refer to him as 'Professor Lazarus', as in this statement by Goebbels to the British press in May 1933:

> The English Jew is of quite a different type from the German Jew. It would never have been possible in England, for example, for a Jewish author to say, as the German Professor Lazarus, calling himself Lessing, did, that the Jewish soldiers had fallen for 'filth', nor for the Jewish literary man in England to compare the head of the state with a wholesale murderer.

The pseudonym and the attributed opinions were 'absolute inventions' by Goebbels, Lessing informed the *Manchester Guardian*. But they were believed in Germany. So too were the Nazi allegations that Einstein had spread 'atrocity propaganda' against Germany abroad.

A mere week later, on 8 September, came international press announcements that a secret Nazi terror organisation, the Fehme (associated with the murder of Rathenau in 1922), had placed a price on Einstein's head: £1,000 according to London's *Daily Herald*, 20,000 marks said the *New York Times*. 'Whether the story is true or not we do not know,' warned *The Sunday Times* on 10 September:

> though nothing that the Nazi hotheads might plan in this line would surprise us. But should it be true, let them take fair warning and think twice of this folly before it is too late. If they should commit this crime against humanity the conscience

> of the whole civilised world will rise against them, and the German Government will find itself execrated and isolated as no German Government has been before or since the war.

By the time this comment appeared, Einstein was again in London. He and his wife had abruptly abandoned their immediate plan following the press announcements to take a long-distance 'cruise to "nowhere"' by ship, as reported in the *New York Times* on 9 September. Instead, Einstein had reluctantly yielded to his wife's terrible worries about his safety – and no doubt to the stress of still-closer police protection, which now included a policeman sleeping beside his bed all night long. On 9 September, he packed a few bags with vital books and papers; caught a boat to England in the company of a visiting British journalist from the *Sunday Express* (at the insistence of Elsa); and went to stay with the suddenly reignited Locker-Lampson.

LOCKER-LAMPSON TO THE RESCUE

The dashing commander had received less than a day's notice of Einstein's arrival, but he rose to the occasion – by immediately arranging to 'hide' Einstein away from London in his thatched holiday hut on a wild heath somewhere in rural Norfolk. Indeed, Einstein's sojourn in England in September–October 1933 would prove to be, in a way, Locker-Lampson's version of his friend Churchill's wartime 'finest hour'. Not only did Locker-Lampson serve Einstein and England well, he also served himself and his public image well.

A bizarre mixture of secrecy and publicity surrounded the entire visit. 'Locker-Lampson liked to pretend he always played a straight bat but he was in fact as slippery as an eel,' in the perceptive and amusing words of local Norfolk historian Stuart

McLaren. (Think of his story of British prisoners of war in Germany playing cricket with Hitler!)

The first local newspaper report of Einstein's arrival, published as early as 11 September in the *Eastern Daily Press*, set the scene well, as Einstein relaxed in his new rural encampment, supervised by his guardian Locker-Lampson:

> It was in a tiny wooden hut, with the sun shining through a window facing the North Sea, that a reporter found Professor Einstein yesterday. Broadly smiling, he seemed not to have a care in the world. No police precautions for his safety had been taken, but Commander Locker-Lampson had arranged for a private guard of friends so that the professor could not be molested.
>
> His first words were a request for a penknife for his pipe. The famous scientist who had overcome many mathematical difficulties had not been able to make his pipe smoke. Then, when it was puffing well, he settled back in his chair and spoke of the Nazi threat against him and of the price that it is said has been put on his head by the Fehme, the German secret society.
>
> 'All I want is peace,' he said, 'and could I have found a more peaceful retreat than here in England? At Le Coq I was always guarded. It was a terrible strain and a great responsibility to be put on the Belgian police. It interfered with my work. My friend has invited me here, and I hope to stay in England for a month. No one will know where I am until October, when I go to America to lecture. I can live quietly working out my mathematical problems.'
>
> Here Commander Locker-Lampson broke in: 'The professor is modest. He is engaged on a new mathematical theory.'

The professor smiled. He did not say what the new theory was. He reiterated what had already been stated, that there was no reason why he should be singled out by the Nazis. . . .

The reporter left him peacefully puffing at his pipe and gazing out over the calm North Sea towards Germany.

The very next day, national newspapers carried a photograph of Einstein with this 'private guard of friends': Locker-Lampson in the foreground (naturally) with a wind-blown Einstein, and a local gamekeeper hovering in the background – the two Englishmen holding guns – plus one of the commander's two female secretaries, apparently attentive to the mathematics of the professor. The exact location was given only as 'near Cromer' in the newspaper reports, but without too much detective work any Nazi agent worth his salt could have worked out where Einstein was hidden: a point that did not escape the satire of the *Daily Express*'s well-known columnist 'Beachcomber'. On 14 September, the columnist reported tongue-in-cheek from 'Cromer, Wednesday Night': 'I was informed, on making enquiries today at the headquarters of the Einstein Defence Force in this town, that it had been decided not to accept the generous offer of the War Office to send two infantry brigades to Fort Lampson.' As the *Observer* diarist straightforwardly observed on 17 September: 'England is not a very good place to hide in. Dr. Einstein, who has come here to escape Nazi persecution, finds his wooden hut photographed in the papers, with full indications of locality, and Cromer Council considers the question of presenting an address. Germany, I suppose, is presumed to be looking the other way.'

Einstein, genuinely modest about his personal reputation, told his wife in a brief letter from London before reaching Norfolk: 'I am going to the countryside, where nobody will recognise me. I have a good feeling in anticipation.' And this

Lime Juice for Health
ROSE'S of course

Daily Express

TUESDAY, SEPTEMBER 12, 1933

Be tempted by
HP SAUCE

EINSTEIN WORKS OUT HIS PROBLEMS
PROTECTED BY ARMED GUARDS

RAPTUROUS!
Enjoy the raptures of a perfect bath by using the finest soap in the world.
BRONNLEY'S
BATH SOAP

Einstein on the front page of the *Daily Express*, September 1933. The caption reads: 'Gamekeepers armed with shot-guns are guarding the little log-hut near Cromer, where Professor Einstein has found a refuge from Nazi threats and peace to work at his mathematical problems. With the famous scientist are his host, Commander Locker-Lampson (who has a sporting rifle handy) and the latter's secretary, Miss B. Howard.'

proved to be true among the locals on Roughton Heath. Neither the gamekeeper, Herbert Eastoe, nor Philip Colman, the son of the local farmer on whose land Locker-Lampson's huts stood, knew who Einstein was. More than half a century later, Colman recalled with a laugh that Eastoe appeared on the farm one day and the following conversation ensued:

> 'Morning, Master Colman,' he said, touching his hat. 'I've come to tell you we've got an ol' Garman up there on the Heath. Them thar Nazi people hev put a price on his head. They'll give £1,000 if you tell 'em where he is.'
>
> 'Ol' Locker is a-guardin' him, along o' me and his secretaries. They've got a rifle and I've got my 12-bore. But Locker wants to hire a horse so he can guard him better. I thought you could rent him Tom, your milk pony. . . .'

Einstein in his Norfolk retreat, September 1933. Most of his time there was spent in solitude, working on mathematical calculations in his hut or occasionally playing his violin outdoors. The photographer is unknown.

As for the name of the man at the centre of this security operation, 'I think,' said Eastoe uncertainly, 'they called him *Einsteen*, or somethin' like that.' When Colman agreed to the suggestion, the hired milk pony soon appeared in a press photograph with Locker-Lampson astride it, looking manly, and Einstein giving the pony's head a gentle pat. Ironically, Colman once found himself being chased on the heath by the gun-wielding commander. 'He was a rich man's pig of a son, but quite likeable in an eccentric sort of way.' Yet, Locker-Lampson had at least some reason for concern, other than a prowling Nazi visitor: the fact that Einstein was 'an ol' Garman' was enough to cause several local villagers – servicemen who had suffered at the hands of the Germans in the First World War – to want to claim the price on his head!

'L.L. is wonderful and keeps everything away,' Einstein wrote to his wife in Le Coq. 'I live here like a hermit, only I do not need to eat roots and herbs.' To his son, Eduard, he described his 'admirable solitude'. As he had hoped back in Belgium, he was now able to spend most of his three or so weeks in Norfolk doing mathematical calculations alone in his hut, and sometimes playing music on a grand piano in another hut or on his violin outdoors. (A third hut was used by Locker-Lampson's two secretaries, plus a cook brought from London, while Locker-Lampson himself occupied a military-style bell-tent.) He also went for country walks. A second armed guard, Albert Thurston, son-in-law of Eastoe, used to follow him to the local post office. 'He would walk across the heath and I would follow him with a gun,' recalled Thurston. 'Mother would wait with the pram on the road and escort him to the post-office while I waited behind the hedge. Then I would escort him back again. I don't think the post-office knew who he was. He would buy sweets: simple things like a child might buy.' Once, Thurston showed Einstein his baby son. 'He loved children. He touched my son on the forehead and said, "Double crown, he'll go a long way."' On another occasion, Einstein invited two local village women to visit him and take tea. But when they discovered his hut full of German newspapers and a chest of drawers full of guns, they took fright and ran away. A contemporary caricature by the political cartoonist David Low captured this unique atmosphere beautifully: it portrayed Einstein as a harmless, diminutive professor with persecuted eyes walking hesitantly beneath a wildly dishevelled halo of hair towards a dark shadow.

Other than local walks, Einstein seems to have left the encampment only a very few times, such as to call with Locker-Lampson on a near neighbour, the senior Conservative politician and future foreign secretary Sir Samuel Hoare, who was sympathetic to the cause of Jewish refugees. And he received hardly

'Professor Einstein'. This classic cartoon by David Low appeared in the *New Statesman and Nation* to illustrate an article on Einstein by John Maynard Keynes published in October 1933, just after Einstein departed Britain for the United States, never to return to Europe.

any invited visitors, just as he and Locker-Lampson had intended. Only two visits were of real significance.

The earlier one was that of Walter Adams, a lecturer in history at University College London (and later director of the London School of Economics). He was secretary of the newly formed Academic Assistance Council. Having driven out to Cromer from London, Adams recalled, 'First we were confronted by one beautiful girl with a gun. Then there was a second one, also with a gun. Finally we saw Einstein who was walking around inside what seemed to be a little hedged compound.' Adams quickly asked Einstein if he would agree to speak on behalf of academic refugees from Germany at the council's first public meeting in London planned for 3 October. Einstein almost as quickly agreed. Whereupon Locker-Lampson went away, picked up the telephone and single-handedly hired the Albert Hall, according to Adams.

VISIT FROM JACOB EPSTEIN

Einstein's second visitor, in late September, was very different. 'Beachcomber' introduced him weirdly in the *Daily Express* as follows:

> A suspicious-looking cow waddled up to the hornworks at Fort Lampson yesterday, and miaowed pitifully.
>
> It was this wrong noise that aroused the sentry's suspicions. He ordered the animal to give the password, which was 'Epstein'.
>
> The cow began to bark.
>
> The alarm was sounded, the fortifications were lined, and Professor Einstein was hustled down a disused well, for safety.
>
> The cow was surrounded and searched. In its pocket the searchers found a betting-slip, a beer-label, two empty quart

bottles, and an ace with the corner nicked off it. At this point the cow said, 'It's only us.'

The front and hind legs came apart, revealing the well-known features of Nervo and Knox. [An English acrobatic dancing duo, part of the original Crazy Gang.]

The guards have been doubled.

Jacob Epstein, the sculptor, came to the not-so-secret encampment on Roughton Heath in the last week of the month, in order to prepare a model for his magnificent bronze bust of Einstein. He left a vivid account of the experience in his autobiography, *Let There Be Sculpture*, beginning with this personal description: 'Einstein appeared dressed very comfortably in a pullover with his wild hair floating in the wind. His glance contained a mixture of the humane, the humorous and the profound. This was a combination which delighted me. He resembled the ageing Rembrandt.'

Working conditions left something to be desired, however. Sittings took place in the hut with the piano, with hardly any space to move. Epstein persuaded Locker-Lampson's secretaries to remove the door, which they did and then facetiously asked if the sculptor would like the roof off as well. 'I thought I should have liked that too, but I did not demand it, as the attendant "angels" seemed to resent a little my intrusion into the retreat of their professor.'

There was also a problem with Einstein himself: not his appearance, but rather his pipe. At the first sitting 'the professor was so surrounded with tobacco smoke from his pipe that I saw nothing. At the second sitting I asked him to smoke in the interval.'

His conversation was 'full of charm and *bonhomie*', wrote Epstein. 'He enjoyed a joke and had many a jibe at the Nazi professors, one hundred of whom in a book had condemned his theory. "Were I wrong," he said, "one professor would have been quite enough." Also, in speaking of Nazis he once said, "I thought I was a physicist, I did not bother about being non-Aryan until Hitler made me conscious of it."'

After the morning sittings, Einstein sat down at the piano to play. Once he took his violin and scraped away outside. 'He looked altogether like a wandering gypsy, but the sea air was damp, the violin execrable, and he gave up. The Nazis had taken his own good violin when they confiscated his property in Germany.' He also watched Epstein at work 'with a kind of naïve wonder and seemed to sense that I was doing something good of him'.

Unfortunately, there was too little time for Epstein to complete the model, because Einstein was due in London for his speech in the Albert Hall and subsequent departure for America; he and Epstein left Cromer for London on the same train with Locker-Lampson. Yet the final bust, created and exhibited later that year in a London gallery, with its gentle smile, philosophical gaze and blazing aureole of hair, is generally regarded as a triumph. (It was, however, mysteriously knocked onto the floor during the exhibition, when the gallery attendants happened to be out of the room, provoking some speculation about a deliberate attack.)

REJECTION OF COMMUNISM

If visitors to Einstein in Norfolk were a rarity, so too were public statements from him while he was 'in hiding'. He turned down all invitations to write articles for British and American newspapers. The only real exception, written on 15 September, concerned his attitude to Communism, rather than Nazism. Provoked by a

Einstein stands beside an unfinished bronze bust of him and its sculptor Jacob Epstein, Roughton Heath, Norfolk, October 1933. The finished bust was eventually placed in the Tate Gallery in London.

Labour Party pamphlet, *The Communist Solar System*, sent to him in Norfolk by friends – and probably encouraged by the strongly anti-Communist Locker-Lampson – the statement was Einstein's attempt to clear his name in both Britain and continental Europe, following its close association with the Communist-inspired *Brown Book of the Hitler Terror* and its misuse by some other Communist-dominated bodies. His statement was published in the *Manchester Guardian* as follows: 'Like other intellectuals who feel it their duty to serve the cause of human progress to the best of their ability, I have been the victim of a misunderstanding as to the true objects of certain organisations which are in truth nothing less than camouflaged propaganda in the service of Russian despotism.' He singled out two organisations that had misused his name, which he had lent to them because he was unaware of their real purpose: the Workers' International Relief and the Anti-War Movement. But here, said Einstein, he would like to make clear that 'I have never favoured Communism and do not favour it now'. In explanation, he concluded: 'any power must be the enemy of mankind which enslaves the individual by terror and force, whether it arises under a Fascist or Communist flag. All that is valuable in human society depends upon the opportunity for development accorded to the individual.'

Unmentioned in his statement was the fact that Einstein had consistently refused to accept invitations to visit Russia, beginning in 1914 – initially because of its history of anti-Jewish pogroms, later because of his doubts about Soviet Communism under Stalin. Such a mention would surely have helped to persuade sceptical readers.

Little was announced in advance about his forthcoming address in the Albert Hall on 3 October, which was to be Einstein's first-ever speech to a general audience on a general subject in English.

On 24 September, two Sunday newspapers carried a brief report about the event, yet gave different titles for the address. According to *The Sunday Times*, 'He does not speak really good English, and his conversation is not easy, but he is writing a speech in German on "England as a sanctuary", and this is being translated for the meeting.' Whereas according to the *Observer* the speech was entitled 'Fair play for the Oppressed', and its report quoted 'one of the organisers' (probably Locker-Lampson) as saying: 'It is not a protest meeting; it is not a political meeting. The professor's speech will be just an appeal from the heart.' But by 27 September, the title had been altered to the more neutral 'Science and Civilisation', according to the *Manchester Guardian*. Its report quoted Locker-Lampson by name. The lecture would be 'purely scientific', he said. 'The fact that Professor Einstein has been driven from Germany and that his savings have been taken should be no reason for the assumption when he speaks here that he intends an attack upon the German Government.' Then the commander added his own twist:

> He has been accused of reckless pacifism and Communism. In that connection may I draw your attention to his recent statement where he says that he has never favoured Communism and does not favour it now? The real reason for his unpopularity with the militants in Germany is not his pacifism, which is only the abhorrence of war held by all right-thinking people, but the fact that during the late war he stood up in Germany and defended England when propaganda was launched against her.

Locker-Lampson was responding to an editorial critical of Einstein published in the conservative *Daily Mail* on 26 September. Headlined 'An unwise agitation', it attacked Einstein's pacifist sympathies and Communist affiliations, and warned him against further annoying the Nazis: 'We venture to put it to Dr Einstein that he would be wise to stop this injudicious agitation in this country against the Nazi regime in Germany. We have every sympathy with the German Jews as such. They are immensely to be pitied. But their treatment will not be improved by Albert Hall denunciations of the Nazis.'

A second *Daily Mail* editorial, 'Meddling', published on 2 October, the day before the Albert Hall meeting, went considerably further. 'Tomorrow there is due to take place at the Albert Hall a mass meeting, nominally to appeal for funds on behalf of the exiles from Germany,' it began. 'Actually, it will everywhere be regarded as a demonstration against the Hitler regime and Nazi policy.' About Einstein, it took note of his recent statement about Communism, and also his recent change of heart about pacifism, and implied that he was either naïve or insincere. 'No doubt the Communists exploited what the anti-Hitler "Brown Book" has called his "Left democratic political views", to produce the impression that he was one of themselves.' Then the newspaper revealed its own Fascist sympathies: 'This would explain why the German Government has intimated that it does not desire his presence on German soil. Herr Hitler will take no risks. He knows from what happened in Russia that, if the Communists seized power, there would be no limit to their violence and bloodshed in Germany.'

MASS MEETING IN LONDON ON BEHALF OF ACADEMIC REFUGEES

Evidently the meeting on 3 October, despite having been arranged in less than two weeks, was set to be controversial and well attended – as Locker-Lampson, its chief publicist (and veteran of Blue Shirts rallies at the Albert Hall), intended. But just in case there had been insufficient advance publicity, Einstein's host may have 'carefully leaked' a last-minute story to Scotland Yard that an attempt might be made on his guest's life. That is, according to Ronald Clark in his Einstein biography: an allegation for which Clark provided no definite evidence. The Scotland Yard detectives apparently received an anonymous communication of 'a plot to assassinate Einstein' from 'members of the League of Gentiles against the Jewish warmongers', the *Jewish Telegraphic Agency* reported.

On the evening itself, hundreds of uniformed officers from the Metropolitan Police stationed in pairs observed the area

'Science and Civilisation'. Einstein speaks to a full house at the Albert Hall, London, October 1933. Behind him is the chairman of the meeting, Lord Ernest Rutherford, and another speaker, Sir Austen Chamberlain (on the right). Outside and inside the hall (concealed from the audience) was a strong police presence in case the meeting was disrupted by British Fascists.

outside the hall, while plain-clothes officers hid in dark corners and mounted police waited in nearby mews and garages. Inside the hall about 1,000 students from the University of London acted as stewards, many of them in cap and gown, with an invisible reserve force of uniformed policemen in case of serious trouble. The multinational audience ranged from large numbers of Jews to a group of Blackshirts from Sir Oswald Mosley's British Union of Fascists and a group of turbanned Indians. Every ticket-holder, before being admitted, was asked to sign a declaration: 'I hereby undertake not to create any disturbance or in any way impede the progress and proper conduct of the meeting.' In the comedic view of 'Beachcomber', writing in the *Daily Express* just after the packed-out meeting, 'It is now permissible to disclose the fact that the presence of 40,000 police in the neighbourhood of the Albert Hall, on the night of Herr Einstein's address, was fully justified.' After all, 'A man in the crowd was heard to say, with true British vigour and independence, that he had a good mind to write to the papers about the meeting. And a woman uttered a protest. According to police evidence, she twice cried out, "It's a scandal!"' That said, according to 'Beachcomber':

> Nobody need have been alarmed. Behind every window in Albert Hall Mansions was a field-gun, camouflaged to look like a pot of geraniums, and two infantry battalions were in readiness in a side-turning off Exhibition Road. A Storm Platoon of Mrs Wretch's Scarlet Shirts came from Fort Lampson, under the command of Quasi-Colonel Laski, and was hidden in the great organ during the address.

Einstein arrived in a taxi with Locker-Lampson only three minutes before the advertised starting time. His public entrance up the gangway below the organ was 'at once dramatic and homely', reported the *Manchester Guardian*, which provided this detailed, atmospheric account:

> Suddenly the organ stopped in the middle of Handel's march from *Rinaldo*. The grey-haired, grey-bearded Bishop of Exeter, followed by Sir James Jeans and the other speakers, made their way slowly up the gangway and took their seats on the platform. Then a pause. Mr Cooley [the official 'chief organiser' of the meeting, an agent of Locker-Lampson], holding back the red-plush curtain, shouted, 'Ladies and gentleman, Lord Rutherford, and Professor Einstein,' and then 'Hip, hip, hooray!' The audience rose to its feet, cheering and applauding. The organ broke out again. The arc lamps grew suddenly stronger, and then, to the accompaniment of flashes from the battery of cameramen crowding the fringes of the platform, the professor appeared – a small figure in a blue suit, his enormous head surrounded with the fluffy nimbus of grey hair, bowing, smiling, and working his graceful hands in delicate, nervous movements. The audience continued to cheer, and, standing before them, the professor continued to bow and smile and yet manage to convey an almost inexpressible sadness and pathos in his deep-brown eyes – a tiny figure against a towering background blinking at each 'summer lightning' flash from the cameramen.

Other well-known speakers included the economist and social reformer Sir William Beveridge, the statesman and Nobel peace laureate Sir Austen Chamberlain, the suffragist Maude Royden and, of course, the event's *éminence grise*, Commander Locker-Lampson. Indeed, Einstein was the only speaker (apart from the Lord Bishop of Exeter) to be advertised without distinguishing initials after his (or her) name – presumably because he was so famous as to need no introduction. As Beveridge remarked in a live broadcast on BBC radio to a national audience that very evening while the Albert Hall meeting was still in session: 'I had never seen him before. Einstein was a legend to me. It is like seeing Christopher Columbus or Julius Caesar.'

Rutherford spoke first, and explained that the Refugee Assistance Committee behind the meeting had recently been formed from four societies: the International Student Service, the Refugee Professionals Committee, the Germany Emergency Committee of the Society of Friends and the Academic Assistance Council, of which he was president. He then set out the purpose of the meeting in unemotional and non-political terms:

> The saving of these refugee students, scholars and skilled professional workers presents great difficulties, and must be approached in no petty spirit of sectional hostility, and with a complete absence of the spirit of national antagonism.
>
> Each of us may have his own private political views, but in this work of relief all such differences of opinion must give way before the vital necessity of effectively serving this great body of learning and skilled experience, which otherwise will be lost to the world. It is in such a spirit that the four Societies are working, and intend to continue to work together. Their sole concern is to relieve suffering, and, regardless of creed, regardless of race, and regardless of political opinion, to save these academic professional workers who are now dependent on the charity of humanity.
>
> I am sure that this is an appeal to which this country will generously respond.

Rutherford especially thanked 'my friend, Professor Einstein, who has made his first public appearance tonight, to plead for help for his refugee colleagues in the hour of their distress'. His speech was followed by the bishop and then by his Cambridge scientific colleague, Jeans. Then it was Einstein's turn, greeted with rousing applause.

With his eyes constantly looking down, Einstein read quietly from his English manuscript, 'as unconcernedly as if lecturing in a classroom', according to the *New York Times*. But he clearly had the attention of his entire audience – more than 10,000 strong – judging by the silence in the hall and the bursts of applause.

He appealed to his listeners – in his hesitant and peculiar but expressive and touching German accent (as can still be heard in a partial recording of his speech) – to give moral and financial support to the growing exodus of desperate, mainly Jewish, academic refugees from Germany. 'It cannot be my task today to act as scourge of the conduct of a nation which for many years has considered me as their own,' he cautiously announced, deliberately avoiding any direct mention of Germany, presumably to avoid giving the slightest impression of a political demonstration against Nazism. However, he said:

> If we want to resist the powers which threaten to suppress intellectual and individual freedom we must keep clearly before us what is at stake, and what we owe to that freedom which our ancestors have won for us after hard struggles. Without such freedom, there would have been no Shakespeare, no Goethe, no Newton, no Faraday, no Pasteur and no Lister [a remark (quoted earlier) that prompted a storm of sympathetic applause]. There would be no comfortable houses for the mass of the people, no railway, no wireless, no protection

against epidemics, no cheap books, no culture and no enjoyment of art for all.

Then he made a radical, idiosyncratic suggestion for encouraging scientific creativity, which perhaps only Einstein, the former patent clerk turned solitary professor, could have come up with. It was based on his recent retreat by the sea in Norfolk, he implied:

> I lived in solitude in the country and noticed how the monotony of a quiet life stimulates the creative mind. There are certain callings in our modern organisation which entail such an isolated life without making a great claim on bodily and intellectual effort. I think of such occupations as the service in lighthouses and lightships. Would it not be possible to fill such places with young people who wish to think out scientific problems, especially of a mathematical or philosophical nature? ... The young scientist who carries on an ordinary practical profession which maintains him is in a much better position – assuming, of course, that this profession leaves him with sufficient spare time and energy. In this way, perhaps a greater number of creative individuals could be given an opportunity for mental development than is possible at present. In these times of economic depression and political upheaval such considerations seem to be worth attention.

This last remark was a tactful and prescient hint that many Jewish academic refugees from Germany might have to adopt new livelihoods, rather than expecting to find equivalent university positions abroad. As Einstein put this in a subsequent statement to the World Union of Jewish Students (of which he was honorary president) before he left London: 'In these difficult times we must explore every possibility of adjusting ourselves to practical needs, without thereby surrendering our love for the things of the spirit or the right to pursue our studies.'

Einstein's lighthouse-keeper suggestion was mostly greeted with enchanted mirth in Britain (though it impressed the politician Hoare as an 'imaginative proposal'). A *Daily Express* cartoonist, in a cartoon entitled 'Stormy Weather', depicted a wild-haired 'Lighthouse Keeper Professor Stan Baldstein' perched alone in his electrically radiant lighthouse, holding a humble candle. A former lighthouse-keeper pointed out in the *Manchester Guardian* that a keeper was legally forbidden to read while on watch, and that a certain clockwork arrangement had to be wound every half-hour, to keep the bell ringing and the light automatically clicking on and off – which would surely inhibit intellectual reflection. As for scientists, both in Einstein's day and also nowadays, most of them tend to regard collaboration, rather

'Stormy Weather'. This cartoon by Sidney 'George' Strube appeared in the *Daily Express* in October 1933. It was inspired by a remark about lighthouse-keepers in Einstein's speech at the Albert Hall.

than isolation, as the key to having good ideas. His own collaborator, Leopold Infeld, commented: 'For him loneliness, life in a lighthouse, would be most stimulating, would free him from so many of the duties which he hates. In fact it would be for him the ideal life. But nearly every scientist thinks just the opposite.' Perhaps Einstein's friend, Born, should have the last word on this subject:

> Einstein expressed over and over again the thought that one should not couple the quest for knowledge with a bread-and-butter profession, but that research should be done as a private spare-time occupation. . . . What he did not consider, however, was the organisational rigidity of almost all professions, and the importance which individual members of a profession attach to their work. No professional pride could develop without it. To be able successfully to practise science as a hobby, one has to be an Einstein.

DEPARTURE FOR AMERICA

The three clear days after the meeting before his departure for the United States on 7 October were somewhat clouded by difficulties with Locker-Lampson and Lindemann, Einstein's two, very disparate, hosts in England. By the end of his stay in Norfolk, Locker-Lampson's personal 'Ether-Atmosphere' must sometimes have struck Einstein more as German *Zwang* – coercion – than English freedom. For example, his English host had the habit in Norfolk of opening his guest's letters, including even letters from Einstein's wife: a fact revealed by Einstein to Yahuda (as mentioned in a shocked letter to Einstein from Yahuda's wife after he had left England). 'Black Swan' Locker-Lampson, whom Einstein had lauded to his wife Elsa for his lack of egoism back in late July, had become something like Black (or Blue) Shirt Locker-Lampson by early October. He would now try to manipulate Lindemann, too.

On 4 October, Lindemann (who had missed the Albert Hall meeting) drove from Oxford to London, where he telephoned Locker-Lampson and expressed a wish to meet Einstein on the following day – presumably to discuss the latter's future relationship with Oxford physics. What happened next is not clear, but no meeting took place on 5 October. Later that day, Einstein wrote a friendly letter to Lindemann: 'I heard that you called me and hoped to see you today. But I did not hear anything, and I suppose you are back in Oxford.' Having congratulated Lindemann on his successfully helping so many refugee physicist colleagues, Einstein looked forward to 'a happy reunion' with Lindemann. But in fact the two of them would never meet again. No doubt Lindemann thought that Locker-Lampson deliberately engineered the botched meeting with Einstein in London. In years to come, Lindemann apparently claimed, according to Christ Church legend, that 'Locker-Lampson frightened Einstein from Europe'.

Supporting evidence for Locker-Lampson's somewhat autocratic behaviour at this time comes from his handling of the funds raised by the London meeting. He and his organiser, Charles Cooley, handed over £3,000 (including a single donation of £1,000) to the Refugee Assistance Committee, yet retained considerable, undeclared funds for their own purposes – including, it would appear, the rapid publication of an illustrated 'souvenir' booklet of the meeting, prominently featuring Locker-Lampson. A worried letter to Beveridge from Walter Adams (who had visited Roughton Heath in mid-September), remarked on 18 December:

> Mr Sieff, who was acting as treasurer when the matter was being discussed, agreed it would be wiser not to press for a

> detailed account, capable of audit, but to treat the payment as a block grant to the fund. Commander Locker-Lampson feels that he was responsible for the meeting and, therefore, for the funds collected and seems to prefer to keep a balance as a fund for further campaign expenses. The irregularity of this position has caused a great deal of irritation and distress and the whole question of the Einstein accounts must be settled if further paralysing delays are to be avoided.

In response, Beveridge told the treasurer on 20 December: 'An amicable settlement is highly preferable to any open rupture. The object of all parties to this unfortunate misunderstanding is the common service of humanity.'

Certainly there is no record of any fond farewell between the commander and the professor as he left London for America. A draft chapter of Locker-Lampson's unpublished memoirs claimed that one of the commander's lady secretaries (who had helped to look after Einstein in Norfolk) drove Einstein by car from London to Southampton and saw him off to America: a forlorn figure to the very end. But this ultimate moment of departure appears to be pure Locker-Lampson fantasy – reminiscent of his supposed first meeting with Einstein in Oxford back in 1921. According to contemporary newspaper reports, an unaccompanied Einstein took the boat train from London to Southampton on 7 October, where, under security, he boarded the liner for New York coming from Antwerp with his wife, his secretary Helen Dukas, and his calculator Walther Mayer on board. In a very brief press statement at a Southampton hotel, a business-like Einstein refused to be interviewed and announced simply: 'I am going to visit Princeton University to carry out a series of scientific investigations. I shall be away for six months. Beyond that I am not making plans at present.'

CHAPTER EIGHT

I Vill a Little T'ink

Science is not and never will be a closed book. Every important advance brings new questions. Every development reveals, in the long run, new and deeper difficulties.

Comment by Einstein in *The Evolution of Physics: The Growth of Ideas from the Early Concepts to Relativity and Quanta*, 1938

Even as he crossed the Atlantic Ocean in October 1933, Einstein busied himself with trying to help other refugees from Nazi Germany. Writing to the Academic Assistance Council in London on 14 October from on board ship to express his satisfaction at the Albert Hall event and the substantial funds it had raised, he brought to the council's attention the names and details of three deserving Jewish academics: a professor of paediatrics now in Holland, a psychiatrist still in Berlin and a physician in Zurich. The psychiatrist, Otto Juliusburger – a friend who had treated Einstein's nephew – wanted to emigrate to Palestine and found a clinic there, Einstein noted, but he had been financially ruined by the German government. If the council were to contact him, he added, it should on no account mention who had suggested Juliusburger's name, because this move would be highly dangerous for him if he were somehow associated with Einstein. (Juliusburger eventually left Berlin at the last minute, in 1941, with Einstein's help and financial support, and died in New York in 1952 at an advanced age.)

About a month after he reached Princeton, he wrote again to Lindemann on the same subject. It was 'hardly justifiable', he said, that he should continue to receive payments from Christ Church, given the current emergency. Might the college offer the money from his annual stipend – £400 per annum for the years 1932–37 – to another foreign scholar in distress?

Lindemann replied on 6 December, after discussion with some colleagues, that such an arrangement would probably be possible. 'On the other hand, we should be very sorry if you abandoned your connections with the college.' He hoped that Einstein would come to stay in Oxford for as long as possible during the summer of 1934, 'especially since Belgium cannot be particularly attractive in the present circumstances'. Then he added, obviously thinking of what he regarded as Einstein's political naïveté (including perhaps the speech at the Albert Hall?):

> I trust you are enjoying America and have not been pestered too much by people who want to exploit you for political ends. I gather in Germany scarcely any of these demonstrations do any good. On the contrary, any activities abroad are made an excuse to intensify the campaign against the Jews remaining. In these matters politicians, even the most well meaning, unless they know the situation in Germany, are apt to be unsafe guides to follow.

Einstein replied quickly, but made no commitment to visit Oxford during the following year. As for politics in the United States, he wrote: 'I have voiced my opinion much less than it may seem, since the press makes a great deal of fuss over me without my intending it or wishing it.' But then he significantly qualified this observation: 'All the same I am of the opinion that a conscientious person who has a certain amount of influence cannot in times like the present keep completely silent, since such silence can lead to wrong interpretation which is undesirable in the present circumstances.'

Here was a hint of what would keep Einstein from returning to Europe. If the American press oppressed him, how much more oppressive would be the European press, given his uniquely symbolic role in opposing the increasing barbarity of Nazism? While he could cope with one Albert Hall meeting, a series of such events would have been a very different and much more stressful matter. Nor would he have a hideaway to retreat to and think about science, away from the pressure of political and media events; an Oxford college, even Christ Church, was far from being such a retreat. So he declined offers of hospitality in England in mid-1934 from both Lindemann and, separately, Locker-Lampson, who was equally keen on Einstein's return for his own, entirely non-scientific reasons.

Nothing came of Lindemann's hopes for another Einstein visit to Oxford. In early May, Einstein officially informed the dean of Christ Church that he would not visit the college that summer and hoped that his stipend might be used in whole or in part to pay one or more distinguished foreign scientists to give brief lecture courses during the term. If this suggestion were agreeable, then the dean might consult Lindemann, and also Erwin Schrödinger, who was then in Oxford, to find out which scientists were available. 'I need scarcely tell you how much I regret my inability to see once more my many friends at Christ Church but I hope to be more fortunate on some future occasion.' And in January 1935, he told Lindemann that he would not visit that year either, 'because if I come to Oxford I must also go to Paris and Madrid and I lack the courage to undertake all this'. He said almost the same thing, around the same time, to his musical friend Elisabeth, Queen of Belgium: 'Sometimes I think back nostalgically to beautiful past hours; they tempt me to make a journey to Europe. But so many obligations would await me there that I cannot summon the courage for such an undertaking.' No doubt, in addition to the demands of anti-Nazi politics, Einstein also had in mind his reluctance to deal with intractable family matters in Europe, in particular the psychiatric illness of his younger son, Eduard, looked after by his ex-wife Mileva. He did not accompany his wife Elsa when she returned to Paris in May 1934 to watch her elder daughter, Ilse, die – despite his fondness for his stepdaughter.

ESTABLISHMENT AT PRINCETON AMONG FELLOW EUROPEAN EXILES

Thus did Einstein's last institutional link with England, and with Europe as a whole, fade away. But at the same time, of course, Europe came to Einstein in America, in the shape of numerous Jewish fellow refugees and non-Jewish visitors to the Institute for Advanced Study. In fact, Einstein's closest human interactions in America were almost exclusively with Europeans, not native-born Americans, until his death in 1955. As noted by an influential English-born physicist, Freeman Dyson, who knew Einstein at Princeton in 1948 and later settled in the United States: 'He had gone through the ritual of naturalisation, but he remained an alien spirit in America.' In fact, Einstein retained his Swiss citizenship when he became a United States citizen in 1940. Despite his admiration for the principles of American democracy, Dyson's summary comment feels true. After all, in late 1939, following the outbreak of war in Europe, Princeton University's freshmen chose Hitler, for the second year running, as 'the greatest living person' in the annual poll of their class conducted by the *Daily Princetonian*. (The German leader received ninety-three votes in the poll; Einstein twenty-seven votes; and Neville Chamberlain, the British prime minister, fifteen votes.) Certainly, Einstein never gave expression to any deep gratitude, or even love, towards America, as he did towards England in 1933.

By way of example of his continuing European Jewish affiliations, he collaborated with Leopold Infeld and Banesh Hoffmann on general relativity, to create the important Einstein–Infeld–Hoffmann equations of motion, published in 1938. Infeld was a Polish-born physicist who left Poland for Cambridge in 1933, and later came to Princeton as a Polish refugee without any academic

Einstein in his study at Princeton, 1951. On the wall is a portrait of Mahatma Gandhi, of whom Einstein said: 'Generations to come, it may well be, will scarce believe that such a one as this ever in flesh and blood walked upon this earth.' Other walls carried portraits of Isaac Newton, Michael Faraday and James Clerk Maxwell. Much of Einstein's time in Princeton was spent alone at home, working on physics, despite his active involvement with American Cold War politics.

position, where his excellent command of English enabled him to co-write *The Evolution of Physics* with Einstein and survive financially on the royalties from sales of the book. Hoffmann was a British-born son of Polish immigrants, educated at the University of Oxford, who earned his doctorate at Princeton University, settled at the City University of New York as a mathematician, and later wrote *Albert Einstein: Creator and Rebel* with Einstein's secretary, Dukas.

Hoffmann had an irresistible anecdote about Einstein in Princeton caught in the act of thinking about physics, accompanied by Infeld and himself:

> Whenever we came to an impasse the three of us had heated discussions – in English for my benefit, because my German was not too fluent – but when the argument became really intricate Einstein, without realising it, would lapse into German. He thought more readily in his native tongue. Infeld would join him in that tongue, while I struggled so hard to follow what was being said that I rarely had time to interject a remark till the excitement died down.
>
> When it became clear, as it often did, that even resorting to German did not solve the problem, we would all pause, and then Einstein would stand up quietly and say, in his quaint English, 'I vill a little t'ink'. So saying he would pace up and down or walk around in circles, all the time twirling a lock of his long, greying hair around his forefinger. At these moments of high drama Infeld and I would remain completely still, not daring to move or make a sound, lest we interrupt his train of thought. A minute would pass in this way and another, and Infeld and I would eye each other silently while Einstein continued pacing and all the time twirling his hair. There was a dreamy, far-away, and yet sort of inward look on his face.

There was no appearance at all of intense concentration. Another minute would pass and another, and then all of a sudden Einstein would visibly relax and a smile would light up his face. No longer did he pace and twirl his hair. He seemed to come back to his surroundings and to notice us once more, and then he would tell us the solution to the problem and almost always the solution worked.

So here we were, with the magic performed triumphantly and the solution sometimes was so simple we could have kicked ourselves for not having been able to think of it by ourselves. But that magic was performed invisibly in the recesses of Einstein's mind, by a process that we could not fathom. From this point of view the whole thing was completely frustrating. But, from the more immediately practical point of view, it was just the opposite, since it opened a way to further progress and without it we should never have been able to bring the research to a successful conclusion.

As Infeld subsequently observed: 'The clue to the understanding of Einstein's role in science lies in his loneliness and aloofness. In this respect he differs from all other scientists I know.' Perhaps Dirac, whom Infeld knew in Cambridge, could be regarded as 'the nearest to Einstein, although the difference between them is still great'.

NUCLEAR FISSION AND THE ATOMIC BOMB

Probably the best-known European Jewish refugee to work with Einstein in America was the Hungarian-born physicist Leo Szilard. Having moved from post-war Hungary to study in Berlin, he got to know Einstein in the early 1920s and together they designed and patented an Einstein–Szilard refrigerator pump in 1927, which was later used for the circulation of liquid sodium coolant in nuclear reactors. With the advent of the Nazi regime, Szilard moved to England in 1933, became involved with the fledgling Academic Assistance Council, and took a job at St Bartholomew's Hospital studying the use of radioactive istopes for medical treatments. While in London – after reading a newspaper article on atomic energy by Rutherford and supposedly just after waiting for a traffic light not far from the British Museum to go green so that he could step off the kerb – Szilard conceived, on 12 September 1933, the idea of the nuclear chain reaction, which would prove so crucial in the atomic bomb project. In 1938, fearing an imminent war with Germany, he emigrated to the United States, where he once again came in contact with Einstein.

In July 1939, Szilard became concerned by reports that German physicists were investigating nuclear fission, very likely with a view to making a bomb. He – accompanied by another Hungarian émigré physicist, Eugene Wigner, a future Nobel laureate – decided to drive out from New York and interrupt Einstein at his summer house in rural Long Island, in order to ask him to intervene politically. It was so tricky to find the address in Peconic, however, that they were about to give up and return to New York when Szilard thought of asking a young boy where Professor Einstein lived. The boy got into their car and took them to him.

Talking to Einstein, Szilard was surprised to discover that he had not considered the possibility of a nuclear chain reaction. That is, the idea of one neutron bombarding a uranium atom, causing it to fission and release two neutrons, which then cause two uranium atoms to fission, producing four neutrons, and so on – and very quickly a concatenation of neutrons and an explosion of atomic energy. 'I never thought of that!' Szilard recalled

Einstein's saying when he told him that Enrico Fermi (a recent physicist refugee from Mussolini's Italy) had just achieved a nuclear chain reaction in his New York laboratory. But as usual Einstein was quick to see the scientific implications of the new idea. And he instinctively shared his visitors' fear that the Nazis might build the bomb first. 'He was willing to assume responsibility for sounding the alarm even though it was quite possible that the alarm might prove to be a false alarm,' said Szilard. 'The one thing most scientists are really afraid of is to make fools of themselves. Einstein was free from such a fear and this above all is what made his position unique on this occasion.'

By 2 August, the threesome had finalised what would become a historic letter from Einstein to President Franklin Roosevelt. Its most dramatic paragraph read as follows:

> This new phenomenon [a nuclear chain reaction] would also lead to the construction of bombs, and it is conceivable – though much less certain – that extremely powerful bombs of a new type may thus be constructed. A single bomb of this type, carried by boat and exploded in a port, might very well destroy the whole port together with some of the surrounding territory.

But Einstein advised that such bombs might possibly turn out to be too heavy to be transported in aircraft.

Einstein's letter was personally delivered to the president through a trusted intermediary after a considerable delay – by which time war had broken out in Europe. Roosevelt responded promptly, but it took well over two years (and another reminder to Roosevelt from Einstein in 1940), plus the Japanese attack on the United States in December 1941, before the Manhattan Project to build the bomb got fully under way.

At this time, during 1941, Infeld – who had now emigrated from the United States to Canada – happened to publish an autobiography, *Quest*. He wrote presciently: 'Very few of the younger generation of physicists are seriously interested in the problems with which Einstein occupies his life. Most of them work in close contact, gathering material, searching for theories, often of a provisional character, to fit the tremendous richness of experimental data in the realm of nuclear physics' – a situation that did not remotely resemble that of solitary young physicist-cum-lighthouse-keepers as fantasised by Einstein in his Albert Hall speech in 1933.

Indeed, Einstein had nothing directly to do with the actual making of the atomic bomb – unlike Szilard and Wigner, who both joined the Manhattan Project. While he was responsible for deriving the equation $E = mc^2$, which he published in 1905, at that time he had absolutely no vision of its use in weaponry. 'It is true that this equation plays an important role in nuclear physics, but to say this made possible the construction of weapons is like saying that the invention of the alphabet caused the Bible to be written,' remarked Abraham Pais. In July 1939, when Szilard met him, Einstein was clearly out of touch with nuclear physics. Despite his letters to Roosevelt, during the Manhattan Project in 1942–45 Einstein was not given a security clearance by the army authorities (probably because of his alleged Communist sympathies) – although he did receive clearance from the naval authorities to work on the theory of explosions – and was kept officially unaware of the project's technical progress right up to the bombing of Hiroshima and Nagasaki in August 1945. So Einstein was certainly not the 'father' of the atomic bomb, as strongly implied on a famous cover of *Time* magazine in 1946, although there is a case for calling him the bomb's 'grandfather'. But after 1945, once he came to know that the German scientists (including

Heisenberg) had achieved no significant progress in building an atomic bomb, Einstein strongly regretted his encouragement of Roosevelt; and for the remainder of his life he was relentlessly opposed to the spread of nuclear weapons.

As well as receiving visitors from Europe, Einstein also kept in contact by letter with those who remained there. His correspondents included Elisabeth, Queen of Belgium, Murray in Oxford, two old friends from Zurich days, Besso and Solovine, and among the major physicists living outside the Third Reich, Born in Britain (Cambridge and Edinburgh) and Schrödinger in Ireland (Dublin).

FRIENDSHIP AND DEBATE WITH MAX BORN ACROSS THE ATLANTIC

The most illuminating of these exchanges was undoubtedly that with Born – most famously, Einstein's 1926 remark to Born about God not playing dice with the universe – covering the period 1916–55, beginning in wartime Germany and continuing after the last personal meeting between Einstein and Born in 1932. Thereafter, they were divided by the Atlantic Ocean. (Born arrived in England in 1933 just after Einstein's departure, and never visited the United States after 1933.) Like Einstein, Born abandoned his German citizenship, becoming a British citizen just days before the outbreak of war in 1939, in Edinburgh, where he had been appointed a professor of physics at the university in 1936. His son and two daughters married and settled down in the new country. But unlike Einstein, Born returned to Germany in 1954 on his retirement, and died in his native land. Their letters range from analysis of quantum mechanics to debate over the German threat to peace, including some fundamental disagreements about physics, politics and life in general, which at times led to long periods of silence between them. Nonetheless, Born, who edited the letters after Einstein's death with the addition of an extensive commentary, concluded the collection with the comment: 'With his death, we, my wife and I, lost our dearest friend.'

It was published after Born's own death as *The Born–Einstein Letters* in 1971, with prefatory material by two Nobel laureates: a foreword by Bertrand Russell and an introduction by Heisenberg, both of whom had known Born and Einstein personally, if from very different angles. Then it appeared in a second edition in 2005, the centenary of special relativity, with a new preface jointly written by Diana Kormos Buchwald, general editor of the Einstein Papers Project, and Kip Thorne, a leading expert on the astrophysical implications of general relativity. They focused on the history of Einstein's scientific ideas over a century, and how 'many of his scientific concerns at the time continue to engage modern physics'. For instance, the Einstein–Infeld–Hoffmann equations of 1938 – 'Einstein's greatest contribution to relativity after 1920' – and also gravitational waves, predicted by Einstein from general relativity in 1916, which were finally confirmed to exist in 2016 by a team including Thorne (for which he shared a Nobel prize in 2017).

To quote Russell's foreword about Born and Einstein: 'Both men were brilliant, humble and completely without fear in their public utterances. In an age of mediocrity and moral pygmies, their lives shine with an intense beauty. Something of this is reflected in their correspondence, and the world is the richer for its publication.'

They agreed on some aspects of Britain and of Germany, but differed considerably on others. For example, in early 1937, Einstein wrote from Princeton to Born in Edinburgh: 'I am extremely delighted that you have found such an excellent sphere of activity, and what's more in the most civilised country of the day. And more than just a refuge. It seems to me that you, with your well-adjusted personality and good family background, will feel quite happy there.' Then he contrasted his own position in the United States: 'I have settled down splendidly here: I hibernate like a bear in a cave, and really feel more at home than ever before in all my varied existence. This bearishness has been accentuated still further by the death of my mate who was more attached to human beings than I.'

Elsa Einstein died in late December 1936 after a painful illness. 'He has been so upset by my illness,' she wrote of her husband not long before her death to her friend Vallentin in Paris. 'He wanders about like a lost soul. I never thought he loved me so much. And that comforts me.' Yet Einstein himself said nothing to others about Elsa's death, except for his minimal remark to Born. 'The incidental way in which Einstein describes his wife's death, in the course of a brief description of his bear-like existence, seems rather strange. For all his kindness, sociability and love of humanity, he was nevertheless totally detached from his environment and the human beings included in it,' Born frankly commented. As Einstein himself honestly admitted, a month before his own death, in a condolence letter to the widow of his lifelong friend Besso: 'What I most admired in [Michele] as a human being is the fact that he managed to live for many years not only in peace but in lasting harmony with a woman – an undertaking in which I twice failed rather disgracefully.'

This difference in attitude towards human relationships between Einstein and Born – who was undoubtedly much more of a family man than Einstein – would be reflected in their attitude to post-war Germans and German responsibility for Nazism. Einstein blamed all Germans for Nazism, whereas Born was willing to draw distinctions between Germans, after the horrors of the war were over. And this was despite the fact that Born had lost thirty-four relatives and friends during the Nazi period, two-thirds of whom had committed suicide rather than face imprisonment in a concentration camp, whereas Einstein had got off much more lightly.

'I did share your opinion, but I have now come to another conclusion,' Born wrote to Einstein in 1950. 'I think that in a higher sense responsibility *en masse* does not exist, but only that of individuals. I have met a sufficient number of decent Germans, only a few perhaps, but nevertheless genuinely decent. I assume that you may have modified your wartime views to some extent.' Not so. Einstein remained adamant – not only about the German masses but also about German intellectuals. He had not changed his attitude to the Germans, he said, which dated from before the Nazi period. According to him, although all human beings were more or less the same from birth, 'The Germans, however, have a far more dangerous tradition than any of the other so-called civilised nations. The present behaviour of these other nations towards the Germans merely proves to me how little human beings learn even from their most painful experiences.'

In 1953, Einstein regretted Born's decision to migrate back 'to the land of the mass-murderers of our kinsmen', although he blamed it partly on the parsimony of the University of Edinburgh, which had failed to provide Born with a pension – unlike Born's former university at Göttingen in Germany. 'But then we know only too well that the collective conscience is a miserable little plant which is always most likely to wither just when it is needed most.'

To which Born replied: 'I only want to tell you that the German Quakers have their headquarters in Pyrmont', that is, the spa town in Lower Saxony where the Borns were planning to retire. 'They are no "mass-murderers", and many of our friends there suffered far worse things under the Nazis than you or I. One should be chary of applying epithets of this sort. The Americans have demonstrated in Dresden, Hiroshima and Nagasaki that in sheer speed of extermination they surpass even the Nazis.' (Later, Born even directly equated 'Hiroshima and Nagasaki on the one hand, and Auschwitz and Belsen on the other.') In response to Einstein's accusation of Scottish parsimony forcing him to return, he remarked: 'You are wrong in casting aspersions on my dear Scots; the inadequate provision for the old age of teachers and professors is quite general all over Britain, and is just as wretched in Oxford and Cambridge. If anyone is to blame it is the Swedes, who could quite well have found out about my contribution to quantum mechanics.' Happily, the following year, 1954, just after Born's return to Germany, the Swedish Academy in Stockholm awarded him a long-delayed Nobel prize (following its earlier awards for quantum mechanics to his collaborator Heisenberg in 1932 and Dirac/Schrödinger in 1933), partly as a consequence of the acceptance of Born's ideas in the intervening period, promoted by Bohr and his Copenhagen school of quantum physics.

On Britain and the Jews, by contrast, Einstein and Born were in definite agreement, both before and after the Second World War. In May 1939, Born wrote to Einstein congratulating him on a speech about Palestine, which had been reported in the British press. He commented:

> Without wishing to defend the wavering and unreliable British policy, I am of the opinion that the Jews could do nothing more stupid than to assume an antagonistic attitude towards the English. The British Empire is still a place of refuge and protection for the persecuted, and particularly for Jews. I also completely subscribe to what you are reported to have said

> concerning the need for and the possibility of coming to an understanding with the Arabs. I am glad that you have said what you did; your voice will be heard. I can only think my own thoughts in silence.

However, by 1948, the time of the expiration of the British Mandate and the foundation of the state of Israel, both Born and Einstein had changed their minds. Born now wrote to Einstein:

> I was very sad when the Jews started to use terror themselves, and showed that they had learned a lesson from Hitler. Also I was so grateful towards my new 'fatherland', Britain, that I expected nothing evil from it. But it gradually dawned on me that our Mr Bevin [Ernest Bevin, the British foreign secretary] is playing a wicked game: first the Arabs are supplied with arms and trained; then the British army pulls out and leaves the dirty business of liquidating the Jews to the Arabs. Of course, I have no proof that it is so. Moreover, I detest nationalism of every kind, including that of the Jews. Therefore I could not get very excited about it. But gradually it has become quite obvious to me that my worst suspicions were correct. A leading article in today's *Manchester Guardian* openly attacks Bevin for doing precisely what I had suspected. I am feeling very depressed, for I am completely powerless and without influence in this country. The main purpose of this letter is to tell you that you have my wholehearted support if you take any action to help. Could you not induce the American government to act before it is too late?

To which Einstein responded in wholehearted agreement: 'Your Palestine letter has moved me very deeply. Without any doubt, you have summed up Bevin's policy correctly. He seems to have become infected with the infamy germ by virtue of the post he occupies.' However, he said, Born had 'rather too optimistic an idea of the opportunities I have to influence the game in Washington. The latter can be summed up with the maxim: never let the right hand know what the left is doing. One thumps the table with the right hand, while with the left one helps England (by an embargo, for example) in its insidious attack.'

As for probability and certainty in physics, Einstein and Born remained in sharp but friendly dispute to the very end. In 1947, while continuing to labour on his unified field theory, Einstein stated his underlying belief to Born, in which he coined a phrase, 'spooky actions at a distance', now familiar to all physicists:

> I cannot make a case for my attitude to physics which you would consider at all reasonable. I admit, of course, that there is a considerable amount of validity in the statistical approach which you were the first to recognise clearly as necessary given the framework of the existing formalism. I cannot seriously believe in it because the theory cannot be reconciled with the idea that physics should represent a reality in time and space, free from spooky actions at a distance. I am, however, not yet firmly convinced that it can really be achieved with a continuous field theory, although I have discovered a possible way of doing this which so far seems quite reasonable. The calculation difficulties are so great that I will be biting the dust long before I myself can be fully convinced of it. But I am quite convinced that someone will eventually come up with a theory whose objects, connected by laws, are not probabilities but considered facts, as used to be taken for granted until quite recently. I cannot, however, base this conviction on logical reasons, but can only produce my little finger as witness, that is, I offer no authority which

> would be able to command any kind of respect outside of my own hand.

After Einstein's death, Born summed up this disagreement elegantly, in words that still resonate today:

> He saw in the quantum mechanics of today a useful intermediate stage between the traditional classical physics and a still completely unknown 'physics of the future' based on general relativity, in which – and this he regarded as indispensable for philosophical reasons – the traditional concepts of physical reality and determinism come into their own again. Thus he regarded statistical quantum mechanics to be not wrong but 'incomplete'.

As for his own view, he explained:

> I am convinced that ideas such as absolute certainty, absolute precision, final truth, and so on are phantoms, which should be excluded from science. . . . The relaxation of the rules of thinking seems to me the greatest blessing which modern science has given us. For the belief that there is only one truth and that oneself is in possession of it, seems to me the deepest root of all that is evil in the world.

A final theme of the Born–Einstein letters concerns isolation as a source of scientific inspiration, and even genius. For Born, it had been a decidedly mixed blessing, but he recognised its value for Einstein. Solitude had been highly productive for Einstein in 1915–16, when he created his theory of general relativity in Berlin. Princeton seems to have encouraged his desire for it – and his concomitant unwillingness to return to the distractions of

Europe. In 1936, Einstein told Born: 'I personally feel very happy here, and find it indescribably enjoyable really to be able to lead a quiet life. It is, after all, no more than one deserves in one's last terms, though it is granted to very few.' And in 1952, he wrote: 'One feels as if one were an Ichthyosaurus, left behind by accident. Most of our dear friends, but thank God also some of the less dear, are already gone.' ('What have you got against being an Ichthyosaurus?' replied Born's wife, Hedwig. 'They were, after all, rather vigorous little beasts, probably able to look back on the experiences of a very long lifetime.') To visitors in Princeton who had known him in Europe, Einstein would apparently often say: 'You are surprised, aren't you, at the contrast between my fame throughout the world, the fuss over me in the newspapers, and the isolation and quiet in which I live here? I wished for this isolation all my life, and now I have finally achieved it here in Princeton.'

ISOLATED FROM, OR INVOLVED WITH, FELLOW PHYSICISTS?

To what extent is this self-drawn and familiar picture of Einstein's isolation in Princeton accurate? Not according to Buchwald and Thorne in their preface to *The Born–Einstein Letters*: 'Actually, Einstein was not isolated from bright colleagues and visitors during his Princeton years. He was in lively contact with many creative physicists and mathematicians . . . and he maintained a voluminous correspondence.'

Perhaps the truth is that both pictures are accurate: Einstein was in personal contact with highly intelligent Princeton colleagues and visitors and in written contact with other physicists (including of course Born) – yet he was also aloof. 'He always has a certain feeling of being a stranger, and even a desire to be isolated,' remarked his biographer Frank in 1948. 'On the other hand, however, he has a great curiosity about everything human and a great sense of humour.'

One of his collaborators, Infeld, gave a fascinating example of how this apparently contradictory combination worked, taken not from his highly theoretical work with Einstein and Hoffmann mentioned earlier, but from his joint book with Einstein on physics for a popular readership, *The Evolution of Physics*, published by Simon & Schuster in New York and Cambridge University Press in England. At this time, in 1937, Infeld (who had fled Poland because of anti-Semitism) had failed to win a fellowship at the Institute for Advanced Study despite Einstein's strong personal recommendation, because Princeton colleagues did not believe in the value of Einstein's work on the unified field theory. Infeld was therefore in serious financial difficulties when he approached Einstein with his idea for a physics book capitalising on Einstein's fame plus Infeld's own knowledge of English. He became uncharacteristically tongue-tied with embarrassment in front of Einstein, as described in his autobiography. After an incoherent explanation of the proposed book, Infeld finally blurted out the remark: 'The greatest men of science wrote popular books. Books still regarded as classics. Faraday's popular lectures, Maxwell's *Matter and Motion*, the popular writings of Helmholtz and Boltzmann still make exciting reading.' Einstein looked at him silently, stroked his moustache with his finger and then said quietly: 'This is not at all a stupid idea. Not stupid at all.' He got up, stretched out his hand and said: 'We shall do it.'

Einstein took the challenge to heart and was increasingly enthusiastic as the work progressed, saying repeatedly: 'This was a splendid idea of yours.' He believed that the fundamental ideas of physics could be expressed in words, commenting: 'No scientist thinks in formulae.' They discussed and revised the manuscript over and over again until it was in its final form, in a remarkable collaboration which captured the complexity of the subject while also making it intelligible to the ordinary reader (unlike Einstein's own short book on relativity, as Einstein well knew). Not once did Einstein try to pull rank over Infeld. 'Then suddenly Einstein lost all interest. His interest lasted exactly as long as our work lasted. It ended the moment our work was finished.' When the advance copies arrived from Simon & Schuster, Infeld took them to Einstein. He was completely uninterested and did not even open the book. 'Once a work is finished his interest in it ceases. The same applies to the reprints of his scientific papers. Later he had to autograph so many copies of our book that automatically, when he saw a blue jacket, he groped for his fountain pen.' But for Infeld – known forever after as the 'man who worked with Einstein' – publication of the book was an adventure that changed both his intellectual outlook and his academic career.

DRAWN INTO POLITICS BY NUCLEAR WEAPONS AND THE COLD WAR

With the evolution of physics into nuclear physics in the 1930s, the dropping of the atomic bomb on Japan in 1945 and the end of the Second World War, Einstein was drawn into American and international politics – whether or not he would have preferred to remain aloof. His only reaction on hearing the radio announcement of the atomic bomb on Hiroshima relayed to him by his secretary Dukas was '*Oj weh*' (Yiddish for 'Woe is me'). But soon he began a public campaign to control atomic and nuclear weapons by calling for a new political ethics. This culminated in his appeal in 1950 against the development of the hydrogen bomb in a nationwide television programme hosted by Eleanor Roosevelt: a broadcast regarded as so subversive by the Federal Bureau of Investigation director, J. Edgar Hoover, that the FBI and the Immigration and Naturalization Service launched a top-secret investigation aimed at revoking Einstein's American citizenship, so that he could be deported from America. (Even US President Dwight Eisenhower was kept in the dark, judging from his eulogy of Einstein after his death: 'Americans are proud that he sought and found here a climate of freedom in his search for knowledge and truth.' He further commented: 'No other man contributed so much to the vast expansion of twentieth-century knowledge.')

Einstein hoped that the fresh horrors of the Second World War and the obvious potential horrors of a nuclear third world war might together be enough to force reform in international affairs. 'We must realise we cannot simultaneously plan for war and for peace,' he told the *New York Times*. As he put it on the occasion of the fifth Nobel anniversary dinner in New York in December 1945, 'The war is won, but the peace is not.' He began his speech: 'Physicists find themselves in a position not unlike that of Alfred Nobel. He invented the most powerful explosive ever known up to his time, a means of destruction par excellence. In order to atone for this, in order to relieve his human conscience, he instituted his awards for the promotion of peace and for achievements of peace.' And he concluded: 'The situation calls for a courageous effort, for a radical change in our whole attitude, in the entire political concept.' He evoked the name of Nobel: 'May the spirit that prompted Alfred Nobel to create his great institution, the spirit of trust and confidence, of generosity and brotherhood among men, prevail in the minds of those upon whose decisions our destiny rests. Otherwise, human civilisation will be doomed.'

Einstein's main practical recommendation for managing nuclear weapons (which he sensibly anticipated the Soviet Union would soon develop) was that they could be controlled only by what he called a 'world government'. This would be an essentially military organisation, to which the world's leading nations would contribute armed forces, which would then be 'commingled and distributed as were the regiments of the former Austro-Hungarian Empire', and which would have the power to enforce international law according to the direction of its representative executive. 'Do I fear the tyranny of a world government? Of course I do. But I fear still more the coming of another war or wars.' The United States, he said, should immediately announce its readiness to commit the secret of the atomic bomb to this world government. And the Soviet Union should be sincerely invited to join it. In September 1947, Einstein proposed his idea in an open letter to the General Assembly of the United Nations. If the UN were to have a chance of becoming such a world government, he said, then 'the authority of the General Assembly must be increased so that the Security Council as well as all other bodies of the UN will be subordinated to it.' (He even grimly suggested to an American friend that 'it might not be altogether illogical to place a statue of the contemptible Hitler in the vestibule of the future palace of world government since he, ironically, has greatly helped to convince many people of the necessity of a supranational organisation'.)

Perhaps needless to say, as the Cold War hotted up in 1947, no leading power was remotely interested in Einstein's world government. It was assailed from all sides. Four top scientists of the Russian Academy replied respectfully but in unequivocal opposition, virtually accusing Einstein of advocating American imperialism. Einstein was not surprised but pleaded in response that:

> If we hold fast to the concept and practice of unlimited sovereignty of nations it only means that each country reserves the right for itself of pursuing its objectives through warlike means. . . . I advocate world government because I am convinced that there is no other possible way of eliminating the most terrible danger in which man has ever found himself.

'World government' enjoyed a brief vogue among a spectrum of American intellectuals – on the right as well as on the left – and then faded from view. So too did the Emergency Committee of Atomic Scientists, a brainchild of Szilard, which Einstein agreed to chair in May 1946. Both fell victim to the Cold War.

More effective was Einstein's opposition to Senator Joseph McCarthy and his 1950s Red Scare in the United States. Einstein helped to turn the tide against the climate of fear and precipitate the decline of McCarthyism. In this period he made a number of public statements and supported several individuals threatened with dismissal from their jobs for having Communist sympathies. But the one that really stirred public controversy was Einstein's letter to a New York teacher of English, William Frauenglass, in May 1953. Frauenglass had refused to testify before a congressional committee about his political affiliations and now faced dismissal from his school. He asked for advice from Einstein, who wrote (no doubt thinking of his experience of German intellectuals in the First World War and under Nazism):

> The reactionary politicians have managed to instil suspicion of all intellectual efforts into the public by dangling before their eyes a danger from without. . . . What ought the minority of intellectuals to do against this evil? Frankly, I can only see the revolutionary way of non-cooperation in the sense of

> Gandhi's. Every intellectual who is called before one of the committees ought to refuse to testify, i.e., he must be prepared for jail and economic ruin, in short, for the sacrifice of his personal welfare in the interest of the cultural welfare of his country. . . . If enough people are ready to take this grave step they will be successful. If not, then the intellectuals of this country deserve nothing better than the slavery which is intended for them.

Mahatma Gandhi was 'the greatest political genius of our time', wrote Einstein in 1952. 'His work on behalf of India's liberation is living testimony to the fact that man's will, sustained by an indomitable conviction, is more powerful than material forces that seem insurmountable.'

When the advice to Frauenglass was published in the *New York Times* with Einstein's permission, he feared that, at the age of seventy-four and in poor health, he might have to go to jail. Immediately, McCarthy told the paper that 'anyone who gives advice like Einstein's to Frauenglass is himself an enemy of America. . . . That's the same advice given by every Communist lawyer that has ever appeared before our committee.' (A week later, he modified 'enemy of America' to 'a disloyal American'.) The *New York Times*, in an editorial, agreed with McCarthy's criticism of Einstein's advice.

At the same time, Einstein received two expressions of support from England. The first was a private cable from Locker-Lampson, sent on the very day of McCarthy's first published statement against Einstein. Long out of contact with Einstein, and now a retired recluse living in London, but still the impulsive romantic he was in 1933, Locker-Lampson recalled their alliance against Nazism: 'Commander Locker-Lampson offers same humble hut as sanctuary in England.' The second was a punchy public letter from Bertrand Russell. It was published after some delay caused by internal debate within the *New York Times*. Russell wrote:

> In your issue of June 13 you have a leading article disagreeing with Einstein's view that teachers questioned by Senator McCarthy's emissaries should refuse to testify. You seem to maintain that one should always obey the law, however bad. I cannot think you have realised the implications of this position.
>
> Do you condemn the Christian martyrs who refused to sacrifice to the emperor? Do you condemn John Brown? Nay, more, I am compelled to suppose that you condemn George Washington, and hold that your country ought to return to allegiance to Her Gracious Majesty Queen Elizabeth II. As a loyal Briton I of course applaud your view, but I fear it may not win much support in your country.

Einstein responded privately to Russell with deep appreciation on 28 June:

> All the intellectuals in this country, down to the youngest student, have become completely intimidated. Virtually no one of 'prominence' besides yourself has actually challenged these absurdities in which the politicians have become engaged. . . . The cruder the tales they spread, the more assured they feel of their re-election by the misguided population.

Hence the fact, he added, that President Eisenhower had not dared to commute the death sentences of the Soviet spies Ethel and Julius Rosenberg – American citizens who had been electrocuted on 19 June – even though Eisenhower 'well knew how much their execution would injure the name of the United States internationally.

> You should be given much credit for having used your unique literary talent in the service of public enlightenment and education. I am convinced that your literary work will exercise a great and lasting influence particularly since you have resisted the temptation to gain some short-lived effects through paradoxes and exaggerations.

THE RUSSELL–EINSTEIN MANIFESTO

No doubt this exchange prepared the ground for what would be the last public act of Einstein's life: the Russell–Einstein Manifesto of 1955. It started with a letter from Russell to Einstein in February 1955, which began:

> In common with every other thinking person, I am profoundly disquieted by the armaments race in nuclear weapons. You have on various occasions given expression to feelings and opinions with which I am in close agreement. I think that eminent men of science ought to do something dramatic to bring home to the public and governments the disasters that may occur. Do you think it would be possible to get, say, six men of the very highest scientific repute, headed by yourself, to make a very solemn statement about the imperative necessity of avoiding war? These men should be so diverse in their politics that any statement signed by all of them would be obviously free from pro-Communist or anti-Communist bias.

Einstein was immediately responsive. In fact he suggested upping the number of signatories to 'twelve persons whose scientific attainments (scientific in the widest sense) have gained them international stature and whose declarations will not lose any effectiveness on account of their political affiliations'. In the United States, the choice would be particularly tricky, he said, because 'this country has been ravaged by a political plague that has by no means spared scientists'. As for obtaining Russian signatures, his colleague L. Infeld, professor at the University of Warsaw, might possibly be of assistance.

Einstein's signature, on 11 April, was the last one he ever gave. It reached Russell only after Einstein's death. The statement was made public at a meeting called by him in London in

The Russell–Einstein Manifesto against nuclear weapons, 1955: cover of a sound recording made by Bertrand Russell after Einstein's death in April. It was Einstein's last, and most enduring, political statement.

July 1955. The other nine signatories, apart from Einstein and Russell, were all scientists, the majority of them physicists: Max Born (from Germany), Percy Bridgman (United States), Leopold Infeld (Poland), Frédéric Joliot-Curie (France), Hermann Muller (United States), Linus Pauling (United States), Cecil Powell (Britain), Joseph Rotblat (Britain) and Hideki Yukawa (Japan). All eleven of them, except for Infeld, received the Nobel prize (twice over in the case of Pauling, for both chemistry and peace). Significantly, there was no signatory from the Soviet Union.

The final paragraph of the manifesto warned:

> There lies before us, if we choose, continual progress in happiness, knowledge and wisdom. Shall we, instead, choose death, because we cannot forget our quarrels? We appeal, as human beings, to human beings: Remember your humanity and forget the rest. If you can do so, the way lies open to a new paradise; if you cannot, there lies before you the risk of universal death.

As Rotblat, the youngest signatory, regretted in an article about 'Einstein's quest for global peace' written shortly before his own death in 2005, this warning 'is as valid today as it was then'. Rotblat had spent the half-century since signing the manifesto in building up the Pugwash Conferences on Science and World Affairs, meeting in the village of Pugwash in Canada with the aim of bringing together intellectuals and public figures to promote dialogue towards reducing the dangers of armed conflict. In 1995, he and Pugwash were jointly awarded the Nobel peace prize.

Einstein himself was lucky with his death. He had once told Infeld: 'if I knew that I should have to die in three hours it would impress me very little. I should think how best to use the last three hours, then quietly order my papers and lie peacefully down.' Soon after writing to Russell, he was taken to a Princeton hospital, still in possession of all his faculties but knowing that his death was imminent. He died early in the morning of 18 April, leaving pages of calculations about his unified field theory beside his bed.

EPILOGUE

An Old Gypsy in a Quaint and Ceremonious Village

Princeton is a wonderful little spot, a quaint and ceremonious village of puny demigods on stilts. Yet, by ignoring certain special conventions, I have been able to create for myself an atmosphere conducive to study and free from distraction.

Letter from Einstein to Elisabeth, Queen of Belgium, November 1933

Einstein's very last interview was focused on Sir Isaac Newton, as mentioned earlier. The interviewer was a historian of science from Harvard University, I. Bernard Cohen, with a burgeoning interest in Newton. Published in *Scientific American* in July 1955, even now Cohen's lengthy article reads as a lively portrait of Einstein, both as a scientist and as a personality. As they sat together in Einstein's Princeton study, observed by the portraits of Faraday and Maxwell (and Gandhi) on its walls, 'His face was contemplatively tragic and deeply lined, and yet his sparkling eyes made him seem ageless. His eyes watered almost continually; even in moments of laughter he would wipe away a tear with the back of his hand. He spoke softly and clearly; his command of English was remarkable, though marked by a German accent,' wrote Cohen. 'The contrast between his soft speech and his ringing laughter was enormous. He enjoyed making jokes; every time he made a point that he liked, or heard something that appealed to him, he would burst into booming laughter that echoed from the walls.'

Just before Cohen left the house, Einstein delightedly showed off a brand-new gadget specially designed for his seventy-sixth birthday on 14 March by a Princeton physics professor, Eric Rogers. It consisted of a small upright plastic tube enclosing a spring, anchored at the bottom of the tube and attached near the top of the tube to a string, from the other end of which hung a little ball draped over the outer part of the tube. The spring was not forceful enough to pull the hanging ball into the tube against the force of gravity acting downwards on the ball. But when Einstein raised the gadget to the ceiling and let it freely accelerate downwards to the floor – like a man falling freely from a rooftop – no gravitational force acted on the ball, and so the spring was now forceful enough to pull the ball into the tube. Thus the gadget demonstrated the equivalence between acceleration and gravity in relativity: 'the happiest thought' of Einstein's life back in the Patent Office in Bern in 1907, two centuries after Newton.

The interview was illuminating about Newton, mostly as a scientist and occasionally as a man. When Cohen brought into the discussion Newton's notorious refusal to publish any acknowledgement of the ideas of Robert Hooke in the preface to his *Principia Mathematica*, Einstein responded: 'That, alas, is vanity. You find it in so many scientists. You know, it has always hurt me to think that Galileo did not acknowledge the work of Kepler.' Later in the discussion he pointed out that vanity may appear in many different forms. A man might often say that he had no vanity, but this too was a kind of vanity because he took such special pride in the fact. 'It is like childishness,' Einstein said. Then he turned to Cohen and let out a booming laugh that filled the room as he remarked, 'Many of us are childish; some of us more childish than others. But if a man knows he is childish, then that knowledge can be a mitigating factor.'

Was Einstein perhaps including himself here? According to Russell, 'I never saw in him any trace, however faint, of vanity or envy, which are vices to which even the greatest men, such as Newton and Leibniz, are prone.' That said, Einstein had an increasing tendency with the passing of the years to write about his creation of relativity without much reference to others whom he had earlier acknowledged as providing important help, such as his close friends Besso, Ehrenfest and Grossmann. 'As with many other major breakthroughs in the history of science, Einstein was standing on the shoulders of many scientists, not just the proverbial giants,' according to a recent study in *Nature*. On the other hand, according to what Einstein told Cohen, his forgetfulness was most probably not due to vanity:

> Einstein said most emphatically that he thought the worst person to document any ideas about how discoveries are made

> is the discoverer. Many people, he went on, had asked him how he had come to think of this or how he had come to think of that. He had always found himself a very poor source of information concerning the genesis of his own ideas. Einstein believed that the historian is likely to have a better insight into the thought processes of a scientist than the scientist himself.

For all its interest, the Einstein–Cohen conversation barely touched on two important aspects of its subject that are key to this book. It contained nothing significant about Einstein's view of Newton's relationship with English history and culture, and nothing at all about Einstein's own relationship with English history and culture, other than his obvious admiration of Newton as a scientist. When Einstein and Cohen discussed Newton's long-running, anti-Trinitarian, linguistic study of theology, Einstein said he regarded this as a 'weakness'. If Newton did not accept the Trinitarian view of Scripture, why did he still believe that Scripture must be true?

> Einstein apparently had little feeling for the way in which a man's mind is imprisoned by his culture and the character of his thoughts is moulded by his intellectual environment. . . . I was struck by the fact that in physics Einstein could see Newton as a man of the seventeenth century, but that in the other realms of thought and action he viewed each man as a timeless, freely acting individual to be judged as if he were a contemporary of ours.

Einstein's attitude here certainly clashes with the strong admiration for English tradition and continuity he had expressed on the bicentenary of Newton's death in 1927, as quoted earlier, which surely motivated Newton's intensive theological studies.

It prompts the question: how much of an Anglophile was Einstein really – and why did he settle in America after 1933 rather than in England? Let us end by considering the evidence.

ANGLOPHILE, OR NOT?

There is a clue in Einstein's conversation about England with C. P. Snow, a visitor in 1937 to Einstein's summer house on Long Island invited by their mutual friend, Infeld, while he and Einstein were working closely together on *The Evolution of Physics*. Einstein talked to Snow of the countries he had lived in. He said he preferred them in inverse proportion to their size. How did he like England? asked Snow. 'Yes, he liked England. It had some of the qualities of his beloved Holland. After all, by world standards, England was becoming a small country.' They talked of the people Einstein had met in England, not only of the scientists, such as Eddington, but also the politicians, such as Churchill. 'Einstein admired him. I said that progressives of my kind wanted him in the government as a token of resistance: this was being opposed, not so much by the Labour Party, but by Churchill's own Tories. Einstein was brooding. To defeat Nazism, he said, we should need every kind of force, including nationalism, that we could bring together.'

Then Snow asked Einstein why, after he abandoned Nazi Germany in 1933, he had not come to live in England. 'No, no!' said Einstein. But why not? 'It is your style of life,' replied Einstein. Suddenly he began to laugh. 'It is a splendid style of life. But it is not for me.' Einstein struck Snow as enjoying some gigantic joke, but what was so funny? Snow was puzzled. What was this mysterious 'style of life'?

When Snow pressed Einstein a little, it appeared that he was thinking of the formality of English life which he had experienced, willy-nilly, during his visits to England. Lord Haldane's private reception at his London house in 1921 with the Archbishop of Canterbury, for example; and of course college dinners with Lindemann and the dons in Christ Church's hall in 1931–33: 'the holy brotherhood in tails'. In other words, butlers and the dreaded dinner-jacket. 'Einstein chortled. He seemed to have a fixed idea that the English, or certainly the English professional classes, spent much of their time getting into and out of formal clothes. Any protests I made were swept aside,' wrote Snow. 'It was then that he introduced me to the word *Zwang*. No *Zwang* for him. No butlers. No evening dress.' And of course no Nazis.

In Princeton, Einstein became well known for walking through the streets in summer dressed in a sweater without a coat and sandals without stockings, eating an ice-cream cone, to the amazement of the other professors, the delight of students, and the disapproval of the more conservative among them. 'If Einstein dislikes his fame and would like to increase his privacy, why does he not do what ordinary people do? Why does he wear long hair, a funny leather jacket, no socks, no suspenders, no collars, no ties?' a colleague of Infeld asked him. Because he wants to restrict his physical needs and thereby increase his freedom to live and to think, answered Infeld.

Privately, Einstein could be downright scathing about America, focusing on its shallowness, conformism and materialism. In 1932, on return to Europe from a stay at the California Institute of Technology, he advised Ehrenfest, who was thinking of leaving Holland to do physics in the United States: 'I must tell you quite frankly that in the long term I would prefer to be in Holland rather than in America, and that I am convinced you would come to regret the change. Apart from the handful of really fine scholars, it is a boring and barren society that would make you shiver.' And in 1950, he wrote from Princeton to

Suzanne Markwalder, a woman he had known as a student in Zurich half a century before, that he had now lived in America for seventeen years without having adopted anything of the country's mentality. 'One has to guard against becoming superficial in thought and feeling; it lies in the air here. You have never changed your human surroundings and can hardly realise what it is to be an old gypsy: it is not so bad.'

Ironically, Princeton happened to be probably the most Anglicised town in the entire United States. 'We might almost believe that we are in Oxford and when the bells ring – and they ring so often here – it makes us think of Westminster, of the heart of England,' Elsa Einstein wrote to Vallentin. 'I have never seen a place in America which looks so un-American.' One of the university's gates was an imitation of the Trinity College gate in Cambridge, but built in stone rather than brick. 'The copy was supposed to be exact, but it looked grotesque whereas the original was beautiful and impressive,' noted Infeld on first arrival in Princeton. Even the physics building, for which modern straight lines and large windows might have been expected, was mock-Gothic.

'The atmosphere of Princeton is exemplary and decorous: Einstein's laughter blew all that away,' remarked an English visitor to his house, the writer and literary critic Sir V. S. Pritchett, who was teaching at the Princeton Graduate School in 1954. 'No small, correct Princeton smile, but a laugh that had two thousand years of Europe in it.' 'What Englishman was it who said that sentence – you know?' Einstein questioned Pritchett. 'You remember? It goes, "When in doubt, act." Now who was that? I like that. It is very good – and very brief. I like it because it is brief, to the point.' He laughed 'with naïve and total delight of mind and body at that, waving his hand, in which he held an empty pipe'. Then he added, speaking in 'excellent English', as Pritchett significantly noted:

> It is nice to talk to Europeans. In Europe, the French, the Germans, and the English think they are so different, but when they meet here, in America, they see they are the same. They do not take themselves so seriously as the Americans. They are humble and modest about themselves. They laugh at themselves, but the Americans don't. They take themselves *au grand sérieux*, like adolescents. They do not say they are unhappy; they say they have problems: that sounds more serious and important. In their scholarship there is a great deal of pedantry. In Europe one can talk. A European like Planck, who was a great friend of mine and a nationalist, the opposite of everything I believe in, could be convinced by argument. He was open to reason.

Clearly, Einstein's Anglophilia, whatever it consisted of, was not the love of England that had inspired the quadrangles and high-table rituals of Christ Church or its colonial equivalent that had motivated the buildings and ceremonies of Princeton University. One would search in vain in Einstein's life and writings for any reverence towards English royalty, aristocrats and clergymen; for any pleasure in English high society, formal social gatherings and grand country estates; for any taste for team sports such as cricket and football; or, for that matter, any passion to read and quote from English literature, such as the works of William Shakespeare, Charles Dickens or Rudyard Kipling (though Einstein certainly enjoyed reading George Bernard Shaw and also H. G. Wells), or any strong desire to play English music, whether it be Henry Purcell, George Frederick Handel (despite his German roots) or Sir Edward Elgar. On the whole, Einstein preferred a simple cup of coffee to the English ritual of taking tea.

A portrait of Einstein in a stained-glass window of Christ Church Hall, Oxford, where he dined in 1931, 1932 and 1933 and was constantly amused by the college's formal ceremonies.

DEPARTURE FROM ENGLAND

At the same time, however, it is intriguing that Einstein's main contacts with politics in England, beyond the politics of science, tended to be among Conservatives more than among Liberals. Lord Haldane, it is true, was a Liberal, but Einstein's relationship with Haldane in 1921 had more to do with Haldane's character and his interest in relativity than with his politics. Lindemann and Locker-Lampson – Einstein's two other hosts in England – were paid-up Conservatives, as were Chamberlain and of course Churchill, who Einstein described as 'eminently wise' after meeting him in the company of Lindemann and Locker-Lampson. By contrast, his brief contacts with Labour progressives such as Lloyd George and Beveridge in England in 1933, and also with Prime Minister Ramsay MacDonald in Berlin in 1931, led no further; moreover Einstein strongly objected to the Palestinian policy of the Labour government post-1945 (as is clear from his exchange with Born about Bevin in 1948).

Fluency in German may have been a facilitating factor in the case of Lindemann and Locker-Lampson, given Einstein's discomfort with speaking English in 1933, before he moved to America. He could talk to and write to both the Oxford professor and the London politician in German, without effort or confusion of meaning. But surely more important was Einstein's agreement with Lindemann and Locker-Lampson on certain values beyond their obvious shared detestation of the Nazi regime – however much the three of them may have differed as personalities.

The most important of these shared values for Einstein and Lindemann was their belief in academic elitism, nurtured by their joint background at the university in Berlin, dating back to their first meeting in 1911. 'As a theoretical physicist Einstein stands alone in this century and perhaps in any century,' Lindemann wrote in his obituary of Einstein in 1955. That was why Lindemann – 'a thorough-going Englishman despite his German name' (as Born noted) – was determined to 'get' Einstein for the physics department at Oxford. He took the same elitist view of the other German-Jewish refugee physicists in 1933: all were plainly at risk from the Nazis, but only the best of them should be found jobs in Oxford (provided that they had an experimental orientation). His campaign for the physicist refugees was an admirable opportunity to save livelihoods and even lives, certainly, but it was also an opportunity to boost Oxford's – and Lindemann's – international reputation.

Einstein, in advising Lindemann whom among his German-Jewish colleagues to invite to Oxford, essentially concurred with Lindemann's elitism. Intellectual excellence always mattered more to him than a scientist's other qualities, however valuable. Hence, at root, Einstein's astonishing rejection of the Hebrew University in Jerusalem in the 1930s. From its beginning, in the early 1920s, he saw the fledgling university as a research institution, which must aim to rival the world's best research universities such as those in Berlin and Cambridge – not as a collegiate educational institution dedicated to building up the skills of poor

Jewish settlers. Mainly because this elitist view failed to prevail in Jerusalem, Einstein resigned from the university's governing body and severely criticised its leadership, including Weizmann. In 1933, while staying at Christ Church with Lindemann, he wrote to a newly jobless Born that he had heard of plans being under consideration to establish a good Institute of Physics in Jerusalem. 'There has been a nasty mess there up to now, complete charlatanism.' But, he added, if in the future he received definite indications that Jerusalem was likely to become serious about research, he would immediately advise Born of the details. 'For it would be splendid if something good were to be created there; it could develop into an institute of international renown.'

However, nothing came of this plan and so Einstein repeatedly refused to accept a professorship from the Hebrew University, or even to revisit Palestine from Princeton. Although, when he turned down the presidency of Israel in 1952, he remarked that his relationship with the Jewish people had become his 'strongest human bond', he clearly valued the pleasures of solitary thinking more highly than human bonds, whether in Jerusalem, Oxford, Berlin or anywhere else in the world. 'Remoteness, a relative absence of intimate personal relationships, is . . . a genuine ingredient of certain types of genius,' noted Isaiah Berlin long after Einstein's death. 'It is certainly true of Einstein, who was himself aware of his absence of contact with human beings; although in his case this certainly did not take the form of a desire for power or glory.'

With Locker-Lampson, by contrast, Einstein's shared understanding was clearly not fundamentally intellectual, but rather emotional. It goes without saying that Einstein appreciated Locker-Lampson's sincere desire for England to show 'fair play' to Jews, especially because Locker-Lampson (unlike Lindemann) had nothing directly to gain from such support. But strange as it may seem, the commander's can-do, gung-ho personality, too, plainly appealed to Einstein. 'When in doubt, act' appeared to be Locker-Lampson's personal motto. (It was officially 'Fear God! Fear Nought!' in the days of the Blue Shirts.) How else can one explain Einstein's willingness to be photographed peacefully disporting himself beside the athletic Locker-Lampson wielding a gun outside his hut in Norfolk – and then to be prominently displayed in British national newspapers? No doubt Einstein was genuinely grateful for the refuge, but surely he was also enjoying Locker-Lampson's melodrama, which one of the newly arrived German-Jewish refugee physicists in Oxford, Kurt Mendelssohn, criticised as a case of 'slight overacting'. (Lindemann must privately have agreed.)

Locker-Lampson's extremism and impulsiveness, as expressed in his urge to cock a snook at Hitler, appealed to Einstein. They chimed with his childhood and adult aversion for authority, for Prussianism, for *Zwang*. And also, it would appear, with his own extreme swing from being an absolute pacifist in 1932 to being a proponent of European rearmament and military conscription in 1933. Einstein must have had some notion of Locker-Lampson's recent affiliation with Fascism (though not, one assumes, his open admiration of Hitler in 1930) – whether from reading British and German newspapers in 1933 or from his friend Yahuda, who distrusted the commander. Even so, he was touched by Locker-Lampson's powerful, and even courageous, declaration of support for the Jews in his House of Commons speech. Furthermore, he sensed that Locker-Lampson's contacts with Churchill and other British politicians offered the best chance of rousing the British government against the Nazi menace. Finally, the success of the Albert Hall event in 1933 (whatever the absentee Lindemann's reservations) – which owed a large debt to Locker-Lampson's drive and organisational skills – was still more a cause for Einstein's appreciation, not criticism, of this eccentric and swashbuckling

Englishman. When the event was over, as we know, Einstein told a waiting journalist: 'I shall leave England for America at the end of the week, but no matter how long I live I shall never forget the kindness which I have received from the people of England.'

So why did Einstein leave Europe, including England, forever in October 1933? His reservations about English formality, expressed in his Oxford diary, to Snow and to others, played some part. So did his insoluble family entanglements with his ex-wife and incurably ill younger son in Zurich. So, too, did his fear of

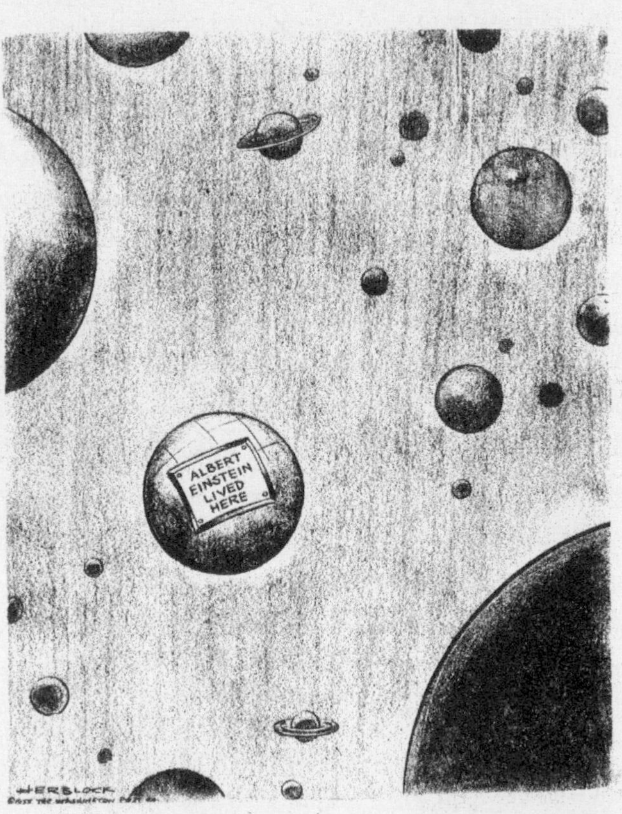

'Albert Einstein lived here'. This famous cartoon by Herbert Lawrence Block (Herblock) appeared in the *Washington Post* just after Einstein's death in Princeton in April 1955.

further entrapment by the anti-Nazi cause, and his expectation of a brutal war with Germany. Most of all, though, he wanted to be in a place where he was absolutely free to think about theoretical physics, either on his own or in conjunction with other leading experts from all over the world, exactly as he chose. The new Institute for Advanced Study in Princeton offered this prospect, without any lecturing, committee or social obligations and with a sufficient salary – unlike established universities such as Oxford and Cambridge. Thus Einstein was 'on the run' not just from the Nazis but ultimately from unwanted human contact: the *Zwang* imposed on him, as he felt, by political meetings, by mass media demands, by conventional academic expectations and by painful family commitments – none of which helped his science. For Einstein, science always took precedence over nation – unlike for his almost equally distinguished physicist friends Planck and Bohr. 'To Bohr one and only one place was home: Denmark. Einstein never fully identified himself with one country or nation; he would call himself a gypsy, or a bird of passage,' wrote Einstein's (and Bohr's) biographer, Pais, who knew both physicists well. 'If I had to characterise Einstein by one single word I would choose *apartness*.'

In *De Profundis*, a gaoled Oscar Wilde remarked: 'Nothing really at any period of my life was ever of the smallest importance to me compared with Art.' From all the available evidence, Einstein felt the same way about Physics.

Notes and References

PREFACE

xi **in England . . . my work** Letter to Frederick Lindemann, 28 Aug. 1927, in Cherwell Papers, file D54, Nuffield College, Oxford.
xi **I love this country** *Daily Telegraph*, 28 July 1933.
xi **the most civilised country** Letter to Max Born, in Born and Einstein: 125.
xii **It just won't stick** Eisinger: 136.
xii **Einstein's English** Infeld: 260.

xii **I cannot write in English** Born and Einstein: 145.
xii **Einstein was an Anglophile** Calaprice, Kennefick and Schulmann: 119.
xiii **I rejoice at the new universe** Holroyd: 611.

PROLOGUE | A WANDERER ON THE FACE OF THE EARTH

2 **See him as he squats** *New Statesman and Nation*, 21 Oct. 1933, in Keynes, *Collected Writings*, vol. 28: 22. See also an earlier article on Einstein by Keynes, controversial for its anti-Semitism, in Keynes, *Collected Writings*, vol. 10: 382–4.
3 **atrocity propaganda** World Committee for the Victims of German Fascism, *The Brown Book of the Hitler Terror*: 236–7.
5 **I really had no idea my head** *Manchester Guardian*, 8 Sept. 1933.
5 **When a bandit** *New York Times*, 9 Sept. 1933.
6 **I shall become a naturalised Englishman** *Daily Express*, 11 Sept. 1933.
6 **there would have been no Shakespeare** 'Professor Einstein' in [Albert Hall]: 5. This souvenir booklet, *Royal Albert Hall: Tuesday October 3rd 1933*, reproduces all of the speeches at the meeting. No publisher is given; the booklet was presumably produced by Oliver Locker-Lampson.
6 **I could not believe that it was possible** *Eastern Daily Press*, 4 Oct. 1933. Einstein's comment appears to have been made to the reporter, who is unnamed.

ONE | THE HAPPIEST THOUGHT OF MY LIFE

10 **Before Maxwell, people conceived** Einstein, *Ideas and Opinions*: 269.
11 **England has always produced** Salaman, 'Memories of Einstein': 23.
11 **It is a pleasure and an honour** Film of Einstein talking at the University of Nottingham, 6 June 1930, at: https://www.youtube.com/watch?v=161UNSza_qk (accessed 6 June 2020).

12 **entirely irreligious** Schilpp, ed.: 3.
12 **speculative brooding** Fölsing: 8.
13 **sergeants** Moszkowski: 223.
13 **Constraint has always been** Vallentin: 20.
13 **Let us return to Nature** Moszkowski: 66.
14 **To punish me** Hoffmann with Dukas: 24.
14 **withdraw to the sofa** Einstein, *CPAE*, vol. 1: xxii.
14 **Einstein was more of an artist** Whitrow: 52.
15 **I can still remember** Schilpp, ed.: 9.
15 **a second wonder** Ibid.
15 **earth-measuring** Einstein, *Ideas and Opinions*: 234.
15 **suspicion against every kind of authority** Schilpp, ed.: 5.
15 **he would never get anywhere** Fölsing: 27.
16 **Hypersensitivity** Einstein, *The Travel Diaries*: 89. He refers to Ernest Kretschmer.
17 **my individual inclination for the abstract** Einstein, *CPAE*, vol. 1, doc. 22: 16.
17 **So far as he was ever at home** Snow: 74.
18 **creating a new theory** Einstein and Infeld: 159.
18 **I'm convinced more and more** ?10 Aug. 1899, in Einstein and Marić: 10.
19 **lazy dog** Seelig: 28.
19 **impudence** 12 Dec. 1901, in Einstein and Marić: 67.
20 **He a model student** Hoffmann with Dukas: 36.
21 **It gave me the opportunity** Clark: 75.
21 **was intrigued rather than dismayed** Rigden: 8.
21 **[Einstein] would carefully study** Jürgen Renn and Robert Schulmann, in introduction to Einstein and Marić: xxii.
22 **three intellectual musketeers** Highfield and Carter: 96.
22 **laughed so much** Ibid.: 102.
22 **far less childish** Ibid.: 97.
23 **Thank you. I've completely solved** Fölsing: 155.
23 **steadfastness** Ibid.: 195.
23 **started from the postulate** 'A Brief History of Relativity', in Robinson, *Einstein*: 42.
24 **misdeed** Einstein, *Relativity*: 10.
24 **The stone traverses** Ibid.: 11.
26 **If I pursue a beam of light** Schilpp, ed.: 53.
26 **We should catch them in a reverse order** Einstein and Infeld: 177.
27 **unjustifiable hypotheses** Einstein, *Relativity*: 32.
27 **required abandoning the idea** 'A Brief History of Relativity', in Robinson, *Einstein*: 44.
28 **Not only do we have no direct experience** Fölsing: 175.
28 **We are accustomed** Einstein, *Ideas and Opinions*: 299.
29 **revolutionary** Robinson, *Einstein*: 52.
29 **Is the world to be described** Rigden: 21.
30 **According to the assumption** Ibid.: 19.
31 **I just read a wonderful paper** ?28 May 1901, in Einstein and Marić: 54.
33 **The views of space and time** Bernstein: 95.
33 **Since the mathematicians pounced** Fölsing: 245.
33 **mysterious shuddering** Einstein, *Relativity*: 56.
33 **'Analytic' or 'algebraically expressed' geometry** Arianrhod: 172.
34 **singularly simple** *Daily Telegraph*, 22 Apr. 1955.
36 **The two sentences** Einstein and Infeld: 224.
36 **I was sitting on a chair** Fölsing: 301.
37 **the happiest thought** Miller: 217.

38 **the idea that the physics in an accelerated laboratory** Hey and Walters, *Einstein's Mirror*: 270.

38 **You understand, what I need to know** Fölsing: 325.

39 **A beam of light carries energy** Einstein and Infeld: 234.

40 **When a blind beetle** Michael Grüning, *Ein Haus für Albert Einstein*, Berlin: Verlag der Nation, 1990: 498.

40 **space was deprived of its rigidity** Einstein, *Ideas and Opinions*: 281.

40 **His idea was that mass and energy** 'A Brief History of Relativity', in Robinson, *Einstein*: 46.

40 **Matter tells space-time** Isaacson: 220.

41 **The examination of the correctness or otherwise** Einstein, *Relativity*: 76–7.

TWO | HATS OFF TO THE FELLOWS! FROM A SWISS JEW

44 **the English have behaved** 9 Mar. 1921, in Einstein, *CPAE*, vol. 12, doc. 88: 71.

45 **The theory of relativity by Einstein** Eve: 353. Rutherford made the comment at the Royal Society of Arts in 1932.

45 **The foundation of general relativity** Eisenstadt: 250.

45 **Einstein had really offended** Clark: 125.

46 **he should not worry** Morrell: 401.

46 **How came it** Harrod: 21.

46 **he did not show the slightest sign** Ibid.: 15.

47 **It was a hot-house Oxford product . . . perfectly futile.** Ibid.: 25–6.

47 **No Anglo-Saxon can understand relativity!** Eve: 193.

47 **In Cambridge during the period 1905 to 1920** Warwick: 358.

48 **I have not been able so far** 20 May 1909, in Einstein, *CPAE*, vol. 5, doc. 162: 121.

48 **The principle of relativity then does not deny** Warwick: 424.

49 **Take electricity out of the world** Fölsing: 159.

49 **the whole electrodynamic properties** Ibid.: 388.

49 **Quietly obeying the law** Cunningham, 'Einstein's Relativity Theory of Gravitation': 355.

50 **The long train of events** Clark: 261.

52 **Unlike the case of British electromagnetic theory** Warwick: 454.

53 **Far from regarding the theory as a threat** Ibid.: 464.

53 **the lies and defamations** Fölsing: 345.

54 **create an organic unity** Stern: 115.

55 **Why are we hated** Fölsing: 366. Einstein's Swiss colleague was Romain Rolland.

55 **dead, except for a few Indians** Stanley, *Practical Mystic*: 136.

56 **To assert that it is our religious duty** Douglas, *The Life of Arthur Stanley Eddington*: 93.

56 **I should like to bring to the notice of the tribunal** Ibid.: 149.

58 **What will it mean if we get** Ibid.: 40.

58 **had he been left to himself** Chandrasekhar: 112.

59 **About 1:30 . . . a second plate.** Stanley, *Practical Mystic*: 106–7.

59 **was a moment which Eddington never forgot** Douglas, *The Life of Arthur Stanley Eddington*: 40.

60 **Through cloud. Hopeful.** Stanley, *Practical Mystic*: 107.

60 **Oh leave the Wise** Douglas, *The Life of Arthur Stanley Eddington*: 43.

60 **They gave a final verdict** Clark: 286–7.

61 **I knew all the time that the theory** Fölsing: 439.

61 **but, you know, he didn't really understand physics** French: 31.

62 **The result is now definite** Fölsing: 440.

62 **The whole atmosphere of tense interest** Bernstein: 119.

62 **A very definite result** Fölsing: 443.

63 **this result is not an isolated one** Chandrasekhar: 116.

64 **Einstein's theories would dominate all physics** Clark: 299.

64 **I was myself a sceptic** Ibid.

64 **Professor Eddington, you must be** Chandrasekhar: 117. The physicist who approached Eddington was Ludwik Silberstein, author of *The Theory of Relativity*, London: Macmillan, 1914.

65 **The description of me and my circumstances** *The Times*, 28 Nov. 1919.

66 **He is famous just now** Ibid.

66 **and during the lecture the hall** *Nature*, 11 Dec. 1919: 385.

68 **Einstein and Epstein** Clark: 301–2.

68 **Its formation was due** Ibid.: 307.

69 **All England has been talking about your theory** 1 Dec. 1919, in Einstein, *CPAE*, vol. 9, doc. 186: 263.

69 **[He] gave a moan** Warwick: 485.

70 **The time has come, said Eddington** Clark: 401–3. The parody was written in 1924. Sadly, there is no record of Einstein's reaction to it.

71 **People here have been talking of nothing else** 26 Nov. 1919, in Einstein, *CPAE*, vol. 9, doc. 177: 151–2.

72 **thank God, the solar eclipse** 12 Dec. 1919, in Lawson: 927. Einstein's original German letter is lost, but was partially published by Lawson in his obituary of Einstein.

72 **Einstein believes his books** Fölsing: 379.

73 **When you send in the matter** 22 Feb. 1920, in Einstein, *CPAE*, vol. 9, doc. 326: 273.

73 **Einstein taught everything is relative** Friedman and Donley: 9.

74 **An hour sitting with a pretty girl** Sayen: 130.

74 **though that would, no doubt** *Manchester Guardian*, 10 June 1921.

74 **Einstein himself has become** *Manchester Guardian*, 10 June 1921, https://www.theguardian.com/science/the-northerner/2016/jun/10/albert-einstein-manchester-university-doctor-of-science (accessed 6 June 2020).

76 **Lord Haldane tells us** Clark: 339–40.

76 **will be found to date back** Haldane: 33.

77 **In a post-war Britain** Ibid.: 336–7.

77 **the less they know about physics** Salaman, 'A talk with Einstein': 370.

77 **Lord Haldane was a man** Sommer: 382.

78 **I was almost terrified by the commotion** Ibid.: 381.

78 **You are in the presence of the Newton** *Nation & Athenaeum*, 18 June 1921: 431. Reports in the *Manchester Guardian* (14 June 1921) and *The Times* (14 June 1921) mention applause for Einstein at the beginning of his lecture, but appear to be less reliable. See also the report in *Nature*, 16 June 1921: 504, and a letter by A. S. Yahuda in *The Times*, 30 Mar. 1933, which mentions only silence from the audience until the end of the lecture.

80 **It is a special joy for me** 'King's College Lecture', in Einstein, *CPAE*, vol. 7, doc. 58: 238.

81 **My lecture is already a little long** *Nation & Athenaeum*, 18 June 1921: 431.

81 **and surely not least for his courage** Letter from A. S. Yahuda in *The Times*, 30 Mar. 1933.

81 **We welcome you twice** *Jewish Chronicle*, 17 June 1921: 26.

82 **I enclose a note** 14 June 1921, in Cherwell Papers, file D53, Nuffield College, Oxford.

82 **They both enjoyed greatly their visit** 15 June 1921, in Cherwell Papers, file D53, Nuffield College, Oxford.
83 **The wonderful experiences in England** 21 June 1921, in Einstein, *CPAE*, vol. 12, doc. 155: 113.
83 **There is no doubt that your visit** 26 June 1921, in Einstein, *CPAE*, vol. 12, doc. 159: 115.

THREE | A STINKING FLOWER IN A GERMAN BUTTONHOLE

86 **A funny lot, these Germans** 17 Apr. 1925, in Fölsing: 549.
87 **For the first time, a world-famous German scholar** Eisinger: 83.
88 **expressing his hope** Ball: 85.
88 **He invented the difference** Born and Einstein: 35.
88 **In contrast to the intractable** Calaprice: 14.
88 **This, however, was no more than one could expect** Ball: 84.
89 **As the speakers went on** Clark: 318.
89 **That was most amusing** Ibid.
89 **I feel like a man lying in a good bed** Fölsing: 463.
90 **Herr Weyland and Herr Gehrcke** 'My Response. On the Anti-Relativity Company', in Einstein, *CPAE*, vol. 7, doc. 45: 197–9.
91 **The attacks on Prof. Einstein** Fölsing: 464.
91 **goaded** Born and Einstein: 33.
91 **Don't be too hard on me** Ibid.: 34.
93 **impudence** Einstein and Marić: 67.
93 **The state, to which I belong as a citizen** Fölsing: 368.
93 **you know that my darling** Letter to Helen Savić, ? Dec. 1901, in Marić: 79.
93 **the virulent anti-Semitism** Rosenkranz, *Einstein before Israel*: 26.
94 **Herr Dr Einstein is an Israelite** Fölsing: 250.
94 **Why are these fellows** Ibid.: 489–90.
94 **was Jewish, but wished he weren't** Isidor Rabi quoted in Cassidy: 32.
94 **unjustified humiliations** Born and Einstein: 17.
95 **not to be got rid of by well-meaning propaganda** Einstein, *Ideas and Opinions*: 182.
95 **History has shown that Einstein** Born and Einstein: 17.
95 **I am neither a German citizen** Clark: 379.
95 **It goes against the grain** Fölsing: 489.
95 **Naturally, I am needed not for my abilities** Ibid.: 495.
96 **lone traveller** Einstein, *Ideas and Opinions*: 9.
96 **they did not make the all-important transition** Rosenkranz, *Einstein before Israel*: 260.
96 **I was fully convinced** Seelig, *Albert Einstein*: 81.
97 **Weizmann's relationship with Einstein** Weisgal and Carmichael, eds: 42.
98 **Einstein and the Zionist movement** Rosenkranz, *Einstein before Israel*: 65.
98 **I was to stir up Einstein . . . Telegram Weizmann that I agree** Clark: 465–6.
99 **To the whole world you are today** 9 Mar. 1921, in Fölsing: 497.
100 **Despite my internationalist beliefs** Ibid.
101 **Recall Einstein's visit** *Jewish Chronicle*, 24 June 1921.
101 **For, I am supposedly among** 6 July 1922, in Einstein, *CPAE*, vol. 13, doc. 266: 212.
102 **The great scholar Albert Einstein** Note 170 in Einstein, *Travel Diaries*: 305.
102 **Harden's statement is certainly awkward** 20 Dec. 1922, in Einstein, *Travel Diaries*: 253.
103 **enlightened colonialism** 'Historical introduction' to Einstein, *Travel Diaries*: 42.
103 **very Wilhelminian** 1 Feb. 1923, in ibid.: 211.
103 **English formality** Ibid.: 213.
103 **a man of kindly disposition** Samuel: 253.

104 **Continue on into the city with Ginsberg** 3 Feb. 1923, in Einstein, *Travel Diaries*: 213–15

105 **The great event has been Einstein** Bentwich: 95–6.

107 **Mount the platform** Clark: 479.

107 **evidently unfamiliar** Samuel: 253.

107 **That evening, well and truly satisfied** 7 Feb. 1923, in Einstein, *Travel Diaries*: 221.

107 **Drive from terraced, very scenic Nazareth** 13 Feb. 1923, in ibid.: 229–31.

108 **Political passions** Nathan and Norden, eds: 640.

109 **You can do nothing, gentlemen** 'The International Character of Science', in Einstein, *CPAE*, vol. 13, doc. 3: 24–5.

110 **I was naturally eager** Nathan and Norden, eds: 58–9.

110 **Although I am not clear at all** Clark: 430.

111 **the situation here is such that a Jew** Nathan and Norden, eds: 59.

111 **I have received your letter** Clark: 431–2.

112 **I have become convinced that the League** Nathan and Norden, eds: 61.

112 **I fully understand your action** Ibid.

113 **the League functions as a tool** Ibid.: 62.

113 **I do not hesitate to tell you** Ibid.: 66.

113 **an exchange of letters** Clark: 441.

113 **Is there any way** Nathan and Norden, eds: 188–90.

114 **It seems to me an utterly futile task** Ibid.: 90.

115 **I am convinced that the international movement** Ibid.: 91.

115 **I feel only contempt** Ibid.: 111–12.

116 **Even if only two per cent** Ibid.: 117.

117 **The next war will, I think** Letter to Herbert Runham Brown, 21 Mar. 1931, in Russell, *Autobiography*, 2: 202

FOUR | GOD DOES NOT PLAY DICE WITH THE UNIVERSE

120 **Quantum mechanics is certainly imposing** Born and Einstein: 88.

121 **I no longer ask whether** 13 May 1911, in Einstein, *CPAE*, vol. 5, doc. 267: 187.

121 **I suppose it's a good thing** 15 Mar. 1922, in Fölsing: 512.

121 **I have thought a hundred times** Pais, *Einstein Lived Here*: 57.

121 **I think I can safely say** Hey and Walters, *The New Quantum Universe*: 1.

121 **The strange landscape** Rovelli: 72.

122 **it was the *law* that was accepted** Whitaker: 100.

123 **the tremendous practical success** 'On the Method of Theoretical Physics', in Einstein, *Ideas and Opinions*: 273.

123 **probably the strangest thing** Fölsing: 154.

124 **That sometimes, as for instance in his hypothesis** Ibid.: 147.

124 **wholly untenable** Pais, *'Subtle is the Lord'*: 357.

126 **If Planck's theory of radiation** Ibid.: 395.

126 **It cannot be denied** Fölsing: 256.

126 **It is my opinion that the next phase** Rigden: 37–8.

126 **one of the landmarks** Schilpp, ed.: 154.

128 **revelation** Fölsing: 390.

129 **Einstein was the first to recognise** Townes: 13.

129 **With this, the light quanta** Fölsing: 392.

129 **leaves the time and direction of the elementary process** Ibid.

130 **Were it not for Einstein's challenge** Jammer: 220.

130 **I find the idea quite intolerable** Born and Einstein: 80.

131 **If one abandons the assumption** Ibid.: 162.
131 **Einstein's moon really exists** Peat: 166.
132 **It was quite a shock for Bohr** Whitaker: 217–18.
134 **wave, or quantum, mechanics** Pais, *'Subtle is the Lord'*: 515.
134 **The conviction prevails** Einstein, *Relativity*: 158.
135 **Ten more papers appeared** Tilman Sauer, 'Einstein's Unified Field Theory Program', in Janssen and Lehner, eds: 281.
135 **like the hermits of old** 5 Jan. 1929, in Fölsing: 604.
136 **Large crowds gather** Pais, *Einstein Lived Here*: 179.
136 **to obtain a formula** Jammer: 57.
137 **Could we not reject** Einstein and Infeld: 257–8.
138 **no trace remains** Steven Weinberg, 'Einstein's Search for Unification', in Robinson, *Einstein*: 108.
139 **He himself had established his name** Abraham Taub, quoted by Christopher Sykes in foreword to Whitrow: xii.
139 **There are two different conceptions** Tagore: 531–2.
140 **we ought to be concerned solely** Heisenberg: 68.
140 **wrong to think that the task** Pais, *Niels Bohr's Times*: 427.
140 **Man defends himself** Tagore: 532.
141 **I have never been able to understand Einstein** Born and Einstein: 151.
141 **Theory fed on observation** Powell: 97.
142 **a spacious castle in the air** 'Einstein's Role in the Creation of Relativistic Cosmology', in Janssen and Lehner, eds: 241.

142 **not justified by our actual knowledge** Clark: 269.
143 **totally abominable** Christopher Smeenk, 'Einstein's Role in the Creation of Relativistic Cosmology', in Janssen and Lehner, eds: 255.
143 **Many theorists saw the phenomenon** O'Raifeartaigh: 31.
143 **biggest blunder** Gamow: 44.
144 **did not go away so easily** Weinberg: 178–9.
144 **Every man has his own cosmology** Douglas, 'Forty minutes with Einstein': 100.

FIVE | A BARBARIAN AMONG THE HOLY BROTHERHOOD IN TAILS

146 **Doctoral ceremony in large hall** 23 May 1931, in Einstein, 'Diary Notes, April–June 1931, Berlin and Oxford', Einstein Archives, Jerusalem: 29–142.
147 **You are the only sort of man** 2 Dec. 1924, in Einstein, *CPAE*, vol. 14, doc. 387: 595.
147 **Everybody knows that Einstein** Russell, *The ABC of Relativity*: 9.
147 **Nature and Nature's laws** John Collings Squire, *Poems in One Volume*, London: Heinemann, 1926: 218.
147 **I think you are the youngest** 5 Nov. 1925, in Einstein, *CPAE*, vol. 15, doc. 102: 183.
147 **makers of universes** *Jewish Chronicle*, 31 Oct. 1930. The speeches by Shaw and Einstein at the dinner can be heard on *Albert Einstein: Historic Recordings 1930–1947*, London: British Library, 2005.
150 **I looked out from the window** Griffiths: 5.
151 **More than any other people** *Nature*, 26 Mar. 1927: 467.
152 **If your father were not** Mendelssohn: 168.
152 **was a man of intuition** Entry on Lindemann, *ODNB*, 3 Jan. 2008.
153 **The Prof., so it went** Harrod: 48.
153 **He was an out-and-out inequalitarian** Entry on Lindemann, *ODNB*, 3 Jan. 2008.
153 **Like many scientists Einstein** *Daily Telegraph*, 22 Apr. 1955.

154 **It has often been asked how** Fort: 200.

155 **It is a disaster** Fox: 2.

155 **The university and the trustees desire** 29 June 1927, in Einstein Archives, Jerusalem: 32–654.

155 **How gladly would I accept** Undated but probably July 1927, in Cherwell Papers, file D54, Nuffield College, Oxford.

156 **During the holidays** 28 Aug. 1927, in Cherwell Papers, file D54, Nuffield College, Oxford.

157 **The movement to induce Prof. Einstein** *Jewish Telegraphic Agency*, 26 Dec. 1930.

157 **two blackboards, plentifully sprinkled** *The Times*, 18 May 1931.

157 **an account of his attempt to derive** *Nature*, 16 May 1931: 765.

159 **the discourse should be in English** *Manchester Guardian*, 28 Apr. 1955. Einstein's remarks were recalled by Mrs K. Haldane.

159 **l'affaire Einstein** Chapman to Lord Lothian, 10 June 1931, in Rhodes Trust Archives, file 2694(2), Rhodes House, Oxford.

159 **he had since discovered** 9 June 1933, in Rhodes Trust Archives, file 2694A, Rhodes House, Oxford.

160 **The lecture was indeed well-attended** 16 May 1931, in Einstein, 'Diary Notes, April–June 1931, Berlin and Oxford', Einstein Archives, Jerusalem: 29–142.

161 **Some of the scientists seem** 13 May 1931, in Rhodes Trust Archives, file 2694A, Rhodes House, Oxford.

163 **your present of two blackboards** 19 May 1931, in Rhodes Trust Archives, file 2694A, Rhodes House, Oxford.

163 **I should be glad if you could come round** 25 May 1931, in Rhodes Trust Archives, file 2694A, Rhodes House, Oxford.

163 **It appears that Einstein stumbled** Cormac O'Raifeartaigh, 'Einstein's Blackboard and the Friedmann-Einstein Model of the Cosmos', https://coraifeartaigh.wordpress.com/2015/12/22/einsteins-blackboard/ (accessed 6 June 2020).

164 **In so far as he understood what Relativity was about** Griffiths: 5.

164 **Atque utinam Mercurius hodie adesset** *Oxford University Gazette*, 3 June 1931: 627.

164 **The doctrine which he interprets** *Oxford Times*, 29 May 1931.

165 **serious, but not wholly accurate** 23 May 1931, in Einstein, 'Diary Notes, April–June 1931, Berlin and Oxford', Einstein Archives, Jerusalem: 29–142.

165 **I had noticed his face lit up** Margaret Deneke, 'Professor Albert Einstein': 4, in Deneke Papers, Lady Margaret Hall, Oxford.

166 **Generations of Oxford undergraduates** Entry on Helena Deneke, *ODNB*, 23 Sept. 2004.

167 **In he came with short quick steps** Margaret Deneke, 'Professor Albert Einstein': 1–3, in Deneke Papers, Lady Margaret Hall, Oxford.

168 **Lady Wylie thought** Ibid.: 4–5.

169 **The guests hastily left the room** 15 May 1931 in Einstein, 'Diary Notes, April–June 1931, Berlin and Oxford', Einstein Archives, Jerusalem: 29–142.

169 **He scrutinised the violin** Margaret Deneke, 'Professor Albert Einstein': 13–14, in Deneke Papers, Lady Margaret Hall, Oxford.

169 **relatively good** White: 287.

169 **the denizen of dimly lit music rooms** Ibid.: 288.

170 **Professor Einstein was still at his breakfast table** Margaret Deneke, 'Professor Albert Einstein': 23–4, in Deneke Papers, Lady Margaret Hall, Oxford.

172 **the holy brotherhood in tails** 2/3 May 1931, in Einstein, 'Diary Notes, April–June 1931, Berlin and Oxford', Einstein Archives, Jerusalem: 29–142.

172 **He was by nature a rebel** Hoffmann and Dukas: 248.

173 **In our governing body** Harrod: 47.

173 **Dr. Einstein, do tell me** Toynbee: 268. According to Arnold Toynbee, Einstein answered Gilbert Murray in Tom Quad: 'I am thinking that, after all, this is a very small star.' However, in a remarkably similar anecdote referring to Murray's house recounted by Murray himself, Einstein answered as I have given: see Nathan and Norden, eds: 70.

174 **Dundas lets his rooms decay** *The Times*, 17 May 1955.

174 **Evening club meal in dinner-jacket** 1 May 1931, in Einstein, 'Diary Notes, April–June 1931, Berlin and Oxford', Einstein Archives, Jerusalem: 29–142.

175 **Silent existence in the hermitage** 2/3 May 1931, in Einstein, 'Diary Notes, April–June 1931, Berlin and Oxford', Einstein Archives, Jerusalem: 29–142.

175 **was a charming person** Harrod: 47.

177 **threw himself into all the activities** Lindemann to Lothian, 27 June 1931, in Cherwell Papers, file D56, Nuffield College, Oxford.

178 **very clever man** 5 May 1931, in Einstein, 'Diary Notes, April–June 1931, Berlin and Oxford', Einstein Archives, Jerusalem: 29–142.

178 **showed that Milne's distinctive approach** Christopher Smeenk, 'Einstein's Role in the Creation of Relativistic Cosmology', in Janssen and Lehner, eds: 253.

178 **excellent institution** 22 May 1931, in Einstein, 'Diary Notes, April–June 1931, Berlin and Oxford', Einstein Archives, Jerusalem: 29–142.

179 **pitiful** 23 May 1931, in Einstein, 'Diary Notes, April–June 1931, Berlin and Oxford', Einstein Archives, Jerusalem: 29–142.

179 **There are so many fictitious peace societies** A. Fenner Brockway, *New World*, July 1931, in Nathan and Norden, eds: 140.

179 **For example, he suggested that** *The Friend*, 12 June 1931: 567.

181 **a fat giant with a red face** 21 May 1931, in Einstein, 'Diary Notes, April–June 1931, Berlin and Oxford', Einstein Archives, Jerusalem: 29–142.

181 **more Egyptian than Greek in character** 26 May 1931, in Einstein, 'Diary Notes, April–June 1931, Berlin and Oxford', Einstein Archives, Jerusalem: 29–142.

181 **The types of humanity in the streets** Margaret Deneke, 'Professor Albert Einstein': 7, in Deneke Papers, Lady Margaret Hall, Oxford.

181 **Make sure you get home** 9 May 1931, in Einstein, 'Diary Notes, April–June 1931, Berlin and Oxford', Einstein Archives, Jerusalem: 29–142.

181 **Soon there will be water-closets** 25 May 1931, in Einstein, 'Diary Notes, April–June 1931, Berlin and Oxford', Einstein Archives, Jerusalem: 29–142.

182 **Long-branched and delicately strung** Isaacson: 361.

182 **tiny moustached and hatted figure** Golding: 182, and extended version in Golding, 'Thinking as a Hobby', http://www.brunswick.k12.me.us/hdwyer/thinking-as-a-hobby-by-william-golding/ (accessed 6 June 2020).

184 **Your kind letter has filled me** 6 July 1931, in Cherwell Papers, file D56, Nuffield College, Oxford.

184 **harmonious community life** 29 Oct. 1931, in Einstein Papers, Christ Church, Oxford.

185 **Dear Dean, I was amazed** 24 Oct. 1931, in Einstein Papers, Christ Church, Oxford.

186 **I think that in electing Einstein** 24 Oct. 1931, in Einstein Papers, Christ Church, Oxford.

186 **a German who has no connection** 2 Nov. 1931, in Einstein Papers, Christ Church, Oxford.

187 **The world at large** *Financial Times*, 2 Feb. 2008.

SIX | THE REALITY OF NATURE AND THE NATURE OF REALITY

190 **Experience can of course guide** 'On the Method of Theoretical Physics', in Kent: 17.
191 **Jews as a race** *Jewish Chronicle*, 20 May 1932.
191 **The gate at Christ Church is locked** Margaret Deneke, 'Professor Albert Einstein': 14, in Deneke Papers, Lady Margaret Hall, Oxford.
192 **when we clean house** Clark: 543.
192 **I am convinced that a military regime** Frank: 273.
193 **Before you leave our villa** Ibid.
193 **As long as I have any choice** *New York World-Telegram*, 10 Mar. 1933.
193 **The raid** Clark: 562.
194 **The concierge of the German embassy** Rowe: 236.
195 **atrocity propaganda** *Jewish Telegraphic Agency*, 14 Apr. 1933.
195 **Even though in political matters** Fölsing: 662.
195 **But now the war of extermination** Ibid.: 664.
195 **Two ideologies** Ibid.
195 **The hours which I was permitted to spend** Ibid.: 729.
195 **in order to maintain public security and order** Grundmann: 297.
197 **Highly Esteemed Professor** Einstein Archives, Jerusalem: 50–804.
198 **despatched their children to Nazi Germany** Boyd: 371.
199 **My first recollection of Herr Hitler** *Daily Mirror*, 30 Sept. 1930.
201 **true** 'Blue shirts and blitzkrieg? It's just not cricket', *The Times*, 18 Mar. 2010.
201 **token of his esteem** Winterbotham: 35.
202 **in more than nickname** *Time*, 6 July 1931.
202 **a Jew and a Communist** Obituary of Locker-Lampson in *New York Times*, 9 Oct. 1954.
204 **I am sitting here in my very pleasant exile** 1 May 1933, in Cherwell Papers, file D57, Nuffield College, Oxford.
204 **there was not much prospect** 4 May 1933, in Cherwell Papers, file D57, Nuffield College, Oxford.
206 **one room** 7 May 1933, in Cherwell Papers, file D57, Nuffield College, Oxford.
207 **You are not a father yourself** 9 May 1933, in Cherwell Papers, file D57, Nuffield College, Oxford.
207 **There is no written evidence** Fölsing: 673.
208 **You know, I think, that I have never had** Born and Einstein: 111–12.
209 **a poor forlorn little figure** Clark: 582.
210 **The sanctuary from personal turmoil** Introduction to Janssen and Lehner, eds: 20.
210 **a reckless overestimation** Fölsing: 561.
211 **perhaps the clearest and most revealing** Pais, *Einstein Lived Here*: 55.
211 **from the chains of the 'merely personal'** Schilpp, ed.: 5.
211 **Strenuous intellectual work** Letter to Pauline Winteler, ? May 1897, in Einstein, *CPAE*, vol. 1, doc. 34: 33.
211 **I believe with Schopenhauer** Einstein, *Ideas and Opinions*: 225.
212 **I wish to preface what I have to say** 'On the Method of Theoretical Physics', in Kent: 12.
213 **If you wish to learn** Ibid.
213 **But this is the common fate** Ibid.: 13.
214 **We honour ancient Greece** Ibid.
214 **Pure logical thinking** Ibid.: 13–14.

214 **the first creator . . . as the ancients dreamed** Ibid.: 15–17.
217 **I still believe in the possibility** Ibid.: 19.
218 **As far as the laws of mathematics refer** Einstein, *The Ultimate Quotable Einstein*: 371.
219 **It was not until several decades later . . . a unified theory of gravity and electromagnetism.** Farmelo: 77–8. The comment by Jeroen von Dongen was made in a personal communication to Farmelo in 2017.
219 **after having ruefully returned** Einstein, *Ideas and Opinions*: 289–90.
220 **Professor Einstein is of all living philosophers** *Manchester Guardian*, 21 June 1933.

SEVEN | ON THE RUN

224 **Through your well-organised work** Einstein, 'Science and Civilisation', in [Albert Hall]: 5. This souvenir booklet, *Royal Albert Hall: Tuesday October 3rd 1933*, reproduces all of the speeches at the meeting. No publisher is given; the booklet was presumably produced by Oliver Locker-Lampson.
225 **rebirth of Germany** Siemens: 124–5.
225 **Murder stalks through Germany** World Committee for the Victims of German Fascism, *The Brown Book of the Hitler Terror*: 312.
225 **a little sprawling Jew** Ibid.: 236–7.
226 **Discovered a much-contested theory** Clark: 572–3.
226 **a bird fascinated by a serpent** Vallentin: 161.
226 **We get as many angry letters** Ibid.: 162.
226 **My husband has not allowed himself** Ibid.: 160.
227 **I need hardly tell you** 31 Mar. 1933, in Einstein Archives, Jerusalem: 51–222.
227 **I now have more professorial chairs** Clark: 574.
228 **There is no need for us to provoke** *Daily Express*, 19 Apr. 1933.
228 **Spain's offer to Einstein** *Jewish Chronicle*, 21 Apr. 1933.
228 **on a fortunate symbiosis** Letter to the editor from Paul S. Riebenfeld, *New York Times*, 1 Nov. 1987.
229 **There is his place** *New York Times*, 30 June 1933.
229 **He answered emphatically** *Jewish Chronicle*, 28 Apr. 1933.
230 **It is completely clear to me** Rosenkranz, *Einstein before Israel*: 230.
230 **Someone has seen Einstein** Einstein Archives, Jerusalem: 123–402.
230 **a friend . . . [who] has seen Professor Einstein abroad** Einstein Archives, Jerusalem: 121–788.
231 **I am going to England tomorrow to speak** Einstein Archives, Jerusalem: 49–566.
233 **He is an eminently wise man** ?22 July 1933, in Einstein Archives, Jerusalem: 143–250.
233 **Person of the Century** See Larres, 'Churchill and Einstein: Overlapping Mindsets', https://winstonchurchill.hillsdale.edu/churchill-einstein-overlapping-mindsets/ (accessed 6 June 2020).
234 **As soon as Hitler took power** Snow: 81.
234 **L. G. was no scientist** Lloyd George: 227.
235 **That leave be given to bring in a bill** 'House of Commons Debates', 26 Jul. 1933, *Hansard*, 280: 2604–6.
237 **Commander Locker-Lampson showed himself** *The Sunday Times*, 30 July 1933.
238 **As a people we are not supposed** *Manchester Guardian*, 27 July 1933.
238 **Members eagerly came forward** *Jewish Chronicle*, 28 July 1933.
238 **Einsteinish Jewish Theatre** *Jewish Telegraphic Agency*, 31 July 1933.

238 **I cannot believe that such a thing** Einstein Archives, Jerusalem: 75–513.
240 **I love this country** *Daily Telegraph*, 28 July 1933.
240 **In the heart of Europe lies a power** Nathan and Norden, eds: 229.
241 **I am sure you will not take it amiss** Ibid.: 230–1.
242 **Under circumstances such as prevailed** Ibid.: 231.
243 **It is the National Socialist leaders** World Committee for the Victims of German Fascism, *The Brown Book of the Hitler Terror*: 195.
244 **is enough to make Hitler's Germany** Ibid.: 162.
244 **anxious that the book should be published** Miles: 96.
245 **They shall not force me to do that** *Daily Express*, 12 Sept. 1933.
245 **I was not responsible for the *Brown Book*** *The Times*, 11 Sept. 1933.
245 **proved to be the author of the book** *Jewish Chronicle*, 8 Dec. 1933.
245 **Belgium was dangerously near Germany** Vallentin: 167.
246 **Why do you assume** Frank: 292.
246 **All sorts of unpleasant surprises** Ibid.: 293.
246 **At the very moment of my arrival** Vallentin: 168.
248 **Professor Lazarus** Letter to the editor from Lessing, *Manchester Guardian*, 26 May 1933.
249 **Locker-Lampson liked to pretend** Personal communication to author from Stuart McLaren, 5 July 2017.
251 **near Cromer** *Daily Express*, 12 Sept. 1933.
251 **I am going to the countryside** 10 Sept. 1933, in Einstein Archives, Jerusalem: 143–260.

252 **Morning, Master Colman** Snelling: 6.
254 **He was a rich man's pig of a son** Ibid.: 7.
254 **L.L. is wonderful** ? Sept. 1933, in Einstein Archives, Jerusalem: 143–643.
254 **I live here like a hermit** ? Sept. 1933, in Einstein Archives, Jerusalem: 143–259.
254 **admirable solitude** 24 Sept. 1933, in Einstein Archives, Jerusalem: 75–960.
254 **He would walk across the heath** *Eastern Daily Press*, 22 Mar. 1979.
256 **First we were confronted by** Clark: 609.
256 **A suspicious-looking cow** *Daily Express*, 29 Sept. 1933.
257 **Einstein appeared dressed** Epstein: 77–8.
260 **Like other intellectuals** *Manchester Guardian*, 16 Sept. 1933.
263 **carefully leaked** Clark: 609.
263 **members of the League of Gentiles** *Jewish Telegraphic Agency*, 4 Oct. 1933.
264 **I hereby undertake not to create any disturbance** Clark: 610.
264 **It is now permissible to disclose** *Daily Express*, 5 Oct. 1933.
265 **at once dramatic and homely** *Manchester Guardian*, 4 Oct. 1933.
266 **I had never seen him before** Notes by William Beveridge for his BBC talk, 'Professor Albert Einstein at the Albert Hall', 3 Oct. 1933, in Beveridge Papers, file 9A/45/4, London School of Economics.
266 **The saving of these refugee students** 'Lord Rutherford' in [Albert Hall]: 2. This souvenir booklet, *Royal Albert Hall: Tuesday October 3rd 1933*, reproduces all of the speeches at the meeting. No publisher is given; the booklet was presumably produced by Oliver Locker-Lampson.
267 **as unconcernedly as if lecturing** *New York Times*, 4 Oct. 1933.
267 **It cannot be my task today** 'Professor Einstein' in [Albert Hall]: 5. See film of Einstein talking at: https://www.youtube.com/watch?v=ZBage5Ff57E (accessed 6 June 2020)
268 **I lived in solitude in the country** Ibid.: 6.
268 **In these difficult times** Clark: 613.

269 **imaginative proposal** Hoare: 240.
269 **Stormy weather** *Daily Express*, 6 Oct. 1933.
270 **For him loneliness** Infeld: 284.
270 **Einstein expressed over and over again** Born and Einstein: 107–8.
271 **I heard that you called me** 5 Oct. 1933, in Cherwell Papers, file D57, Nuffield College, Oxford.
271 **Locker-Lampson frightened Einstein** Clark: 613.
271 **Mr Sieff** Cooper: 78.
272 **An amicable settlement** Ibid.: 80.
272 **I am going to visit Princeton University** *Manchester Guardian*, 9 Oct. 1933.

EIGHT | I VILL A LITTLE T'INK

274 **Science is not and never will be** Einstein and Infeld: 308.
275 **hardly justifiable** 21 Nov. 1933, in Einstein Archives, Jerusalem: 16-383.
275 **On the other hand, we should be very sorry** 6 Dec. 1933, in Einstein Archives, Jerusalem: 16-384.
276 **I have voiced my opinion** 17 Dec. 1933, in Einstein Archives, Jerusalem: 16-382.
277 **I need scarcely tell you** 9 May 1934, in Einstein Archives, Jerusalem: 78–555.
277 **because if I come to Oxford** 22 Jan. 1935, in Einstein Archives, Jerusalem: 16-388.
277 **Sometimes I think back nostalgically** 16 Feb. 1935, in Fölsing: 686.
278 **He had gone through the ritual** Dyson: 14.

278 **the greatest living person** *New York Times*, 28 Nov. 1939.
279 **generations to come** Einstein, *The Ultimate Quotable Einstein*: 124.
280 **Whenever we came to an impasse** Whitrow: 75. A shorter version of the anecdote appears in Hoffmann and Dukas: 231.
281 **The clue to the understanding** Infeld: 274.
282 **I never thought of that!** Rhodes: 305.
283 **This new phenomenon** Rosenkranz, *The Einstein Scrapbook*: 74.
284 **Very few of the younger generation** Infeld: 276.
284 **It is true that this equation** Pais, *Einstein Lived Here*: 229.
286 **With his death, we, my wife and I** Born and Einstein: 229.
286 **many of his scientific concerns** Ibid.: xiii.
286 **Einstein's greatest contribution to relativity** Ibid.: xx.
286 **Both men were brilliant** Ibid.: xxxiii.
286 **I am extremely delighted** Ibid.: 125.
287 **He has been so upset by my illness** Vallentin: 175.
287 **The incidental way in which Einstein** Born and Einstein: 127.
287 **What I most admired in [Michele]** Letter to Vera and Bice Besso, 21 Mar. 1955, in Pais, *Einstein Lived Here*: 25.
288 **I did share your opinion** Born and Einstein: 182.
288 **The Germans, however** Ibid.: 185.
288 **to the land of the mass-murderers** Ibid.: 195.
288 **I only want to tell you** Ibid.: 200.
289 **Hiroshima and Nagasaki on the one hand** Ibid.: 201.
289 **You are wrong in casting aspersions** Ibid.: 200.
289 **Without wishing to defend** Ibid.: 134.
290 **I was very sad when the Jews started** Ibid.: 174.
290 **Your Palestine letter has moved me** Ibid.: 174–5.
291 **I cannot make a case for my attitude to physics** Ibid.: 155.
292 **He saw in the quantum mechanics of today** Ibid.: 199.

292 **I am convinced that ideas** Greenspan: 302.
293 **I personally feel very happy here** Born and Einstein: 122.
293 **One feels as if one were an Ichthyosaurus** Ibid.: 188.
293 **What have you got against being an Ichthyosaurus?** Ibid.: 190.
293 **You are surprised, aren't you** Frank: 356.
293 **Actually, Einstein was not isolated** Born and Einstein: xiii.
293 **He always has a certain feeling** Frank: 354.
294 **The greatest men of science** Infeld: 310–11.
294 **This was a splendid idea** Ibid.: 312.
295 **Once a work is finished** Ibid.: 318.
295 **man who worked with Einstein** Ibid.: 320.
295 ***Oj weh*** Pais, *Einstein Lived Here*: 219.
296 **Americans are proud** Jerome: 218.
296 **No other man contributed** *New York Times*, 19 Apr. 1955.
296 **We must realise we cannot simultaneously** *New York Times*, 23 June 1946.
296 **The war is won, but the peace is not** Einstein, *Ideas and Opinions*: 115–17.
297 **commingled and distributed** Ibid.: 130.
297 **Do I fear the tyranny** Ibid.: 120.
297 **the authority of the General Assembly** Pais, *Einstein Lived Here*: 234.
297 **it might not be altogether illogical** Nathan and Norden, eds: 231.
298 **If we hold fast to the concept** Einstein, *Ideas and Opinions*: 146.
298 **The reactionary politicians** Ibid.: 33–4.
299 **the greatest political genius** Einstein, *The Ultimate Quotable Einstein*: 124–5.
299 **anyone who gives advice like Einstein's** Pais, *Einstein Lived Here*: 238.
299 **That's the same advice** Jerome: 240.
299 **a disloyal American** Ibid.
299 **Commander Locker-Lampson offers** 14 June 1953, in Einstein Archives, Jerusalem: 41–214.
300 **In your issue of June 13** *New York Times*, 26 June 1953.
300 **All the intellectuals in this country** 28 June 1953, in Russell, *Autobiography*, vol. 3: 59.
301 **In common with every other thinking person** 11 Feb. 1955, in Nathan and Norden, eds: 623–4.
301 **twelve persons whose scientific attainments** 16 Feb. 1955, in ibid.: 625–6.
303 **There lies before us, if we choose** Robinson, *Einstein*: 206.
303 **is as valid today as it was then** Ibid.
303 **if I knew that I should have to die** Infeld: 294.

EPILOGUE | AN OLD GYPSY IN A QUAINT AND CEREMONIOUS VILLAGE

306 **Princeton is a wonderful little spot** 20 Nov. 1933, in Clark: 643.
307 **His face was contemplatively tragic** 'Einstein's Last Interview', in Robinson, *Einstein*: 212–13.
308 **the happiest thought** Miller: 217.
308 **That, alas, is vanity** 'Einstein's Last Interview', in Robinson, *Einstein*: 215.
308 **It is like childishness** Ibid.: 221.
308 **I never saw in him any trace** Preface to Nathan and Norden, eds: xiv.
308 **As with many other major breakthroughs** Janssen and Renn: 300.
308 **Einstein said most emphatically** 'Einstein's Last Interview', in Robinson, *Einstein*: 217.
309 **weakness** Ibid.: 221.

309 **Einstein apparently had little feeling** Ibid.: 221.

309 **Yes, he liked England** Snow: 87.

311 **the holy brotherhood in tails** 2/3 May 1931, in Einstein, 'Diary Notes, April–June 1931, Berlin and Oxford', Einstein Archives, Jerusalem: 29–142.

311 **Einstein chortled** Snow: 87.

311 **If Einstein dislikes his fame** Infeld: 293.

311 **I must tell you quite frankly** 3 Apr. 1932, in Fölsing: 647–8.

312 **One has to guard against** 23 Dec. 1950, in Seelig: 40.

312 **We might almost believe that we are in Oxford** Vallentin: 170–1.

312 **The copy was supposed to be exact** Infeld: 243–4.

312 **The atmosphere of Princeton is exemplary** Pritchett: 568.

314 **eminently wise** Letter to Elsa Einstein, ?22 July 1933, Einstein Archives, Jerusalem: 143–250.

315 **As a theoretical physicist Einstein stands alone** *Daily Telegraph*, 22 Apr. 1955.

315 **a thorough-going Englishman** Born and Einstein: 112.

316 **There has been a nasty mess** Ibid.: 111.

316 **strongest human bond** Rosenkranz, *Einstein before Israel*: 273.

316 **Remoteness, a relative absence** Letter to Anthony Storr, 29 Sept. 1978, in Berlin: 84.

317 **slight overacting** Mendelssohn: 174. I have slightly rephrased the original for grammatical reasons but not altered its sense.

318 **I shall leave England for America** *Eastern Daily Press*, 4 Oct. 1933.

319 **To Bohr one and only one place** Pais, *Einstein Lived Here*: 39.

319 **If I had to characterise** Ibid.: 55.

319 **Nothing really at any period of my life** Andrew Robinson, *Genius*: 77.

Bibliography

Press coverage of Einstein is extensively cited in the text and in the Notes and References.

[Albert Hall], *Royal Albert Hall: Tuesday October 3rd 1933*, London: publisher unknown, 1933 [souvenir booklet containing speeches by Einstein and others]

[Anon.], 'Einstein', *Nation & Athenaeum*, 18 June 1921: 431–2

Arianrhod, Robyn, *Einstein's Heroes: Imagining the World through the Language of Mathematics*, Cambridge: Icon Books, 2004

Ball, Philip, *Serving the Reich: The Struggle for the the Soul of Physics under Hitler*, London: Bodley Head, 2013

Bentwich, Helen Caroline, *Tidings from Zion: Helen Bentwich's Letters from Jerusalem, 1919–1931*, ed. Jenifer Glynn, London: I. B. Tauris, 2000

Berlin, Isaiah, *Affirming: Letters 1975–1997*, ed. Henry Hardy and Mark Pottle, London: Chatto & Windus, 2015

Bernstein, Jeremy, *Einstein*, 2nd edn, London: Fontana Modern Masters, 1991

Beveridge, W. H. B., *A Defence of Free Learning*, London: Oxford University Press, 1959

Bird, J. Malcolm, ed., *Relativity and Gravitation*, London: Methuen, 1921

Bonner, Thomas Neville, *Iconoclast: Abraham Flexner and a Life in Learning*, Baltimore: Johns Hopkins University Press, 2002

Born, Max and Albert Einstein, *The Born–Einstein Letters*, London: Macmillan, 2nd edn, 2005

Boyd, Julia, *Travellers in the Third Reich: The Rise of Fascism through the Eyes of Everyday People*, London: Elliott and Thompson, 2017

Brian, Denis, *Einstein: A Life*, New York: Wiley, 1996

Brockman, John, ed., *My Einstein: Essays by Twenty-Four of the World's Leading Thinkers on the Man, His Work, and His Legacy*, New York: Pantheon, 2006

Bronowski, Jacob, *The Ascent of Man*, London: Little, Brown, 1973

Brose, Henry, *The Theory of Relativity: An Introductory Sketch Based on Einstein's Original Writings*, Oxford: B. H. Blackwell, 1919

Calaprice, Alice, *The Einstein Almanac*, Baltimore: Johns Hopkins University Press, 2005

Calaprice, Alice, Daniel Kennefick and Robert Schulmann, *An Einstein Encylopedia*, Princeton: Princeton University Press, 2015

Cassidy, David C., *J. Robert Oppenheimer and the American Century*, New York: Pi Press, 2004

Chandrasekhar, Subrahmanyan, *Truth and Beauty: Aesthetics and Motivations in Science*, Chicago: University of Chicago Press, 1987

Clark, Ronald W., *Einstein: The Life and Times*, pbk edn, New York: HarperCollins, 2011

Collins, Jodie, 'Clear Out the Reds! Anti-Communism and the Conservative Right: the Case of Oliver Locker-Lampson, 1926–1933', MA Modern History thesis, University of Leeds, 2016, https://jodebloggs.wordpress.com/2016/10/21/clear-out-the-reds-anti-communism-and-the-conservative-right-the-case-of-oliver-locker-lampson–1926–1933/ (accessed 7 Nov. 2018)

Cooper, Ray, *Retrospective Sympathetic Affection: A Tribute to the Academic Community*, Leeds: Moorland, 1996

Crockatt, Richard, *Einstein and Twentieth-century Politics*, Oxford: Oxford University Press, 2016

Cunningham, Ebenezer, *The Principle of Relativity*, Cambridge: Cambridge University Press, 1914

—— 'Einstein's Relativity Theory of Gravitation', *Nature*, 104, 4 Dec. 1919: 354–6

Dongen, Jeroen van, *Einstein's Unification*, Cambridge: Cambridge University Press, 2010

Douglas, A. Vibert, 'Forty Minutes with Einstein', *Journal of the Royal Astronomical Society of Canada*, 50:3, 1956: 99–102

—— *The Life of Arthur Stanley Eddington*, London: Nelson, 1956

Dry, Sarah, *The Newton Papers: The Strange and True Odyssey of Isaac Newton's Manuscripts*, New York: Oxford University Press, 2014

Dyson, Freeman, 'Einstein as a Jew and a Philosopher', *New York Review of Books*, 7 May 2015: 14–17

Eddington, Arthur Stanley, *Report on the Relativity Theory of Gravitation*, Physical Society, 1918

Einstein, Albert, *The Collected Papers of Albert Einstein* (*CPAE*), vols 1–15, various editors, Princeton: Princeton University Press, 1987–

—— *Ideas and Opinions*, ed. Carl Seelig, New York: Three Rivers Press, 1982

—— *Mein Weltbild*, Amsterdam: Querido Verlag, 1934

—— *Relativity: The Special and the General Theory*, trans. Robert W. Lawson, London: Routledge Classics, 2001

—— *The Travel Diaries of Albert Einstein: The Far East, Palestine & Spain, 1922–1923*, ed. Ze'ev Rosenkranz, Princeton: Princeton University Press, 2018

—— *The Ultimate Quotable Einstein*, ed. Alice Calaprice, Princeton: Princeton University Press, 2011

Einstein, Albert and Sigmund Freud, *Why War?*, Paris: International Institute of Intellectual Cooperation, 1933

Einstein, Albert with Leopold Infeld, *The Evolution of Physics: The Growth of Ideas from the Early Concepts to Relativity and Quanta*, Cambridge: Cambridge University Press, 1938

Einstein, Albert and Mileva Marić, *Albert Einstein/Mileva Marić: The Love Letters*, ed. Jürgen Renn and Robert Schulmann, Princeton: Princeton University Press, 1992

Eisenstadt, Jean, *The Curious History of Relativity: How Einstein's Theory of Gravity was Lost and Found Again*, Princeton: Princeton University Press, 2006

Eisinger, Josef, *Einstein on the Road*, New York: Prometheus, 2011

Epstein, Jacob, *Let There Be Sculpture: An Autobiography*, London: Michael Joseph, 1940

Eve, A. S., *Rutherford*, Cambridge: Cambridge University Press, 1939

Farmelo, Graham, *The Universe Speaks in Numbers: How Modern Maths Reveals Nature's Greatest Secrets*, New York: Basic Books, 2019

Fölsing, Albrecht, *Albert Einstein: A Biography*, London: Penguin, 1998

Fort, Adrian, *Prof: The Life of Frederick Lindemann*, London: Jonathan Cape, 2003

Fox, Robert, 'Einstein in Oxford', *Notes and Records*, 9 May 2018: 1–26, http://rsnr.royalsocietypublishing.org/content/early/2018/05/09/rsnr.2018.0002 (accessed 7 Nov. 2018)

Fox, Robert and Graeme Gooday, eds, *Physics at Oxford 1839–1939: Laboratories, Learning, and College Life*, Oxford: Oxford University Press, 2005

Frank, Philipp, *Einstein: His Life and Times*, London: Jonathan Cape, 1948

French, A. P., ed., *Einstein: A Centenary Volume*, London: Heinemann, 1979

Friedman, Alan J. and Carol C. Donley, *Einstein as Myth and Muse*, Cambridge: Cambridge University Press, 1985

Galison, Peter L., Gerald Holton and Silvan S. Schweber, eds, *Einstein for the 21st Century: His Legacy in Science, Art, and Modern Culture*, Princeton: Princeton University Press, 2008

Gamow, George, *My World Line: An Informal Autobiography*, New York: Viking, 1970

Gimbel, Steven, *Einstein: His Space and Times*, New Haven: Yale University Press, 2015

Golding, William, 'Glimpses', *Reader's Digest*, Aug. 1968: 182

Gordin, Michael D., *Einstein in Bohemia*, Princeton: Princeton University Press, 2020

Greenspan, Nancy Thorndike, *The End of the Certain World: The Life and Science of Max Born*, Wiley: Chichester, 2005

Griffiths, John G., 'Albert Einstein at Winchester 1931', *Trusty Servant*, 1986: 5

Grundmann, Siegfried, *The Einstein Dossiers: Science and Politics – Einstein's Berlin Period*, trans. Ann M. Hentschel, New York: Springer, 2005

Gutfreund, Hanoch and Jürgen Renn, *The Formative Years of Relativity: The History and Meaning of Einstein's Princeton Lectures*, Princeton: Princeton University Press, 2017

Haldane, R. B., *The Reign of Relativity*, London: John Murray, 1921

Harrod, R. F., *The Prof: A Personal Memoir of Lord Cherwell*, London: Macmillan, 1959

Heisenberg, Werner, *Physics and Beyond: Encounters and Conversations*, London: Allen & Unwin, 1971

Hey, Tony and Patrick Walters, *Einstein's Mirror*, Cambridge: Cambridge University Press, 1997

—— *The New Quantum Universe*, Cambridge: Cambridge University Press, 2003

Highfield, Roger and Paul Carter, *The Private Lives of Albert Einstein*, London: Faber & Faber, 1993

Hitchings, Glenys with Del Styan, *Locker-Lampson: Einstein's Protector* (Cromer Museum Brief History Guide, 15), Cromer: Cromer Museum, 2010

Hoare, Samuel (Viscount Templewood), *Nine Troubled Years*, London: Collins, 1954

Hoffmann, Banesh with Helen Dukas, *Albert Einstein: Creator and Rebel*, New York: Viking, 1972

Holroyd, Michael, *Bernard Shaw: The One-volume Definitive Edition*, London: Chatto & Windus, 1997

Iliffe, Rob, *Priest of Nature: The Religious Worlds of Isaac Newton*, New York: Oxford University Press, 2017

Infeld, Leopold, *Quest: An Autobiography*, New York: Chelsea Publishing, 1980

Isaacson, Walter, *Einstein: His Life and Universe*, London: Simon & Schuster, 2007

Jammer, Max, *Einstein and Religion: Physics and Theology*, Princeton: Princeton University Press, 1999

Janssen, Michel and Christoph Lehner, eds, *The Cambridge Companion to Einstein*, Cambridge: Cambridge University Press, 2014

Janssen, Michel and Jürgen Renn, 'Einstein was No Lone Genius', *Nature*, 527, 19 Nov. 2015: 298–300

Jeans, James Hopwood, *The Mathematical Theory of Electricity and Magnetism*, Cambridge: Cambridge University Press, 1908

Jerome, Fred, *The Einstein File: J. Edgar Hoover's Secret War Against the World's Most Famous Scientist*, New York: St. Martin's Press, 2002

Kent, Paul, *Einstein in Oxford: Celebrating the Centenary of the 1905 Publications*, Oxford: Oxford Physics, 2005

Kennefick, Daniel, *No Shadow of a Doubt: The 1919 Eclipse that Confirmed Einstein's Theory of Relativity*, Princeton: Princeton University Press, 2019

Keynes, John Maynard, *The Collected Writings*, vol. 10 ('Essays in Biography'), London: Macmillan and St. Martin's Press, 1972

—— *The Collected Writings*, vol. 28, ed. Donald Moggridge, Cambridge: Macmillan and Cambridge University Press, 1982

Larmor, Joseph, *Aether and Matter*, Cambridge: Cambridge University Press, 1900

Larres, Klaus, 'Churchill and Einstein: Overlapping Mindsets', 22 Nov. 2016, https://winstonchurchill.hillsdale.edu/churchill-einstein-overlapping-mindsets/ (accessed 7 Nov. 2018)

Lawson, Robert W., 'Obituary' [of Einstein], *Nature*, 175, 28 May 1955: 926–7

Lindemann, Frederick A. (Lord Cherwell), 'The Genius of Einstein', *Daily Telegraph*, 22 Apr. 1955

Livens, George Henry, *Theory of Electricity*, Cambridge: Cambridge University Press, 1918

Lloyd George, Frances, *The Years That Are Past*, London: Hutchinson, 1967

Marić, Mileva, *The Life and Letters of Mileva Marić, Einstein's First Wife*, ed. Milan Popović, Baltimore: Johns Hopkins University Press, 2003

Mendelssohn, Kurt, *The World of Walther Nernst: The Rise and Fall of German Science*, London: Macmillan, 1973

Miles, Jonathan, *The Nine Lives of Otto Katz: The Remarkable True Story of a Communist Super-spy*, London: Bantam Press, 2010

Miller, Arthur I., *Einstein, Picasso: Space, Time and the Beauty that Causes Havoc*, New York: Basic Books, 2001

Morrell, Jack, *Science at Oxford 1914–1939: Transforming an Arts University*, Oxford: Oxford University Press, 1997

Moszkowski, Alexander, *Conversations with Einstein*, London: Sidgwick & Jackson, 1972

Murray, Gilbert, *An Unfinished Autobiography*, ed. Jean Smith and Arnold Toynbee, London: George Allen & Unwin, 1960

Nathan, Otto and Heinz Norden, eds, *Einstein on Peace*, New York: Schocken, 1960

O'Raifeartaigh, Cormac, 'Einstein's Steady-State Cosmology', *Physics World*, Sept. 2014: 30–3

Pais, Abraham, *Einstein Lived Here*, Oxford: Oxford University Press, 1994

—— *Niels Bohr's Times in Physics, Philosophy and Polity*, New York: Oxford University Press, 1991

—— *'Subtle Is the Lord': The Science and Life of Albert Einstein*, New York: Oxford University Press, 1983

Peat, F. David, *Einstein's Moon: Bell's Theorem and the Curious Quest for Quantum Reality*, Chicago: Contemporary, 1990

Powell, Corey S., *God in the Equation: How Einstein Transformed Religion*, New York: Free Press, 2003

Pritchett, V. S., 'A Memory of Einstein', *New Statesman and Nation*, 23 Apr. 1955: 568

Rhodes, Richard, *The Making of the Atomic Bomb*, New York: Simon & Schuster, 1986

Rigden, John S., *Einstein 1905: The Standard of Greatness*, Cambridge, MA: Harvard University Press, 2005

Robinson, Andrew, *Einstein: A Hundred Years of Relativity*, Princeton: Princeton University Press, 2015

—— 'Einstein in Oxford', *Christ Church Matters*, 36, 2016: 36–7

—— 'Einstein in Oxford', *Physics World*, June 2019: 32–6

—— 'Einstein Said That – Didn't He?', *Nature*, 557, 3 May 2018: 30

—— *Genius: A Very Short Introduction*, Oxford: Oxford University Press, 2011

—— 'Thus Spake Albert', *Aeon*, Mar. 2018, https://aeon.co/essays/why-do-we-love-to-quote-and-misquote-albert-einstein (accessed 7 Nov. 2018)

Rosenkranz, Ze'ev, *Einstein before Israel: Zionist Icon or Iconoclast?*, Princeton: Princeton University Press, 2011

—— *The Einstein Scrapbook*, Baltimore: Johns Hopkins University Press, 2002

Rothenstein, William, *Men and Memories*, vol. 2, London: Faber & Faber, 1932

Rovelli, Carlo, *The Order of Time*, London: Allen Lane, 2018

Rowe, David E., 'Einstein and Relativity: What Price Fame?', *Science in Context*, 25:2, 2012: 197–246

—— and Robert Schulmann, eds, *Einstein on Politics: His Private Thoughts and Public Stands on Nationalism, Zionism, War, Peace, and the Bomb*, Princeton: Princeton University Press, 2007

Russell, Bertrand, *The ABC of Relativity*, rev. edn, London: Allen & Unwin, 1958

—— *The Autobiography of Bertrand Russell*, vols 1–3, London: Allen & Unwin, 1967–69

Salaman, Esther, 'Memories of Einstein', *Encounter*, Apr. 1979: 19–23

—— 'A Talk with Einstein', *The Listener*, 8 Sept. 1955: 370

Samuel, Herbert, *Memoirs*, London: Cresset Press, 1945

Sayen, Jamie, *Einstein in America: The Scientist's Conscience in the Age of Hitler and Hiroshima*, New York: Crown, 1985

Schilpp, Paul Arthur, ed., *Albert Einstein: Philosopher-Scientist*, Evanston: The Library of Living Philosophers, 1949

Scientific American, 'Beyond Einstein' (special issue on Einstein), Sept. 2004

Seelig, Carl, *Albert Einstein: A Documentary Biography*, London: Staples Press, 1956

Siemens, Daniel, *Stormtroopers: A New History of Hitler's Brownshirts*, New Haven: Yale University Press, 2017

Snelling, Steve, 'A Refuge in Norfolk', *Eastern Daily Press (Magazine)*, 21 Mar. 1998: 6–9

Snow, C. P., *Variety of Men*, London: Macmillan, 1967

Sommer, Dudley, *Haldane of Cloan: His Life and Times, 1856–1928*, London: Allen & Unwin, 1960

Stanley, Matthew, *Einstein's War: How Relativity Triumphed amid the Vicious Nationalism of World War I*, New York: Dutton, 2019

—— *Practical Mystic: Religion, Science, and A. S. Eddington*, Chicago: University of Chicago Press, 2007

Stern, Fritz, *Einstein's German World*, London: Penguin, pbk edn, 2001

Tagore, Rabindranath, *Selected Letters of Rabindranath Tagore*, ed. Krishna Dutta and Andrew Robinson, Cambridge: Cambridge University Press, 1997

Townes, Charles, *How the Laser Happened: Adventures of a Scientist*, New York: Oxford University Press, 1999

Toynbee, Arnold, *Acquaintances*, Oxford: Oxford University Press, 1967

Vallentin, Antonina, *Einstein: A Biography*, London: Weidenfeld & Nicolson, 1954

Warwick, Andrew, *Masters of Theory: Cambridge and the Rise of Mathematical Physics*, Chicago: University of Chicago Press, 2003

Weinberg, Steven, *Dreams of a Final Theory: The Search for the Fundamental Laws of Nature*, London: Hutchinson Radius, 1993

Weisgal, Meyer W., and Joel Carmichael, eds, *Chaim Weizmann: A Biography by Several Hands*, New York: Atheneum, 1962

Whitaker, Andrew, *Einstein, Bohr and the Quantum Dilemma*, Cambridge: Cambridge University Press, 1996

White, Peregrine, 'Albert Einstein: The Violinist', *Physics Teacher*, 43, May 2005: 286–8

Whitrow, G. J., ed., *Einstein: The Man and His Achievement*, New York: Dover, 1967

Winterbotham, F. W., *The Nazi Connection*, New York: Harper & Row, 1978

World Committee for the Victims of German Fascism, *The Brown Book of the Hitler Terror and the Burning of the Reichstag*, London: Victor Gollancz, 1933

Index

Aarau (Switzerland) 17
Academic Assistance Council (UK) 256, 266, 275, 282
Action Française (journal) 228
Adams, Walter 256, 271
Albert Hall (London, UK) 6, 201, 224, 256, 258, 260, 262–70, 271, 275, 276, 284, 317
Albright, William F. 107
All Souls College (Oxford, UK) 46
Allen, Carleton 159–60
America *see* USA
Anderson, John George Clark 185–7
anti-relativity movement (Germany) 87–91, 98, 101
anti-Semitism 3, 13, 87, 88, 93–6, 98, 100, 194, 200, 201, 202, 225–6, 228, 230, 294, 320
Anti-War Movement 260
Antwerp (Belgium) 193, 272
Argentina 86, 87
Arianrhod, Robyn 33
Aristotle 48, 116, 149
Arnold, C. H. 209
Ashmolean Museum (Oxford, UK) 181
atomic bomb 282–5, 295
atomic theory (of Einstein) 21–2
Auschwitz (Poland) 289
Austro-Hungarian Empire 297

Bach, Johann Sebastian 168
Balfour, A. J. 97, 98
Balfour Declaration (1920) 98
Ball, Philip 88
Balsam, Artur 169
Barker, Ernest 77–8, 81
'Beachcomber' (columnist in *Daily Express*) 251, 256–7, 264
Beer, Gavin de 161
Beethoven, Ludwig van 54, 166, 167
Belgium 5, 6, 54, 231, 233, 241, 254, 275, 277, 285
  Einstein in 3, 35, 133, 193–4, 196, 204, 220, 226, 240, 245–7
Belsen (Germany) 289
Bentwich, Helen 105, 107
Bentwich, Norman 105, 106, 107
Bergmann, Hugo 105
Bergson, Henri 110
Berlin, Isaiah 97, 316
Berlin (Germany) 3, 87, 101, 157, 179, 182, 183, 193, 196, 204, 205, 206, 226, 275, 281, 316
  Einstein in 11, 13, 34, 40, 50, 54, 61, 64, 65, 89, 91, 92, 95, 96, 98, 102, 124, 135, 144, 155, 156, 184, 192, 292, 314
Berlin, University of 54, 55, 65, 88, 152, 315
Berlin Goethe League 93
Berliner Tageblatt (newspaper) 89
Bern (Switzerland) 17, 20, 22, 34, 36, 48, 308
Besso, Michele 23, 28, 121, 129, 135, 285, 287, 308
Bethe, Hans 205–6
Beveridge, William 265, 266, 271, 272, 314
Bevin, Ernest 290, 314
Big Bang theory 143
Blackshirts (UK) 264

Blake, Robert 152–3
Block, Herbert Lawrence 318
Blue Shirts (UK) 201, 263, 271, 317
Blumenfeld, Kurt 98–9
Bodleian Library (Oxford, UK) 174
Bohr, Niels 74, 122, 123, 127–9, 130, 131, 132, 133, 134, 137, 140, 217, 289, 319
Bolshevism 198
Bolton, Lyndon 69
Boltzmann, Ludwig 294
Bonaparte, Napoleon xiii, 89
Born, Hedwig 293
Born, Max
- and Britain xii, 286–7, 289, 315
- career 285, 288, 289
- Jewishness 94, 95, 289–91, 316
- and Nazism 88, 91, 208, 287–9
- personality 286, 287
- physics 19, 45, 90, 120, 121, 123, 130–1, 133, 139, 141, 153, 210, 217, 270, 291–2
- politics 289–90, 303, 314

Born–Einstein Letters, The 286–93
Bose, Satyendra Nath 129–30
Bose–Einstein statistics 130
Bowen, Edmund 162
Brahms, Johannes 166, 167, 191
Brasenose College (Oxford, UK) 185
Bridgman, Percy 303
British Museum (London, UK) 282
British Patent Office 69
British Union of Fascists 264
Brockway, A. Fenner 179
Broglie, Louis de 123, 131, 133, 217
Bronowski, Jacob 11
Brooklyn Eagle (newspaper) 243
Brose, Henry 68, 72
Brown, Robert 22
Brownian movement 21–2, 125
Brownshirts (Germany) 225, 246
Brown Book of the Hitler Terror, The 225, 242–5, 247, 260, 262
Brüning, Heinrich 192
Brussels (Belgium) 34, 36, 124, 133, 194
Buchwald, Diana Kormos 286, 293
Burnett, W. G. E. 187
Busch, Adolf 166, 167

Caesar, Julius 266
Calaprice, Alice xii
California Institute of Technology (Pasadena, USA) xiii, 184, 193, 311
Cambridge, University of (UK) xii, 11, 47–53, 55, 56, 62, 63, 66, 69, 71, 74, 154–5, 165, 177, 191, 209, 267, 278, 281, 285, 289, 312, 315, 319
Canada 284
Canterbury, Archbishop of *see* Davidson, Randall
Caputh (Germany) 192–3, 195, 196
Carroll, Lewis 70, 173
Cavendish Laboratory (Cambridge, UK) 11, 48, 52, 209
Ceylon 103
Chamberlain, Austen 199, 234, 263, 265, 314
Chamberlain, Neville 278
Chandrasekhar, Subrahmanyan 58
Chaplin, Charlie 2, 225
Chapman, R. W. 159
Chartwell (UK) 232–3
Christ Church (Oxford, UK) 46, 152, 153, 156, 159, 160, 170–5, 180, 182, 183–7, 191, 203, 204, 208, 209, 212, 271, 275, 277, 311, 313, 314, 316
Churchill, Winston 152, 153, 154, 176, 198, 199, 230, 231–4, 249, 310, 314, 317
City University of New York (USA) 280
Clarendon Laboratory (Oxford, UK) 152, 206
Clark, Ronald 45, 52, 77, 89, 263
Cohen, I. Bernard 307–9
Cold War xii, 279, 297–8
Collège de France (Paris) 227, 228
Colman, Philip 252, 254
Columbus, Christopher 266
Communism 3, 195, 202, 244–5, 258, 261–2, 284, 296, 298–9, 301
Compton, Arthur 122, 133
Cooley, Charles 265, 271
Coote, Henry 68
Copernicus, Nicolaus 36, 78, 116, 124, 141, 149
Coptic music 181
cosmological constant 142, 143–4, 157, 163
Cotswolds (UK) 181

Cottingham, E. T. 58, 59–60
Cromer (UK) 2, 3, 5, 251, 252, 256, 258
Crommelin, A. C. D. 58, 63
Cunningham, Ebenezer 48, 49, 50, 52, 55
Curie, Marie 34, 35, 38, 110, 111, 133
Czechoslovakia 5, 248

Daily Express (newspaper) 245, 251, 252, 256–7, 264, 269
Daily Herald (newspaper) 248
Daily Mail (newspaper) 261–2
Daily Mirror (newspaper) 199–201, 202
Daily Princetonian (newspaper) 278
Daily Telegraph (newspaper) 68, 153, 240
Daudet, Léon 228
Davidson, C. R. 58
Davidson, Randall 76, 311
Debye, Peter 90, 133
Deneke, Helena 166, 170
Deneke, Margaret 166–70, 172, 175, 181, 182, 191–2
Denmark 319
Deutsche Tageszeitung (newspaper) 194
Dickens, Charles 313
Dirac, Paul 123, 133, 134, 138, 217, 219, 281, 289
Dodgson, Charles Lutwidge *see* Carroll, Lewis
Dongen, Jeroen van 219
Dover (UK) 207
Dresden (Germany) 289
Dreyfus Affair (1894–1906) 228
Drummond, Eric 110
Dublin (Eire) 285
Dudden, Frederick Homes 164
Dukas, Helen 272, 280, 295
Dulong, Pierre 124–5
Dundas, Robert Hamilton 173–4
Durrell, C. V. 150
Dyson, Frank 52, 56–7, 58, 60, 62, 63, 64, 76
Dyson, Freeman 278

Eastern Daily Press (newspaper) 250–1
Eastoe, Herbert 4, 252, 254
Eddington, Arthur
  astronomy 47, 50, 52–3, 57–61, 144
  career 52, 177, 191, 310
  education 52–3
  humour 60, 64, 70–1, 136, 173
  leads solar eclipse expedition (1919) 51, 56–64, 72, 76
  lecturer on relativity 66, 69–70, 90, 91
  pacifism 55–7
Edinburgh, University of (UK) 76, 285, 286, 288
Ehrenfest, Paul 61, 91, 121, 133, 308, 311
Einstein, Albert
  academic career and honours 19–20, 34–5, 147, 148, 164–5, 184, 220, 227–8, 278
  aloofness 20, 268, 270, 281, 292–4, 295, 319
  Anglophilia xi, xii, 6, 11, 44, 83, 151, 155, 156, 224, 233, 240, 310–13, 318
  appearance and dress 172, 182–3, 209, 237, 257–8, 265, 280–1, 307, 311
  birth 12
  in Britain xi, 2, 3, 4, 5–7, 74–83, 149–51, 157–83, 191–2, 208–10, 212–13, 219–21, 231–8, 239, 249–72
  childhood 12–15
  citizenship 3, 16–17, 34, 54, 93, 95, 193, 194, 196, 227, 231, 236, 240, 278
  death 303–4
  death threats against xii, 3, 5, 87, 101–2, 246–9
  diaries xii, 16, 86, 103, 104, 107, 146, 160, 165, 169, 172, 174, 176, 178, 180, 182, 318
  education 13–17, 19, 20, 22
  and English language xii, 159, 212–13, 267, 312
  fame xi, 62–3, 66, 68–9, 73–5, 81, 87, 91, 99, 101, 102, 104, 135–6, 147, 149, 163, 209, 220, 227, 246, 251–2, 266, 293, 294, 295, 296, 311, 318
  health 155, 156, 299
  on human relationships 16, 20, 195, 268–70, 280–1, 287–8, 292–5, 308, 316, 318–19
  humour 19, 22, 55, 65–6, 89, 104, 107, 130, 144, 146, 149, 168, 172, 174, 175, 181, 182, 213, 247, 257–8, 268, 269, 293, 306, 307, 308, 310, 312, 313

Einstein, Albert (contd)
 Jewishness xi, 12, 15, 65, 88, 93–6, 99–101, 103–8, 116, 147, 191, 195, 206, 226, 228–30, 231, 238, 240, 260, 268, 275, 278, 316
 marriages and children 17, 18, 20, 207, 211, 226, 246–7, 277, 287, 318
 mathematics/physics *see* relevant entries, e.g., cosmological constant; quantum concept/theory; relativity
 and music 6, 22, 80, 105, 106, 167–9, 175, 191, 193, 236, 253, 254, 258
 and Nazism *see* Nazism
 pacifism 53, 55–7, 87, 108, 114–17, 177, 179, 180, 195, 240–2, 243, 261, 262, 301–3
 patent-office employment 20–1, 23, 34, 36, 48, 69, 182, 268, 308
 philosophy 15, 113–14, 131, 134, 139–41, 173, 211–12, 298–9, 315, 319
 and politics *see* entries for individuals, institutions, movements, nations, e.g., Hitler, Adolf; League of Nations; Zionism; USA
 and portraiture 6, 170–2, 258, 259
 religion 15, 61, 95, 120, 140, 141, 180, 211, 285, 309
 and sailing 5, 180, 195–6
Einstein, Alfred 169
Einstein, Eduard (AE's son) 207, 254, 277, 318
Einstein, Elsa (AE's second wife) 3, 5, 74, 75, 76, 102, 105, 106, 193, 204, 208, 220, 226, 233, 245–7, 251, 254, 270, 272, 277, 287, 312
Einstein, Hermann (AE's father) 12, 20
Einstein, Ilse (AE's step-daughter) 226, 277
Einstein, Maja (AE's sister) 13, 14, 16
Einstein, Margot (AE's step-daughter) 226
Einstein, Pauline (AE's mother) 12, 20, 62
Einstein Papers Project (USA) xiii
Einstein Society (House of Commons, UK) 68
Einstein–Infeld–Hoffmann equations 278, 286
Einstein–Szilard refrigerator 281–2
Eisenhower, Dwight 296, 300
electronic theory of matter (ETM) 48–9, 63
Elgar, Edward 313
Elisabeth, Queen (of Belgium) 193, 277, 285, 306
Elizabeth II, Queen (of UK) 300
Emergency Committee of Atomic Scientists 298
Epstein, Jacob 6, 256–8, 259
equivalence principle 37–8, 39, 307
ether (aether) 18, 21, 26, 28, 30, 48, 49–50, 52, 63, 64, 197, 270
Ettlinger, Lionel 231, 238
Euclid 15, 40, 46, 47, 81, 165, 214
Evans, Arthur 181
Evolution of Physics, *The* (Einstein and Infeld) xii, 17–18, 137, 274, 280, 294–5, 310
Exeter, Bishop of 265, 267

Faraday, Michael 6, 11, 25, 34, 65, 80, 147, 267, 279, 294, 307
Farmelo, Graham 219
Farnborough (UK) 152
Fascism 196, 201, 225, 260, 262, 263, 264, 317
Federal Bureau of Investigation (USA) 296
Fehme secret society (Germany) 248, 250
Fermi, Enrico 283
Feynman, Richard 121
Fiedler, Hermann 176, 181
First World War 3, 4, 17, 50, 53–7, 65, 68, 77, 78, 88, 97, 108, 109, 114, 179, 199–200, 201, 237, 254, 298
Fischer, Emil 109
Fisher, H. A. L. 155, 161
Fitzgerald, Edward 60
Fitzgerald, George 28
Fitzgerald, Lady 181
Flexner, Abraham 156, 228
Fölsing, Albrecht 12, 207, 210
Foot, Michael 210
Fort, Adrian 154
France 110, 111, 112, 113, 123, 179, 220, 226, 227, 228, 240, 241, 242, 303, 313
Frank, Philipp 246, 294

Frauenglass, William 298–9
Freud, Sigmund 113
Friedmann, Alexander 142–3, 163
Friend, The (magazine) 179–80

Galileo Galilei xiii, 37, 78, 116, 141, 149, 214, 218, 308
Gamow, George 144
Gandhi, Mahatma 139, 279, 299, 307
Gehrcke, Ernst 88–90, 91
Geneva (Switzerland) 34, 111, 114, 231
George V, King (of UK) 164
Gerber, Paul 89
German Emergency Committee of the Society of Friends 266
German League for Human Rights 115
Germany
  before 1933 12–16, 53–5, 65, 66, 76–7, 78, 87–96, 98–9, 101, 102, 108, 110, 112, 151–2, 179, 184, 192
  in 1933 and after 5, 193–5, 198, 199–201, 202, 203, 208, 210, 221, 225–7, 231, 235–6, 238, 240–2, 245, 248, 261, 262, 267, 276, 287–9
Ginsberg, Asher 104
Glasgow, University of (UK) 204, 205, 219, 220, 230
Goebbels, Josef 3, 226, 248
Goethe, Johann Wolfgang von 6, 54, 267
Golding, William 182–3
Gollancz, Victor 244–5
Göring, Hermann 245
Göttingen University (Germany) 76, 288
gravitational redshift 39
gravitational waves 286
Greece 29, 54, 76, 214
Griffiths, John 149–51, 164
Griffiths, Robin 151
Grigg, James 187
Grossmann, Marcel 20, 36, 40, 308
Gunfield (Oxford, UK) 166–7, 170, 172, 175, 191
Gunther, Robert 161–3

Haber, Fritz 44, 54, 94, 95, 97, 99–100
Habicht, Conrad 22
Haldane, John Scott 159
Haldane, Richard 75–80, 82–3, 101, 147, 155, 159, 197, 198, 311, 314
Hamburg (Germany) 149
Handel, George Frederick 168, 265, 313
Harden, Maximilian 102
Hardy, Godfrey Harold 177
Harrod, Roy 46–7, 153, 173, 175
Hartog, Philip 230
Hawking, Stephen 23, 27, 40
Haydn, Joseph 167, 169
Hebrew University (Jerusalem) xiii, 65, 96, 97, 98–9, 100, 107, 227, 229–30, 315–16
Heisenberg, Werner 123, 131, 133, 134, 217, 285, 286, 289
Heisenberg uncertainty principle 131–2, 217
Helmholtz, Hermann von 294
Heraclitus 165
Herbert Spencer lecture (Einstein) *see* 'On the Method of Theoretical Physics'
Herman, Robert 52
Herriot, Édouard 220
Hertz, Heinrich 19, 25, 31, 48, 49
Herzl, Theodor 107
Hey, Tony 38
Hindenburg, Paul von 192
Hiroshima (Japan) 284, 289, 295
Hitler, Adolf 3, 55, 88, 157, 160, 192, 198, 199–202, 225, 226, 228, 231, 234, 241, 244, 250, 258, 262, 278, 290, 297, 317
Hitler Youth 196
Hoare, Samuel 255, 269
Hoffmann, Banesh 172–3, 278, 280–1, 294
Holland 50, 91, 227, 275, 310, 311
Hong Kong 103
Hooke, Robert 308
Hoover, J. Edgar 296
House of Commons (London, UK) 196, 234–8, 317
Howard, Marjory 4, 252
Hubble, Edwin 143, 163
Humason, Milton 143
Hume, David 22
Hungary 281, 282
Hurst, Claude 212

Hyades (star cluster) 57
hydrogen bomb 295

Immigration and Nationalization Service (USA) 296
Imperial College (London, UK) 181
India 55, 69, 129, 175, 264, 264, 299
Infeld, Leopold xii, 137, 270, 278, 280, 281, 284, 294–5, 302, 303, 310, 311, 312
Institute for Advanced Study (Princeton, USA) 156, 227, 228, 278, 294, 319
International Student Service 266
Israel xi, 93, 96, 97, 108, 192, 228, 290, 316
Italy 16, 179, 201, 283

Japan 283, 295, 303
  Einstein in 87, 101, 102, 103, 105
Japan Advertiser (newspaper) 102
Jeans, James 35, 48, 52, 147, 265, 267
Jerusalem (Israel) xiii, 97, 103, 104, 106, 107, 108, 229, 316
Jewish Chronicle (newspaper) 101, 191, 228, 229, 238
Jewish Telegraphic Agency 157, 263
Joachim, Joseph 167
Joliot-Curie, Frédéric 303
Joseph, H. W. B. 45–6, 154
Juliusburger, Otto 275
Junkers, landed nobility (Germany) 192

Kant, Immanuel 54, 192
Katz, Otto 244
Kennefick, Daniel xii
Kepler, Johannes 15, 116, 141, 149, 308
Kerr, Philip 160, 177
Keynes, John Maynard 2, 255, 320
Kiel (Germany) 102
King's College (London, UK) 77–8, 81–2, 198
Kipling, Rudyard 313
Kretschmer, Ernest 321
Kube, Wilhelm 192

Labour Party (UK) 210, 260, 314
Lady Margaret Hall (Oxford, UK) 166–7, 170
Langevin, Paul 90
Larmor, Joseph 49, 52, 90
laser 129
Laue, Max von 90
Lawson, Robert 71–3, 323
Le Coq sur Mer (Belgium) 196, 204, 208, 210, 226, 229, 231, 238, 245–7, 250, 254
League of Nations 109, 110, 111, 113, 180, 231, 236, 238
League of Nations Disarmament Commission 114
League of Nations International Committee on Intellectual Cooperation 109–14, 173, 180, 227
League of Nations Society (Oxford, UK) 178
Leers, Johann von 226
Leibniz, Gottfried Wilhelm 308
Leiden, University of (Holland) 50, 61
Leishman, J. B. 173
Lemaître, Georges 143
Lenard, Philipp 31–2, 54, 88–9, 90, 114
Lessing, Theodor 5, 247–8
Levi-Civita, Tullio 90
Lindemann, Adolph 181
Lindemann, Frederick
  birth and education 151–2
  career 152
  and Churchill 152, 153, 154, 230, 233, 234
  encounters Einstein for first time 34, 35
  host of Einstein in UK 82, 83, 144, 146, 149–50, 155, 156, 159, 160, 165, 174, 175, 176, 177, 178, 180, 181, 183–4, 187, 198, 204–8, 212, 227, 270–1, 275–7, 311, 315–16, 317
  and Nazism 205–6, 276, 315
  personality 153–4, 315
  physics 46–7, 68, 152–3
  politics 153, 314
Lister, Joseph 6, 267
Livens, G. H. 49
Lloyd George, David 234, 314
Locker-Lampson, Oliver Stillingfleet
  birth and education 197–8
  career 198, 199
  and Churchill 198, 199, 230, 230, 231, 233, 249

contacts Einstein for first time 196–7, 204
host of Einstein in UK 4, 221, 230, 231, 233–40, 249–52, 254–6, 257, 258, 260, 261, 262–3, 264, 265, 270–2, 277, 299
and Nazism 199–202, 235–6, 238, 315
organises Albert Hall event with Einstein 256, 261, 262–3, 264, 265, 271–2, 317, 320
personality 198, 199, 249, 254, 271, 316–18
politics 198, 199, 234–7, 238, 260, 314
sympathy for Jews 202, 235–7, 238, 240
Lodge, Oliver 64
London, Fritz 205–6
London (UK) 62–3, 67, 72, 91, 92, 98, 103, 115, 136, 161, 166, 181, 196, 197, 201, 204, 230, 241, 244, 247, 248, 254, 256, 258, 259, 275, 282, 299, 302, 315
Einstein in xiii, 5, 6, 75–82, 101, 116, 147, 198, 220, 224, 231, 233, 235, 239, 240, 249, 251, 263, 264–72, 311
London, University of (UK) 264
London School of Economics (UK) 256
Lorentz, Hendrik 28, 34, 35, 49, 61, 80, 90, 91, 110, 133
Lothian, Lord *see* Kerr, Philip
Low, David 255
Luitpold Gymnasium (Munich) 13

Macauley, Charles Raymond 243
McCarthy, Joseph 298, 299, 300
MacDonald, Ramsay 314
Mach, Ernst 21, 22, 23
McLaren, Stuart 249
Madrid, University of (Spain) 227, 277
Magnes, Judah 230
Manchester (UK) 75, 147
Manchester, University of (UK) 74, 97, 100, 127
Manchester Guardian (newspaper) 74–5, 208, 220, 238, 248, 260, 261, 265, 269, 290, 323
Manhattan Project (USA) 283, 284
'Manifesto to the cultured world' (1914) 53–4, 65
'Manifesto to the Europeans' (1917) 54, 114
Marić, Mileva (first wife of Einstein) 17, 18, 19, 20, 22, 31, 93, 207, 277, 318
Marienbad (Czechoslovakia) 248
Markwalder, Suzanne 312
Marley, Dudley 244
Marx Brothers 220
Maxwell, James Clerk 10, 11, 18, 19, 21, 25, 26, 28, 34, 47, 65, 80, 92, 128, 136, 279, 294, 307
Mayer, Walther 204, 210, 272
Mendelssohn, Kurt 317
Mercury (planet) 53, 164, 165
Michanowski, Ethel 182
Michelson, Albert 50
Milan (Italy) 16, 26
Millikan, Robert 122, 124
Milne, Edward Arthur 177–8
Minkowski, Hermann 19, 32–3, 36, 39
Minoan civilisation (Crete) 181
Morley, Edward 50
Mosley, Oswald 264
Moszkowski, Alexander 96
Mount Wilson Observatory (USA) 143
Mozart, Wolfgang Amadeus 105, 167, 177
Muller, Hermann 303
Munich (Germany) 13, 16, 17
Munich Putsch (1923) 199
Murray, Gilbert 110, 111–13, 173, 175, 226–7, 285, 328
Museum of the History of Science (Oxford, UK) 161–3
Mussolini, Benito 201, 202, 283

Nagasaki (Japan) 284, 289
Nation & Athenaeum (magazine) 78
Nature (journal) 49, 66, 157, 308, 323
Nazareth (Israel) 107
Nazism
development of 55, 81, 88, 95, 114, 153, 184, 192, 194–6, 198, 199–202, 225–6, 282, 289, 315
and Einstein xii, 2, 3–5, 7, 55, 88, 108, 117, 186, 192–6, 203, 205–6, 208, 209, 221, 225–7, 229, 231, 232, 234, 235–6, 238, 240–9, 250, 251, 252, 254,

257–8, 262, 267, 275, 276, 277, 283, 287, 288, 298, 299, 310, 311, 317, 319
Nernst, Walther 34, 35, 54, 123–4, 152
Nervo and Knox 257
Netherlands, the *see* Holland
New College (Oxford, UK) 177
New Statesman and Nation (magazine) 2, 255
New York City (USA) 230, 272, 275, 282, 283, 298
New York Herald Tribune (newspaper) 136
New York Times (newspaper) 5, 63, 73, 135, 136, 139, 229, 248, 249, 267, 296, 299
Newton, Isaac xi, 6, 11, 14, 15, 21, 47, 49, 62, 63, 65, 66, 68, 73, 77, 78, 116, 147, 148, 149, 151, 267, 279, 307–9
Newtonian physics 10, 18, 25, 26, 27, 28, 29, 34, 36, 37, 40, 41, 58, 60, 61, 80, 123, 126, 136, 165, 214–16, 218
Nicholas II, Tsar (of Russia) 198
Nicolai, George Friedrich 54
No More War Movement (UK) 115
Nobel, Alfred 296
Norfolk (UK) 3, 198, 249–60, 268, 270, 272, 317
Northcliffe, Alfred 66
Nottingham, University of (UK) 11
nuclear weapons 285, 295, 296, 297, 301, 302

Observer (newspaper) 251, 261
O'Raifeartaigh, Cormac 143, 163
Olympia Academy (Bern, Switzerland) 22, 227
'On the Method of Theoretical Physics' (Einstein) 159, 160, 191, 191, 208, 209–19
Oppenheimer, J. Robert 94
Ostwald, Wilhelm 20
Oxford (UK) xi, 5, 72, 144, 149, 197, 227, 228, 230, 271, 272, 275, 276, 277, 285, 316, 317
  Einstein in 82, 146, 148, 150, 154–87, 190–2, 198, 203, 204–18, 236, 312, 314, 318
Oxford, University of (UK) 34, 45–7, 68, 82, 97, 144, 148, 154–6, 157–9, 164–5, 177, 205–6, 208, 209, 210, 212, 227, 228, 280, 289, 315, 319
Oxford Chamber Music Society 167
Oxford Times (newspaper) 158–9, 164–5
Oxford Union 210
Oxford University Press 159, 160

Page, Denys 212
Pais, Abraham 211, 284, 319
Palestine 87, 95, 96, 97–8, 191, 230, 236, 238, 275, 289–91, 316
  Einstein in 87, 100, 103–8, 229
Papen, Franz von 192
Paris (France) 5, 226, 227, 228, 231, 277, 287
Pasadena (USA) 184
Pasteur, Louis 6, 267
Pauli, Wolfgang 126, 133
Pauling, Linus 303
Peat, David 131
Peconic (USA) 282
Petit, Alexis 124–5
photoelectric effect 31, 122, 124
Planck, Max 34, 35, 54, 61, 62, 72, 90, 101, 114, 124, 133, 135, 153, 195, 211, 313, 319
Planck's quantum theory 30, 32, 122, 125–6, 128, 129, 132
Plato 165
Poincaré, Henri 22, 28, 34, 35, 153
Poland 226, 278, 294, 303
Ponsonby, Arthur 241–2
Pope, Alexander 147
Powell, Cecil 303
Powell, Corey 141–2
Poynton, A. B. 164–5
Prague (Czechoslovakia) 34, 37, 65, 105
Princeton (USA) 156, 227, 228, 312, 319
  Einstein in xii, 11, 94, 172, 230, 275, 278–81, 286, 292–4, 304, 306, 307, 311, 312, 316, 318
Princeton University (USA) 228, 272, 278, 280, 313
Principe (West Africa) 58–61, 63
Pritchett, V. S. 312–13
Prussia 13, 94, 192, 194, 196, 317

Prussian Academy of Sciences (Germany) 3, 34, 109, 124, 135, 193, 195, 204, 205
Ptolemy 116, 149
Pugwash Conferences on Science and World Affairs (Canada) 303
Punch (magazine) 68
Purcell, Henry 168, 313
Pyrmont (Germany) 288
Pythagoras 116, 149

Quakers 53, 55, 71, 179, 288
quantum concept/theory 12, 21, 28–32, 35, 121, 122, 123–30
quantum mechanics 117, 120, 123, 130–5, 137, 138, 140, 141, 210, 217, 218, 285, 289, 291–2

Radium Institute (Vienna, Austria) 71
Rathenau, Walther 5, 87, 101, 102, 108, 111, 248
Refugee Assistance Committee 266, 271
Refugee Professionals Committee 266
relativity
- fame of xi, 44, 63, 65, 66, 67, 68, 69, 70, 72–5, 76, 77, 78, 79, 96, 100, 107, 148, 154, 155, 157, 158, 164, 165, 173, 181, 197, 204, 226, 238, 295, 314
- general theory (1915–16) 6, 11, 18, 20, 29, 32–4, 36–41, 45–50, 51, 52, 53, 56, 57–63, 64, 80–1, 90, 91, 121, 123, 126, 127, 129, 134, 135, 136, 138, 141, 142, 144, 150, 178, 216, 218–20, 278, 286, 292, 308
- special theory (1905) 12, 19, 23–8, 36, 48, 64, 124

Relativity: The Special and the General Theory (Einstein) 72
Renn, Jürgen 21
Rhodes, Cecil 154
Rhodes House (Oxford, UK) 146, 156, 157, 158, 159, 161–3, 168, 208, 212
Rhodes Memorial Lectures (Oxford, UK) 154–63, 175
Rhodes Trust (UK) 154, 155, 156, 160, 162, 177
Riemann, Bernhard 40, 217, 219
Rigden, John 21, 29
Rizzi, F. 170–2
Roaf, Douglas 180
Rogers, Eric 307
Röhm, Ernst 225
Rolland, Romain 322
Roosevelt, Eleanor 296
Roosevelt, Franklin 283, 284, 285
Rosenberg, Alfred 201
Rosenberg, Ethel and Julius 300
Rosenfeld, Léon 132
Rosenkranz, Ze'ev 93, 96, 98
Rotblat, Joseph 303
Rothenstein, William 92
Rothschild, Lionel 98, 116
Roughton Heath (UK) 5, 252, 257, 259, 271
Rovelli, Carlo 121
Royal Astronomical Society (UK) 50, 56, 60, 62, 76
Royal College of Art (UK) 92
Royal Greenwich Observatory (UK) 52
Royal Society (UK) 56, 62, 63, 64, 147, 151, 162
Royden, Maude 265
Ruskin College (Oxford, UK) 178
Russell, Bertrand xii, 29, 55, 116–17, 147, 286, 300–3, 304, 308
Russell–Einstein Manifesto (1955) xii, 301–3
Russia (and Soviet Union) 95, 178, 181, 198, 260, 297, 302
Russian Academy 297
Rutherford, Ernest 34, 35, 45, 47, 74, 153, 208–9, 263, 265, 266–7, 282, 322
Rutherford–Bohr model of atom 122, 127–8
Ryle, Gilbert 212

St Bartholomew's Hospital (London, UK) 282
Salaman, Esther 11
Salzburg (Austria) 34, 126
Samuel, Beatrice 106
Samuel, Herbert 103, 106, 107
Schleicher, Kurt von 192
Schopenhauer, Arthur 211
Schrödinger, Erwin 123, 131, 133, 134, 205, 217, 277, 285, 289
Schubert, Franz 166

Schulmann, Robert xii, 21
Schumann, Clara 166
Schumann, Robert 166
'Science and Civilisation' (Einstein) 224, 261–2, 263, 267–8
Scientific American (magazine) 69, 307
Searle, G. F. C. 48, 52
Second World War 167, 283, 289, 295, 296
Sentinels of Empire *see* Blue Shirts
Shakespeare, William 2, 6, 267, 313
Shaw, George Bernard xiii, 76, 116, 147, 147, 313
Sheffield (UK) 71
Sheldonian Theatre (Oxford, UK) 148, 156, 157, 164–5
Siemens, Daniel 225
Silberstein, Ludwik 323
Simon, Franz (Francis) 206
Sitter, Willem de 50, 52, 61, 142, 143
Smith, J. A. 45–6, 154
Smuts, Jan Christiaan 156, 159
Snow, C. P. 17, 234, 310–11, 318
Sobral (Brazil) 58, 61, 62, 63
solar eclipse (1919) 51, 57–62, 76, 81
Soldat-Roeger, Marie 166, 167–8, 191
Solf, Wilhelm 102
Solovine, Maurice 22, 227, 285
Solvay Congresses (Brussels, Belgium) 34, 35, 82, 124, 132–4, 139, 152
Sommerfeld, Arnold 35, 55, 90, 91, 205–6
South America 87
Southampton (UK) 149, 272
space-time 32–3, 36, 40, 41
Spain 228
Spinoza, Baruch de 22
Squire, John 147
Stalin, Joseph 244, 260
Stark, Johannes 88
Stern, Otto 121
Strube, Sidney 'George' 269
Sunday Express (newspaper) 249
Sunday Times, The (newspaper) 237, 248, 261
Surrey (UK) 198, 233
Swabians 12
Swedish Academy (Stockholm, Sweden) 134, 289
Swiss Patent Office (Bern) 20–1, 23, 34, 36, 48, 308
Swiss Polytechnic (Zurich) 17, 19, 20, 26, 32, 65
Switzerland 34, 54, 55, 62, 64, 65, 66, 110, 196, 207, 240, 278
  Einstein in xi, 7, 12, 16–20, 38, 69, 93
Szilard, Leo 281–3, 284, 298

Tagore, Rabindranath 139–40
Talmud, Max 15, 16
Tate Gallery (London, UK) 6, 259
Tel Aviv (Israel) 104
Tennyson, Alfred 197
Thomson, J. J. 47, 48, 63, 76
Thorne, Kip 286, 293
Thurston, Albert 254–5
Time (magazine) 201–2, 233, 284
Times, The (newspaper) 53, 63, 64–6, 67, 73, 81, 82, 136, 157, 160, 174, 202, 213, 323
Todd, Thelma 220
Tom Quad (Oxford, UK) 173, 203
Townes, Charles 129
Townsend, John Sealy 177
Tovey, Donald 166, 191
Toynbee, Arnold 328
Trinity College (Cambridge, UK) 66, 312
Trinity College (Oxford, UK) 178
Trusty Servant (magazine) 149
Turkey 227

Ubbelohde, Alfred 180
Ulm (Germany) 12
unified field theory (of Einstein) 5, 135–8, 157, 291–2
United Nations 297
United Nations Educational, Scientific and Cultural Organisation (UNESCO) 109
USA xii, 6, 7, 64, 97, 169, 226, 240, 250, 258, 270, 272, 289
  Einstein in xi, xii, 74, 87, 95, 98, 99, 100, 121, 172, 179, 255, 276, 278, 281, 282, 283, 284, 285, 287, 290, 296, 297, 298, 299, 301, 302, 303, 310, 311–12, 313, 318
University College (London, UK) 256
University College (Oxford, UK) 164
University Museum (Oxford) 208–9
Ussishkin, Menachem 107

Vallentin, Antonina 13, 226, 245, 246–7, 287, 312
Versailles peace conference (1919) 112, 179, 199
Vienna (Austria) 38, 71
Völkischer Beobachter (newspaper) 238, 245

Wadham College (Oxford, UK) 82, 152, 177
Walker, Ernest 166
Walters, Patrick 38
War Resisters' International 115, 116–17, 179, 241
Warsaw, University of (Poland) 302
Warwick, Andrew 47, 53
Washington, George 300
Washington DC (USA) 291
Washington Post (newspaper) 318
Weber, Thomas 201
Weimar Republic (Germany) 87, 93
Weinberg, Steven 138, 144
Weizmann, Chaim 96–9, 108, 229, 230, 316
Wells, H. G. 313
Westminster Abbey (London, UK) 77, 312
Weyland, Paul 88–90
Wheeler, John Archibald 40
Whitaker, Andrew 122
White, Henry Julian 159, 175, 183–6
Whitehead, Alfred North 62, 76
Whitrow, Gerald 14
Why War? (Einstein and Freud) 113–14
Wien, Wilhelm 47, 54,
Wigner, Eugene 282, 284
Wilde, Oscar 198, 319
Wilhelm II, Kaiser (of Germany) 76, 93, 103
Wilkinson, Ellen 244–5
Williams, W. H. 70
Winchester (UK) 149–50
Winchester College (UK) 149–51, 164
Women's International League for Peace and Freedom 114
Woolsthorpe (UK) 11
Workers' International Relief 260
World Committee for the Victims of German Fascism 225
World Union of Jewish Students 268
Wren, Christopher 164
Wylie, Francis 161, 168

Yahuda, Abraham 230, 233, 240, 270, 317, 323
Young, Thomas 29
Yukawa, Hideki 303

Zionism 65, 87, 95, 96–100, 104, 107, 108, 229
Zurich (Switzerland) 14, 17, 18, 19, 23, 34, 54, 94, 207, 227, 275, 285, 312, 318
Zurich, University of (Switzerland) 19, 20, 32, 34, 93
Zwicky, Fritz 136